D1765977

Arts Leadership

International Case Studies

Jo Caust
Editor

Arts Leadership: International Case Studies
1st edition, 3rd printing

Editor: Jo Caust

Cover designer
Christopher Besley, Besley Design.

ISBN: 978-0-7346-1169-7

Copyright

Text copyright © 2013 by Tilde Publishing and Distribution.
Illustration, layout and design copyright © 2013 by Tilde Publishing and Distribution.

Under Australia's *Copyright Act 1968* (the Act), except for any fair dealing for the purposes of study, research, criticism or review, no part of this book may be reproduced, stored in a retrieval system, or transmitted in any form or by any means without prior written permission from Tilde Publishing and Distribution. All inquiries should be directed in the first instance to the publisher at the address below.

Disclaimer

All reasonable efforts have been made to ensure the quality and accuracy of this publication. Tilde Publishing and Distribution assumes no responsibility for any errors or omissions and no warranties are made with regard to this publication. Neither Tilde Publishing and Distribution nor any authorised distributors shall be held responsible for any direct, incidental or consequential damages resulting from the use of this publication.

Published by:
Tilde Publishing and Distribution
PO Box 72
Prahran VIC 3181 Australia
www.tup.net.au

Contents

Dedication

To Max with thanks.

About the editor

Associate Professor Josephine (Jo) Caust currently holds an honorary position as Principal Fellow at the University of Melbourne, Australia, and was formerly Associate Professor in Arts and Cultural Management at the University of South Australia. She holds a BA degree in drama from Flinders University, a Graduate Diploma in Arts Administration from City University London, an MA in Communication Studies from The University of South Australia, and a PhD in Arts Management and Policy from The University of South Australia.

As an academic from 1997 to 2011, Jo led the post-graduate program in Arts and Cultural Management at the University of South Australia. During this time she published more than 50 papers and articles worldwide, and established the *Asia Pacific Journal of Arts Management* to provide publishing opportunities for researchers in the region. She has also worked in the arts sector for over thirty years as an arts practitioner, arts manager and consultant, and is presently Director of her own consulting company JoCaustArts.

About the contributors

Professor William J Byrnes is the Associate Provost & Dean of Graduate Studies at Southern Utah University in the USA, where he is also an adjunct professor in the MFA Arts Administration program. His textbook, *Management and the Arts*, now in its fourth edition, is widely used in arts and culture management courses around the world. He is a member of the Editorial Advisory Committee of the *Asia Pacific Journal of Arts and Cultural Management*, and has lectured on arts management in China, Singapore and Japan, as well as in several countries in Europe.

Sylvie Cameron has been active in the cultural field for over 20 years. In 1996, she completed a Graduate Diploma in the Management of Cultural Organizations (DESSGOC) at HEC Montréal. From 2002 to 2007, she served as Director of the Board of Montreal Museum Directors and as Director of the Musée d'art contemporain de Montréal Foundation. In 2009, she completed a Masters in Management (MSc) at HEC Montréal.

Associate Professor Josephine Caust is a Principal Fellow at the University of Melbourne and Director of her own arts consulting company, JoCaustArts. Previously she directed the Arts and Cultural Management Program at the University of South Australia and founded the *Asia Pacific Journal of Arts and Cultural Management*. She has also worked in the arts sector for over thirty years as an arts practitioner, arts manager and consultant.

Suyin Chew is the Head (School of Arts Management) at LASALLE College of the Arts in Singapore. Her current research interests include documenting the leadership and management of dance companies and the creative process of artists. As a dancer, she has enjoyed working in unconventional spaces using text and visual art. Suyin is currently undertaking a PhD.

Professor Milena Dragićević Šešić is a professor at the University of Arts Belgrade where she holds the UNESCO Chair in Cultural Policy and Management (Intercultural Mediation in the Balkans). She was previously the Rector of the University of Arts Belgrade. Milena has published numerous papers, and written a number of books on art and cultural management and policy.

Dr Patrick Furu is academic director at Hanken & SSE Executive Education, as well as assistant professor at the Department of Management and Organisation, Hanken School of Economics in Helsinki, Finland. His research has dealt with managing organisational knowledge in multinational corporations, leadership models in jazz bands, and corporate governance in medium-sized enterprises.

Associate Professor Hilary Glow is Director of the Arts and Entertainment Management Program at Deakin University in Melbourne, Australia. She researches issues around cultural policy and its impact on artists, arts practices and organisations. Current research investigations are focused on audience engagement and active arts audiences in the performing arts, and public arts programs for children and young people. She is the co-author of a book on the Australian Indigenous performing arts, *Your Genre is Black: Indigenous Performing Arts & Policy* (2009).

Dr Helle Hedegaard Hein has a MSc and PhD, and is affiliated with the Department of Management, Politics and Philosophy at Copenhagen Business School. Her research interests include the management and motivation of highly specialized creative employees. She is the author of several books and articles on the subject, and her latest book is on Primadonna Management (in Danish). Forthcoming research projects focus on the motivation and management of professionals, on talent management, and on creativity and creative work processes.

Professor Robert Hewison has an MA, a MLitt, and a DLitt (Oxon). He is Professor in Cultural Policy and Leadership Studies at City University London, and is also an Associate of the 'think tank' Demos. He is a critic and cultural historian who has published widely on aspects of 19th- and 20th-century British culture. With John Holden, he helped to devise the Clore Leadership Programme, and has contributed to several Demos reports in the field of cultural policy. Robert has written on theatre and the arts for the Sunday Times since 1981.

Professor John Holden, MA (Oxon), MA (Soton), is a Visiting Professor in Cultural Policy and Management at City University London, and an Associate of the 'think tank' Demos, where he was Head of Culture from 2000 to 2008. He has Masters degrees in law and in art history. John's main professional interest is in the development of people and organizations in the cultural sector, and he has developed a theme of work around the topic of cultural value and democratic culture.

Samuel Jones, BA (Cantab), MA (London), is an Associate at the 'think tank' Demos. Sam's interests include the arts, museums and galleries, and creativity, and his primary interests are culture, the arts and international and intercultural communication. He is also a co-author of *Cultural Diplomacy*, and has developed work on the international activity of cultural organizations.

Irina Khizhinskaya has a degree in theatre management. Her main teaching and research subjects are information technology and personnel management in theatre. In addition to her work at Interstudio, she serves as Executive Director of the 'KukArt' International Puppet and Mix Theatre Festival and the Christmas Parade Theatre festival, and undertakes various consulting activities.

Professor Laurent Lapierre holds the Pierre Péladeau Chair in Leadership at HEC Montréal. He teaches courses on leadership, management of arts enterprises, and cultural industries. His research interests include leadership and the influence of managers' personalities on their management style and the role of management behavior in an organization's performance. He has served as editor of the journal *Gestion:Revue internationale de gestion*, and is a board member and an executive committee member of the Canada Council for the Arts.

John Fangjun Li worked at the Shanghai Audio-Visual Press and the Shanghai Oriental Radio Station as music producer and marketing manager for six years. He was also Associate Professor in Arts Management at the China Conservatory of Music and taught at the Beijing Academy of Contemporary Music. He is presently a PhD candidate at Macquarie University in Australia, studying the evolution and development of China's music industry.

Dr Kate MacNeill is a senior lecturer in the School of Culture and Communication at the University of Melbourne. Her doctorate explored issues of performativity, identity and contemporary art in Australia. Kate is a member of the board of Melbourne Fringe, and in 2010 was a visiting scholar at UC Berkeley at the Beatrice Bain Research Group. She is the program head of graduate studies in arts and cultural management and, together with Ann Tonks, is undertaking research on co-leadership in the Australian major performing arts companies.

Dr Guy Morrow works in research and development for the arts industries. He recently developed the Australian band Boy & Bear's career with his co-manager Rowan Brand. In 2010 he worked as a visiting scholar at New York University where he studied artist management practices in the global economy with the International Music Managers' Forum. Guy Morrow is a lecturer at Macquarie University in Australia, researching music business and arts management.

Maria Naimark has a degree in theatre management. Her main teaching and research interests lie within cultural policy and theatre management. For ten years Maria Naimark ran the independent theatre Monplaisir, which she created. Currently, along with her work at Interstudio, she consults widely, and, as an independent producer, cooperates with a number of international arts and cultural projects.

Associate Professor Donatella de Paoli is Associate Professor in Arts Management within the Department of Leadership and Organizational Behaviour at the Norwegian Business School in Oslo, Norway. Her research interests include: management, organization and marketing of arts and culture; how aesthetics, art and culture can be used as a resource within the business sector; and the development of creative industries and culture. She has authored several books and numerous articles on her areas of interest.

Dr Wendy Reid is a faculty member in the Department of Management at HEC Montréal, with a doctorate in organizational behaviour from York University in Toronto. She is also trained as a cellist, and has an MBA. With a 25-year career in the management of dance, music, museums and broadcasting in Canada, her research interests now focus on the nonprofit sector and the arts in the areas of leadership and governance. She also teaches cultural management at HEC.

Ann Tonks is General Manager of the Melbourne Theatre Company, with occasional diversions into teaching arts management and into researching arts leadership with Dr Kate MacNeill at the University of Melbourne. She is a Senior Fellow at the University of Melbourne, is currently Deputy President of Live Performance Australia, and was previously a senior manager at the Australian Broadcasting Corporation.

Foreword

This project began out of conversations between Donatella de Paoli and myself when I was Visiting Professor at the BI School of Management in Oslo in late 2010. Initially we hoped to do it together, but the logistics became too challenging and so it became a solo project. Nevertheless, it is a true collaboration, with the contributors giving me the privilege of being the curator. It has been a pleasurable journey, aided by the tremendous support and encouragement from both the contributors and those at Tilde University Press. Everyone was enthusiastic about the project at the start, which made the process much easier from my perspective. I would like to thank everyone at Tilde, particularly Rick Ryan who steered the project through with much good humour and unfailing support, Felicity Caterer whose contribution has been critical in the final stages, and Maureen Robins who thought the idea was worth pursuing in the first place. Finally I would like to thank all the contributors for generously providing the wonderful stories in this collection.

Introduction

The making of art is seen as a mystery by many. While artists are portrayed as heroes, anti-heroes or naughty children, the reality of their working lives is not always visible. In fact, the making of art is hard work and requires commitment, discipline, creativity and skill from all those involved. In this book there are many stories from around the globe of outstanding individuals and organizations pursuing the goal of making art. Some stories are about survival against all odds, others are about bringing change to create better possibilities. Then there are stories of how people make art and lead others along the way. This book highlights different approaches to arts leadership. While leadership in the context of the arts shares characteristics with other domains, there are aspects of the arts and cultural environment that distinguish it. For instance, governments are often involved as either funders or stakeholders and they can influence an arts organization's structure and practice. The outcomes of arts practice are often intangible, yet they can also be subject to intense scrutiny from the media and public. And for leaders in the arts it is usually the art that motivates them, not extrinsic rewards.

Many texts focus on only one region or even one country, so the intent in this book is to provide the reader with a broader range of case studies from different regions and countries. While it cannot include every region and culture, it does provide a flavour of different cultural, organizational, government and art form approaches to leadership in the arts and cultural sector from across the globe. There are eleven countries represented here and fourteen case studies. The same structure is used for each study, but each researcher has brought their own approach. If the text is to be used as a teaching tool, there are questions at the end of each chapter that relate to each case study.

The book is divided into four parts:

- Part I: Leadership and the Individual
- Part II: Leadership in Different Organizational Contexts
- Part III: Leadership and Organizational Change
- Part IV: Leadership as an Artistic Process

These headings describe the primary focus of the individual case studies but several of them reflect aspects of the other areas too.

Part I: Leadership and the Individual

Part 1 reflects the concept of 'heroic' leadership but it also demonstrates leadership that is unflinching in the face of seemingly insurmountable obstacles. Interestingly all three case studies in this part are from what was known as the

Eastern Bloc and two are set in contemporary Russia. They reflect how individuals, and the organisations they lead, have had to adapt to changing political and social environments to survive. In each case the individual shows remarkable courage, determination and creativity to work within systems that do not necessarily understand or support their endeavours.

The first case study is Sylvie Cameron and Laurent Lapierre's *Mikhaïl Piotrovsky and the State Hermitage Museum*. This is the story of the Director of the Hermitage Museum, Mikhaïl Piotrovsky, and the changes he had to introduce to ensure the Museum's ongoing existence after the end of 'Perestroika' in the early 1990s. The Hermitage houses an extraordinary artistic and cultural collection. The Museum itself has great historical significance in the Russian cultural landscape but it is also of immense international importance. However the change in the political environment of Russia at the end of the 20th century meant the Museum lost most of its state financial support. This could have been a catastrophe for the Museum. Piotrovsky believed deeply in the importance of the institution, to not just Russia, but to the world at large, so he came up with several means to reform and renew the institution and continue to employ its staff, as well as take care of its collection. Some of his actions may seem contentious historically, given the engagement by the Hermitage with other institutions such as the Guggenheim. Nevertheless Piotrovsky did succeed in keeping the doors open, as well as finding new income streams to support the institution into its next era.

The second case in this part is set in Serbia. It is written by Milena Dragicevic and entitled *The leadership style of Mira Trailović: An entrepreneurial spirit in a bureaucratic world*. This is an incredible story about an arts leader who managed to achieve the most remarkable things in a climate that neither supported her desires nor understood her objectives. It is a story of adaption, networking, creativity and resilience. It seems nothing ever defeated her while she kept creating and doing important artistic work. Trailović was an artistic innovator as well as a consummate political operator. She even outwitted the Soviet regime when it was determined to stop any one seeing her company's work in Moscow. When political pressure got too close she would change tack and re-program or bring in others to defend the work, closer to the seat of power. In this way she managed for more than three decades to produce outstanding artistic work. Clearly Trailović provided a role model in Serbia that lives on in those who worked with her or were taught by her, and she has left the most enduring cultural legacy.

This final paper in this part is again set in Russia. It is written by Irina Khizhinskaya and Maria Naimark and entitled *Vladimir Misharin: Charisma and innovation in the modern Russian arts scene*. This, again, is a fascinating story of an arts leader and entrepreneur who is transformative in his approach to his role. Vladimir Misharin started his career working with young people and then kept doing this throughout his different career manifestations. This has meant that he has passed on skills and knowledge to following generations as well as developing the capacity base of many of the places where he has worked. With a belief system that said nothing was impossible he found ways to improve every organization he worked with, so that by the time he left there was a well of knowledge and skills that would keep the organization succeeding for a long period afterwards. Much of his approach is that of a change agent who brings the organization/institution into the contemporary environment to make it alive, responsive and doing important work. His current focus is the city of Sochi and its various venues and organizations involved in producing the performing arts. As they are hosting the next Cultural Olympiad for the Winter Olympic Games, Misharin is working hard at ensuring that the city and its cultural organizations perform to their utmost to ensure the success of the event.

Part II: Leadership in Different Organizational Contexts

Part II presents examples of particular models of leadership prevalent in the arts, as well as an exploration of different approaches and strategies for approaching leadership in the arts. This includes discussion about generational change, different art form approaches, strategy driven leadership and finding appropriate solutions to revitalise arts organizations.

The first case study in this part, *The Utah Shakespeare Festival: An evolving arts leadership partnership* by William Byrnes, relates the story of the Utah Shakespeare Festival in the United States of America. The focus of this study is the approach taken by the Festival, recently, to change its executive and artistic leadership. The Festival has a 50-year history, and there has been stability in the leadership roles for much of that time. The Board of the Festival has a desire to both maintain their core audience as well as the style of work they are doing. There is a challenge underpinning this, given that the majority of their local audience comes from a strong Mormon background with conservative social views. The Board has decided to promote two long term actor/directors from the Festival to the role of co-artistic directors to maintain a sense of continuity. Structurally, the co-artistic directors report to the managing director who has also only recently moved into the top role. Thus, it is a triumvirate leadership model that runs the Festival – a slight variation on the dual leadership model – and so the complexities of the three working together to realise a shared vision is challenging. Reading between the lines, there is also a sense that the new leadership is under close scrutiny from the Board, so any kind of failure (or veering from the received script) may not be tolerated.

The second paper in this part is by Kate MacNeill and Ann Tonks. In *Leadership in Australian arts companies: One size does not fit all*, the authors consider different organizational and leadership models common within Australia for different art forms. While some organizations have a single leader, others do not. They note that an approach that is common in arts organizations, the dual or co-leadership model – where the artistic functions are primarily done by one individual and the management functions are primarily done by another – is mostly represented in collaborative art forms such as dance and theatre. MacNeill and Tonks then explore how this structure works in different companies. In some cases this means that both leaders report directly to the board, and in other companies only one leader does, and the other reports to or through the senior nominated leader. Who is the nominated leader then creates an interesting discussion, as this varies between art forms and even within art forms. This discussion also implicitly raises a question: does it matter who is the nominated leader in terms of the organizational and/or artistic outcomes?

The next case study is a little different from the others, as its subject is more related to ideas around 'creative industries' than to purely arts or cultural practice. In John Fangjun Li and Guy Morrow 's paper *Strategic leadership in China's music industry: A case study of the Shanghai Audio Visual Press*, the focus is on one particular music recording organization, the Shanghai Audio Visual Press (SAVP), which is located in Shanghai, China. This is the story of how the company's co-leaders developed a strategy to re-align their company to make it different from other companies in the field. They made a critical decision to change their organizational vision and structure to create a unique and different approach in the market place. As a result of their successful strategic decisions, they positioned the organization as the dominant force in music distribution in the recorded music industry in China. An additional aspect of this study that makes it unusual, is that the SAVP is a state-owned enterprise – a model that is unfamiliar in the West. So, while the co-leadership described here makes strategic decisions from a purely market model, the organization is actually still part of the state and presumably competing with other state owned enterprises.

The final case study in this part is Wendy Reid's paper, *Dual executive leadership in the Arts: Rémi Brousseau, Pierre Rousseau and Le Théâtre Denise-Pelletier*. This time the setting is Montréal in Canada and the company is a theatre group that focuses on work for young people. While acknowledging that dual leadership models are common, particularly in the performing arts, Reid observes that often these relationships are conflict ridden. In this case study however she explores a situation where conflict is not present but instead there is a harmonious and successful professional relationship that is producing good artistic outcomes. From Reid's description there is a sense of two quite different individuals, who made a conscious decision to work together as dual-leaders, and then made that relationship succeed because of their shared passion for the work. It is clear though, for this to occur, the individuals involved have to be mature and not ego dominated, as well as being able to establish good communication channels from the outset. This is what seems to have happened in this case and it therefore represents a good role model for succeeding in dual leadership.

Part III: Leadership and Organisational Change

This part addresses three different approaches to organizational and cultural change with varying degrees of success. Each case is different in terms of its focus but all three demonstrate the complexities and challenges for leaders in implementing change and getting the outcomes they desire.

The first paper in this part by Donatella De Paoli is set in Norway and discusses the extraordinary ongoing story of the creation of their new National Museum of Art. It is titled, *Leadership and changing management: The case of the Norwegian National Museum of Art* and provides both a documentation and analysis of the events that have taken place over the past decade to create a new national institution from several already existing institutions. In the process of this forced marriage, leaders have come and gone and the problems with the amalgamation have been a subject of continued public interest and regular airing in the Norwegian media. It would seem the change process was flawed from the beginning because the key stakeholders were not part of the planning or decision making. However it is a wonderful case study in how not to bring about a successful institutional merging. It is also instructive about leadership and how right leadership choices need to occur if the outcomes are going to work. It addresses flaws in decision making by politicians, bureaucrats and boards as well as the institutional leaders themselves. It also shows how critical it is, that leaders bring their followers with them, if the change they are implementing is going to be sustained.

In '*Cultural leadership and audience engagement: A case study of the Theatre Royal Stratford East*' Hilary Glow looks at the approach taken by the leadership of the Theatre Royal at Stratford East in London to change the way they relate to their audience as well as the way they approach their creative process. Theatre leadership, in this framing, reflects a hierarchical model that encourages a passive relationship with its audience. This interpretation of the audience as disenfranchised, if the artist is making their work without including the audience's view, might be seen as a provocative reading in the context of making art. In the Stratford East example with their The Open Stage project, the Artistic Directors and performers have directly engaged with their local community to include them in the process of both choosing what the theatre does and how they do it. Glow sees this project as an ambitious attempt to change conventional models of arts leadership, making artistic leadership a participatory and inclusive process rather than one that is exclusive and privileged. It will be interesting to see what outcomes are produced from this process.

The final paper in this part, *Leadership and transformation at the Royal Shakespeare Company* by Robert Hewison, John Holden and Samuel Jones, reviews how the leaders of the Royal Shakespeare Company (RSC) in England went about changing the culture of the RSC to bring about both a change in company practice as well as in the work produced. The authors note that while the RSC had had a glorious history through the second half of the 20th century, at the beginning of the 21st century it was facing a serious crisis where the future of the company was in peril. The new Directors decided that if the organization was going to survive the whole culture of the company had to change, both from the top down and from the ground up. They did this by embracing the concept of the 'ensemble' to include the whole operation of the RSC, not just in the rehearsal room. The process was one of integration instead of separation, matching the structure and organization of the company with the kind of work it was striving to do. Hewison *et al.* were in a sense part of the process too, as they observed and documented the outcomes of this transformative experience as participative observers. This case study is a positive and successful example of how to achieve cultural and organizational change as well as involve everyone in owning the outcome.

Part IV: Leadership as an Artistic Process

In this part, there is an exploration of the way artist leaders work in terms of their approach to creating work and collaborating with others, while also bringing their artistic or creative process to all aspects of their leadership. Understanding how artists work has been a long term fascination for many writers and researchers. More recently it has been the subject of much attention in the generic management and leadership literature. Possibly the most common reference is to orchestras and the relationships between its musicians, as well as the relationship between the conductor and the orchestra. In the four case studies in this part, there is a focus on artist leaders in dance, theatre, music, visual and community arts. The studies address how they work with other artists, develop new work, collaborate successfully and work within the broader context of the arts environment.

Helle Hein has done a deep analysis of how theatre directors work in her study, *'Learning from creative work processes in the theatre: Stepping into character'*. Working in Denmark she studied the approach of two different theatre directors in staging plays at the Royal Danish Theatre in Copenhagen. Her aim was to discover what other leaders might learn from the creative process of two different directors in their process of taking a play from rehearsal to performance. The two directors in the study are quite different in their creative process, which thereby brings different outcomes in terms of the relationship with other artists. A point of difference however is that one was doing a new work and the other was doing a classic. With a new work there usually needs to be a lot more work-shopping and re-working, so essentially the rehearsal process is bound to be different. This does not detract from the value of the study however as Hein's observation of the directors' creative processes is rich and deep. As both directors produced successful productions, artistically and commercially, Hein's study also illustrates that there is not one way to direct successfully.

The second study is set in Singapore and focuses on two artist-leaders working together to make a cross discipline dance, visual art and theatre project. Titled *'Co-leading the creative process through collaboration'* the author, Suyin Chew, examines why the artists decided to work together, the way they then developed their new work, and the outcomes of their collaboration. Initially three artists were leading the collaboration but with the departure of one, artists from other disciplines were invited to participate but with the two initial leaders determining the vision and the process. The final outcome was seen by the participants and the audience as truly cross discipline with no sense of one art form dominating. In addition the artists describe a collaborative process, where they were constantly working off each other, as well as the other artists involved, to bring the work to fruition. Chew argues also that cross discipline work such as this might be the way forward in the making of new art. Again it shows that for successful collaboration to occur between two artist leaders there needs to be both a shared vision as well as a commitment from both leaders to make the collaboration work.

The next paper in this part is by the editor, Jo Caust, and is called *Thriving or surviving: Artists as leaders of smaller arts organizations*. It is set in Australia and considers three different arts leaders working in small arts organizations in three different art form contexts; dance, community arts and theatre. With limited resources available to them, leaders of small arts organizations have to be resourceful and multi-skilled to keep their organization afloat. In this paper each leader describes how they lead their organization as well as undertake their arts practice. It seems collaboration with other artists is a key to all their processes as well as part of their work practice in running their organizations. They talk about the details of their creative process where the focus is on developing new and original art work. While each individual leader demonstrates a deep passion and commitment to producing work, they also discuss how critical it is to engage others in the process so that everyone involved commits to and owns the outcomes of the work. The study provides an insight into the creative process and how these art leaders go about making new work.

The final paper is Patrick Furu's *The art of collaborative leadership in jazz bands*. This paper focuses on the process of collaborative leadership when jazz musicians work together. While Furu is from Finland, the data for the study has been gathered both from Finland and from other international settings. Furu's study is directed towards mainstream leaders to encourage them to understand how collaboration, creativity and improvisation work successfully together in a jazz band. He notes how each musician is already an expert in their craft, and that all the musicians share a language and usage of common musical terms to communicate. However, the fascinating aspect of jazz music is the way the musicians can work together sharing the leadership while producing a piece of art that is totally improvised in the moment of playing together. The art comes about from the musicians playing and experimenting together; it does not occur on its own and it is not pre-planned. It relies on the expertise of each of the musicians as well as on the combined capacity to work together as a team successfully. Furu notes that the act of creation relies on trust and respect between the musicians, so that even if things do go awry, they are able to work together to steer their performance back on track. Everyone is a leader and everyone is an artist.

Final comment

It has been a wonderful experience working with different international researchers in the field to put this collection together and I am very grateful for their commitment and involvement in the project. I hope you all enjoy the case studies as fascinating stories in addition to the learning role that case studies can play for researchers, arts managers and leaders.

Jo Caust

Part I

Leadership and the Individual

Chapter 1

Mikhaïl Piotrovsky and the State Hermitage Museum

SYLVIE CAMERON AND LAURENT LAPIERRE

The State Hermitage Museum is one of the most conservative museums in the world, successfully preserving the spirit and symbolism of 18th and 19th century Russia. In this respect, it represents a living memorial to this period in Russia's history. Many important events in the history of the Russian Empire took place within the walls of the Winter Palace, which is also where the Empire met its demise. (...) But what makes the Hermitage even more exceptional, perhaps, are its magnificent collections, which reflects the diversity of peoples and cultures and which are in perfect harmony with the building's architecture and lavish interiors. The Museum has outstanding collections of works by Rembrandt, Leonardo da Vinci, Matisse, Rubens, as well as Scythian and Greek works in gold, Buddhist frescoes, Islamic and Oriental objects, as well as Greek and Roman antiquities (Piotrovsky 2003).[1]

Background

Introduction

The Hermitage, one of the oldest and most prestigious museums in the world, was founded during the reign of Catherine the Great in 1764, and over the centuries has amassed a permanent collection of three million objects. Not only is the Hermitage one of the oldest museums in the world, but it has one of the most tumultuous histories. In addition to numerous historical events, the Hermitage

---

[1]Piotrovsky M. 2003, 'The Hermitage through the Centuries', *Museum International* (UNESCO, Paris), number 217, p. 9.

was forced to protect its buildings and collections against the Nazi invasion during World War II. By packing up part of the collection for evacuation by train to the Ural mountains, and by physically occupying the premises in an attempt to guard the buildings, the museum's employees managed to protect this invaluable cultural treasure.

As Mikhaïl Piotrovsky, director of the museum, has stated in interviews[2], the Hermitage is more than a symbol of Russian culture; it is a symbol of Russia as a state. However, the museum was not spared the political, economic, and social upheavals that swept through Russia in the latter part of the 20th century. Indeed, with the end of perestroika in the early 1990s, the Hermitage's management was forced to rapidly find alternative solutions in response to the massive withdrawal of state funding. This represented a radical break with over two centuries of the museum's history, and took place in a context of crisis and political turmoil that affected all sectors of Russian society. This other 'revolution' severely tested the museum's ability to adapt to change. However, the many resources of the museum's staff and the formidable talents and skills of its director, constituted a force to be reckoned with.

The State Hermitage Museum: Buildings and collections

The museum covers a total area of 184,317 square metres, with 60,100 metres divided among 1,170 galleries. It comprises a vast complex of 11 buildings: the Winter Palace, the Small Hermitage, the Old Hermitage, the New Hermitage, the Hermitage Theatre, the Reserve House of the Winter Palace, the Menchikov Palace, the General Staff Building, the Museum of Porcelain and the Museum of Heraldry, as well as the Staraya Derevnya Restoration and Storage Centre, an ultramodern space open to the public. Eight of these buildings are located in the historic centre of St Petersburg.

The collection houses approximately three million objects, including 16,700 paintings, 12,500 sculptures, 300,000 objects of applied art, 620,000 works on paper, 725,000 archaeological artefacts and 1,125,000 numismatic objects.

Over two centuries of Russian history

Upon her accession to the throne in 1762, Catherine II, known as Catherine the Great, decided to make the new Winter Palace her official residence. This masterpiece of Baroque architecture, commissioned in 1741 by Empress Elizabeth and designed by the Italian architect Bartolomeo Carlo Rastrelli, received its first collection as a museum in 1764, with the hanging of 225 paintings acquired by Catherine the Great from JE Gotzkowski, a merchant from Berlin. From that moment on, the museum's collections would expand rapidly, leading to a continual need for new exhibition space. In 1769 the collection was enriched by

---

[2] All quotations in this article are from three interviews conducted with Mikhaïl Piotrovsky in Montreal and St. Petersburg between January and April 2006.

600 new paintings purchased from Count Heinrich von Bruhl, including works by Rembrandt, Rubens, Watteau and Poussin. Three years later, in 1772, Catherine acquired the 400-piece collection of Pierre Crozat, including masterpieces by Raphael, Giorgione, Titian, Rembrandt, Rubens, Van Dyck, Poussin, Watteau, Boucher and Chardin. In 1779, the purchase of George Walpole's English collection from Houghton Hall provoked such an outcry in England that the works had to be shipped to St. Petersburg in great haste. The acquisition of Count Baudouin's collection of 119 paintings in 1784 made it possible to further enrich the Hermitage's collection with 17th-century French and Italian paintings. Catherine commissioned the construction of the Small Hermitage, followed by the Great Hermitage (known today as the Old Hermitage), in order to house her ever expanding collections.

Archaeology and science: Over 150 years of influence

While imperial purchases of art continued into the 19th and 20th century, archaeological excavations across the Russian Empire as well as Egypt soon emerged as a new method of acquisition, becoming an invaluable source of treasures for the museum. The Hermitage's 20th-century archaeological missions were extremely fruitful, and while gradually enriching its collections with the numerous objects discovered during digs, the museum also strengthened its ties with Russian scientific institutions. In fact, the museum's archives, publications, departmental libraries, and central library have all become key elements of the Hermitage's activities. It is therefore not surprising to learn that the Hermitage's directors have traditionally been scholars and scientists – Iosif Orbeli, Mikhaïl Artamonov, Boris Piotrovsky, and the current director (and member of the Academy of Sciences) Mikhaïl Piotrovsky.

A museum of world culture

The collections of the Hermitage Museum cover a rich diversity of cultural fields including Oriental art, Classical Antiquity, Western European art, Russian art, archaeology, numismatics, and arms and armour. This variety makes the Hermitage itself a microcosm of cultural diversity. While conscious of its status as a museum of world culture, the Hermitage also symbolizes Russia's attitude towards art and culture, as well as its openness and its excellence on the cultural stage. Thus, while confirming the universalist ideal of the world's great museums, the Hermitage is also a monument to the importance of national culture in the fulfilment of this ambition.

The challenges

Crisis of the 1990s

The early 1990s, which marked the end of 'perestroika' and was a period of transition to a market economy, was a time of major upheaval in Russia. During these difficult years, the country and its population were exposed to unprecedented changes at the political, economic and social levels. Politically, the fall of the Communist regime brought with it the dismantling of long-standing decision-making structures. Economically, it eliminated the state monopoly that had characterized the Soviet period. The country faced the huge challenge of having to construct a new state and promote a new economic and political culture, all in short order. In a country with no democratic precedents or references, this proved to be a difficult task.

The Hermitage in the context of crisis

All this turmoil naturally had enormous repercussions for the Hermitage. Though the museum had repeatedly demonstrated an ability to overcome even the most difficult situations, having survived a major fire, in 1837, two world wars and a civil war, the fall of the Soviet Union presented new challenges, one of the most daunting of which was the need for major restructuring in response to the political and economic changes taking place. While culture was generously funded under the socialist state, this situation changed completely after the fall of the Soviet Union. As a result, the Hermitage lost close to 90 percent of its revenue. This drastic decline in funding, from US$20 million before the crisis to US$2 million during the crisis, created a veritable state of emergency within the institution. The museum was barely able to cover basic wages and operating costs. With nearly two thousand employees and its vast collection, it poured its energy into finding solutions to its precarious situation while struggling to maintain its normal, day-to-day operations. It was intent on continuing to meet the expectations of its traditional Russian clientele while seeking alternative funding solutions and engaging in innovative management processes. Many other Russian institutions collapsed during the shift to a market economy, but the Hermitage not only managed to survive the transition (its 2004 budget was US$40 million, including nearly US$27 million in renewed state funding), it was even able to forge new avenues of expansion throughout the Western world.

The Hermitage team

The State Hermitage Museum has over 2,200 employees, including nearly 400 curators, 100 conservators, 450 education employees, 50 information technology workers, over 100 administrative employees and more than 1,000 labourers, maintenance workers and security guards. The director is supported by seven assistant directors who are responsible for the following sectors:

- research,
- exhibitions and development,
- conservation,
- finance and administration,
- personnel,
- construction and investments, and
- maintenance.

In addition, the museum has 49 departments, each headed by a curator.

At the helm: Mikhaïl Piotrovsky

In 1991, at the peak of the crisis and following the death of his father, who had run the Hermitage from 1964 to 1990, Mikhaïl Piotrovsky was invited to join the museum staff as director of research. One year later he was appointed director of the State Hermitage by government decree.

> At the time I think I represented the compromise candidate the state was seeking, in order to maintain a balance between the past and future in this fragile period of transition for the Hermitage. I would ensure both continuity and change. Because I was from outside the institution, I could provide a new perspective on the situation, but, at the same time, I would ensure continuity within the institution, because, as my father's successor, I represented the pursuit of his work.

Mikhaïl Piotrovsky was born in 1944 in Armenia, which at that time was a republic of the Soviet Union. In 1966 he obtained a degree in Arabic studies at the Oriental Faculty of Leningrad State University, later earning a doctorate. In 1967 he joined the Leningrad branch of the Institute for Oriental Studies, where he worked until 1991. Piotrovsky has taken part in archaeological excavations in the Caucasus, Central Asia and Yemen. He is the author of more than 200 scholarly works on various aspects of the Arabic world, including archaeology, Islamic mythology, and the political and spiritual history of Islam and Arab culture. Although a veteran academic, in 1992 Piotrovsky was thrown into the completely new role of museum director. This is how he explains the transition:

> In reflecting on my situation and that of my predecessors as director of the State Hermitage Museum, I realized that every director of the Hermitage in the 20th century had been an archaeologist. I came to the conclusion that archaeological training was a good preparation for the role of museum director, regardless of the political regime ... At the intellectual level, they have to be able to plan and develop excavation strategies. They also need strong organizational skills in order to meticulously prepare expeditions, including travel and accommodation for numerous people. At the diplomatic level, they need to negotiate at every step to secure the authorizations required in foreign territories. And, finally, they have to be able to raise funds from both public and private sources, and then produce reports that emphasize the quality of the results of their missions, in the hope of creating a climate favourable to their pursuit the following year...In fact, the archaeologist must be...a businessman, a scientist and a politician.

Approach

The Hermitage director and crisis management

In joining the institution at a time of major upheaval, Piotrovsky accepted the challenges that awaited him. He describes the situation facing Russia and the museum during the 1990s:

[handwritten margin notes: "Unesco intervention — valuing high art?" "crisis less less essential focus ×" "gets micro (?) to reduce"]

...trary to what the media would have had us believe, the crisis that Russia ...ured did not destroy it. The fall of the Soviet regime marked the end of a ...od, not the end of Russia. At the beginning of the crisis, all the essential ...nents were already in place: the collections, buildings, traditions, experts, ...etera. Moreover, the problems we already faced under the Soviet regime ...e the same problems facing all museums today, such as dealing with ...ng attendance and the need to modernize our conservation facilities. So, ...ally, we were thrown into the same situation as other museums. The ...y real difference was the extreme precariousness of our situation. The ...e basically cut off all of our funding and told us to turn to the free ...ket.

...ut the most difficult years of the crisis, the director adopted a ...ent approach that was guided by several key principles:

...he central mission,

...a strong work ethic,

...openness to opportunities, and

...upholding of traditions.

...some of his responses to these four key principles:

...on

The most essential thing then, as now, was to constantly remind ourselves of the objective … to preserve the Hermitage and its exceptional world heritage. The Hermitage is more important than anything else. The Hermitage belongs not only to Russia but to the entire world. In the day-to-day life of large institutions such as the Hermitage, people often tend to complicate things, causing them to lose sight of the essential objectives of their institution. Petty internal politics get in the way of action. Periods of crisis have this in common: they bring you back to the essentials; they disrupt the daily routine, forcing people to forget about the divergences that were paralysing action. At the Hermitage, everyone's efforts were suddenly focused on the central mission: the museum and its preservation.

The work

What happened was not the result of a miracle, but rather of hard work – a lot of hard work. Thanks to our hard work. Not once throughout all these difficult years did we refuse anyone entry to the museum. We worked hard, but we also worked differently. This was an important aspect of our strategy. We encouraged everyone to focus on their preferred field. We also asked them to come up with solutions to our financial crisis. People knew that they held the fate of the museum in their hands and that its survival depended on their efforts and initiatives. For nearly ten years, I gave free rein to all the initiatives and new ideas proposed by the people at the museum. The only criterion was that the projects comply with the legal framework in place. That was all. The watchword was: let's try it. Today things have changed, but throughout those years I never said no. We acted seriously and collectively, with dedication, honesty and inventiveness.

Openness to opportunity

> *Of course, on top of working hard, we also had to take advantage of opportunities that would help us adapt to the market. On the one hand, at the same time as it withdrew funding, the state granted us new powers that opened up possibilities for self-financing that had been inaccessible before. For example, the Russian federal government passed a law granting the State Hermitage Museum exclusive rights over the use of its collections, buildings, image, name, reproduction of the works in its collections, the museum's interiors and the research work of its staff, as well as ownership of all the museum's trademarks. This yielded immediate benefits, which we continue to reap today. On the other hand, we received donated assistance from McKenzie, a leading international consulting firm that helped us identify openings in the market. We immediately followed their recommendation to set up a development department. (…) We also benefited from the incredible support of our counterparts in other leading world museums. Despite being in competition with each other, museums form one big family. They opened their doors to us and helped us understand their governance structures, which are set up to satisfy both public and private financial backers. Some museums even introduced us to their boards of directors and identified their donors, including people who could eventually provide aid to the Hermitage. And, finally, we had the support of UNESCO, which acted as an intermediary in order to help us forge new partnerships with states and major institutions. Moreover, UNESCO established an international network of Friends of the Hermitage, thus lending its political weight in order to favour long-term solutions.*

Upholding of traditions

> *To this, I would add that the Hermitage and its traditions made all the difference in seeing us through the crisis. Traditions have helped the Hermitage survive the crises it has faced throughout history. That is why I did not want to abandon the museum's traditions. (…) It was important that we preserve the spirit of the museum while learning new ways of doing things, playing to our strengths and developing new skills without renouncing our past, without provoking a rupture with the previous decades.*

Outcomes

The Hermitage in an era of change

New business processes

The institutional changes discussed by Piotrovsky as a means of dealing with the crisis took place gradually. Existing management models were unsuitable for the Hermitage's situation and the political and economic environment to which it was striving to adapt in the early 1990s. The museum had to adapt its approaches to fit the Russian reality. Several management criteria typical of Western museums had to be rejected. For example, Westerners considered the Hermitage overstaffed because it had more curators than comparable museums in Europe. But the Hermitage's director refused to layoff staff, citing its moral obligation to its employees, particularly at a time of severe economic recession. Thus the museum embarked on its re-organization with an overriding concern for its personnel, its collections and its buildings. New business processes were, however, gradually introduced in four priority areas: fundraising, financial management, marketing and merchandising, and information technology.

Fundraising

In response to the withdrawal of state funding, the Hermitage had no choice but to seek alternative sources of financing. In this regard, it was faced with two challenges: introducing new practices in the museum's activities, and raising funds and finding donors. A Development Department was created to give the Hermitage the tools necessary to carry out fundraising. The first task of the new department was to learn how to operate within the museum. The second was to deal with the problem of an extremely limited donor base in Russia. Philanthropy was still a novel concept in the Russia of the 1990s, but an even greater problem was the fact that Russian companies were struggling with the challenges of the economic transition, and profits were meagre. The Development Department thus shifted its focus to foreign companies with a presence in Russia. This strategy brought its own set of problems, however. For example, the accounting processes left over from the Soviet era did not quite meet the standards of Western donors, [...] tailed proposals, cost estimates, donor recognition and annual [...] measures had to be taken to improve management transparency [...] donors.

[...] ment

[...] cts of the museum's fundraising efforts directed at foreign [...] he adoption of new financial practices. Although the government [...] e Hermitage to comply with specifically Russian accounting [...] from the Soviet era, the museum's management has also [...] rent rules to meet the requirements of foreign donors, in [...] standards in effect within the European Union. In reorganizing [...] e Hermitage has benefited from the support of UNESCO and the [...] national. Customized, 'mixed' software has been put in place to [...] th the Russian system and international accounting standards. [...] has also installed a computerized ticket-counting system, [...] e accurate accounting of ticket-generated revenue. To further [...] ency and fiscal responsibility, the Hermitage publishes its annual [...] and English – the first cultural institution in Russia to do so. In [...] port, the Hermitage remained faithful to its own vision: while [...] seum's activities and financial situation, it also devotes much [...] ork of its researchers, the achievements of its staff and the archaeological expeditions carried out during the year.

Marketing and merchandising

The design and production of marketable items inspired by the Hermitage collections is an important component of the museum's marketing strategy. It is also a means for the museum to generate funding for its educational activities and ongoing development. This merchandising strategy serves as well to promote the Hermitage and its collections. Over the years, the Hermitage has entered into agreements with several organizations, including the Metropolitan Museum of Art in New York, which is licensed to manufacture reproductions of objects and paintings from the Hermitage collections. However, despite selling numerous licences throughout the world, the Hermitage has granted no exclusive rights, and it exercises strict control over the production of all merchandise, which is protected by copyright. An International Merchandising Committee formed of members of the museum staff as well as international merchandising experts, has been set up in order to streamline the Hermitage's international merchandising activities.

As part of its international merchandising program, the Hermitage created an online boutique offering unique products, thus building even stronger links between the museum's commercial activities and its international clientele. In organizing the boutique's auxiliary activities, such as the stocking of merchandise and the delivery of orders, the Hermitage has benefited from the experience of other museums, including the Louvre, the Metropolitan Museum of Art and the Guggenheim. Moreover, in order to meet the strong American demand for the Hermitage's products, as well as expectations of fast delivery, the museum has circumvented the administrative delays of Russian customs by establishing ties with a supplier based in California.

Information technology

Information technology has played a central role in the changes that have transformed the institution's business processes. Four major IT projects have been implemented with the assistance of IBM: an image-creation studio, a museum information system, an IT study centre and a website. The site, at www.hermitagemuseum.org, is a sophisticated one in the international museum community and receives more than 7,000 hits daily. The curators of the Hermitage work closely with the Information Technology Department on all matters related to the development of the site. Information technology has enabled the Hermitage to make its collections accessible to the entire world. Thus, in addition to resolving many of the immediate problems facing the museum in the 1990s, the implementation of IT has given new momentum to its research and educational missions.

UNESCO support

UNESCO already had a longstanding collaboration with the Russian Federation dating back to the organization's founding in 1946. However, UNESCO intensified its support in the wake of the political and economic changes that plunged Russia into a state of chaos in the 1990s. For example, UNESCO has provided support for staff training through conferences and exchange programs, coordinated international cooperation by establishing ties with the international museum community and created an international network of charitable organizations dedicated to the preservation of the Hermitage.

International advisory board

In 1994 UNESCO and the Hermitage management jointly set up an International Advisory Board of leading museum directors and world-renowned experts. In 2006, this board was presided over by Neil MacGregor, Director of the British Museum, and was made up of the following members: Mikhaïl Piotrovsky, Director of the Hermitage; Edmund P Pillsbury, Director of the Meadows Gallery, Dallas; Reinhold Baumstark, Director of the Bayerische Staatsgemael-desammlunge, Munich; Irène Bizot, former head of the Réunion des Musées Nationaux, Paris; Mounir Bouchenaki, Assistant Director-General for Culture, UNESCO; Anne d'Harnoncourt, Director of the Philadelphia Museum of Art; Henri Loyrette, President-Director, Musée du Louvre, Paris; Ronald de Leeuw, Director of the Rijksmuseum, Amsterdam; Anna Maria Petrioli Tofani, Director of the Uffizi Gallery, Florence; and Stuart Gibson, Coordinator of the Hermitage-UNESCO project. The International Advisory Board meets once a year in St Petersburg.

Friends of the Hermitage abroad

Under the direct sponsorship of UNESCO, the Hermitage has succeeded in establishing an international network of Friends of the Hermitage branches. The objectives were to generate financial support and to promote the museum and its collections throughout the world. The network was established in 1994 and includes both private and corporate membership. Four organizations are currently active: the Dutch Friends of the Hermitage, the American Friends of the Hermitage, the Canadian Friends of the Hermitage and the UK Friends of the Hermitage.

International development: The branches

In the 1990s, taking its cue from other leading world museums, the Hermitage embarked on an ambitious mission to expand its markets by opening branches abroad. The quality of the Hermitage's collections was a key factor in the success of its bid to enhance its visibility on the world stage. The Hermitage currently has four branches abroad.

The Hermitage-Amsterdam Exhibition Centre. The Foundation Hermitage Friends in the Netherlands had existed for several years. Due to the active support of the president of the Foundation Ernst Veen, although the project is still under development, exhibition halls covering approximately 500 square metres have been open to the public since 2004, at the site of a historic mansion dating from 1683.

Somerset House in London. The idea of creating exhibition rooms for the Hermitage in one of London's palaces took place in 1998 with the help of Lord Rothschild. The Hermitage Rooms in Somerset House is a total floor area of over 411 square metres which allow the museum to present rotating exhibitions from its collections.

The Hermitage-Guggenheim Exhibition Center in Las Vegas. The creation of the Hermitage-Guggenheim Exhibition Center in Las Vegas was the result of a long-term collaboration with Thomas Krens, Director of the Solomon R. Guggenheim Foundation. A total floor area of 5,920 square metres is located in the Venetian Resort Hotel Casino in the center of Las Vegas. Exhibitions mounted at the Las Vegas branch of the museum are subsequently shown at the Hermitage in St. Petersburg and at the Guggenheim museums in New York, Bilbao and Venice.

The Hermitage-Kazan Exhibition Center in Tatarstan. In August 2005, the Hermitage and the Kazan Kremlin Museum-Park signed a long-term cooperation agreement. The Hermitage-Kazan Exhibition Center in Tatarstan is the most recent branch of the Hermitage and is distinguished by its educational vocation. The center's state-of-the-art technology allows for the multifunctional use of the premises for exhibitions, lectures, conferences, scholarly meetings and educational museum programs.

Local development

Another major project that is central to the Hermitage's development strategy focuses on the local environment and the urban revitalization of St. Petersburg. Known as the Greater Hermitage Project, this US$150 million undertaking is sponsored by UNESCO, the World Bank and the Russian government. With its holistic vision of sustainable development, the Greater Hermitage Project will ensure that the Hermitage takes its rightful place among the great museums of the 21st century. One of the principal elements of the Greater Hermitage Project is the conversion of the General Staff Building into a museum. Designed by the architect Carlo Rossi, this neoclassical building comprises a succession of small, interconnecting rooms with a total floor area of approximately 38,200 square metres. It will be converted into 800 exhibition rooms for the display of 19th- and 20th-century works from the permanent collection, including Impressionist masterpieces, as well as 21st-century works, in partnership with leading world museums. The project will culminate with the creation of a vast museum complex around Palace Square, to include both exhibition galleries and visitor services. To make up for the lack of works representing the latter half of the 20th century in the Hermitage collection, a long-term partnership was reached with the Guggenheim Museum.

Piotrovsky describes the global funding of the Greater Hermitage Project:

> *As usual, we have no money. But, having made it through 10 years without money while still managing to survive and grow, we are optimistic. On the one hand, we can count on the revenue generated by auxiliary activities such as the boutique and restaurant, which could bring in US$1 million annually*

to support this building's operations. On the other hand, we have a loan from the World Bank. This loan was actually granted to the Russian government, which is why the state is paying for the architectural design of the project. At US$21 million, this represents the bulk of our fundraising. In addition, we are planning a vast international campaign that will involve special teams working out of the museum and the participation of our international network of Friends of the Hermitage. In addition to seeking major donations, we will be offering to sell space within the new museum. Each room will have a value attributed to it, in exchange for which it will be named after the donor. This approach was not possible in the Winter Palace, but it works well for the rooms in the General Staff Building. (...) The completion of the project is planned for 2014, the year of the 250th anniversary of the Hermitage.

The 21st century

Despite having survived the crises of the 1990s, the Hermitage today faces many of the same challenges that confront other leading world museums at the start of the new millennium. All are grappling with fundamental questions concerning the meaning of the museographic presentation of cultures, means of funding, partnership strategies, and the fine balance between traditional methods of disseminating knowledge and the use of communication technologies. The clash of ethical, strategic, organizational, commercial and political choices places the museum director in a constant state of emergency. Piotrovsky describes some of these challenges below:

Institutional challenges

Democratization of the institution:

I think the main challenge facing all of the world's leading museums is that of appealing to as broad an audience as possible. Museums are the most democratic of all cultural institutions. They offer an opportunity for everyone– from the expert to the layperson – to satisfy their curiosity. In this regard, the Hermitage is an extraordinary museum, because it caters to very diverse segments of the public, both scholarly and non-scholarly. The question that arises, then, is how to respond to the diversity of these constituencies without losing our personality. That is why I say that today's museums are situated somewhere between the Church and Disneyland, the challenge being to find a balance between the two. We have to try to position ourselves between the world of knowledge and the world of entertainment. Fundamentally, museums belong to the world of knowledge and a museum like the Hermitage has an enormous responsibility in this regard. (...) This is a challenge facing all levels of the institution. The museum must strive to be as democratic a cultural institution as possible while at the same time fulfilling its scholarly and educational responsibilities.

Funding:

> *Funding represents another major challenge shared by all of the leading world museums. While several of these museums have access to public funding, all must rely on private funding to meet the many needs of their institution. Balance is also important when it comes to funding, but, once again, that balance is hard to achieve. In our case, funding was the most crucial battle waged in the 1990s. Because our survival depended on it, we poured all of our energy into this battle. But, as is the case for most museums, funding continues to be one of our top priorities. Indeed, despite the re-establishment of state funding and the private donations to which we now have access, the museum still operates with budgets that fall short of its needs.*

Human resources:

> *In the course of the Hermitage's history, the staff has repeatedly played a determining role in the museum's survival, most recently during the crisis of the 1990s. However, their dedication, which owes much to their Russian heritage, is being put to the test by the new economic context in Russia. Indeed, new paradoxes have emerged that pose a threat to the institution. Despite all our efforts to pay our employees salaries that are at times triple those of other museums, the market economy has imposed a new realty: a professor at the Hermitage now earns less than a secretary working for a private firm. In light of this, I believe it is essential to maintain a high level of motivation within the museum. ...I always remind people that the museum offers them a unique opportunity to be part of a prestigious cultural institution that is emblematic of the whole of Russia as well as of the cultural diversity of the world.*

Management models:

> *When it comes to museum management, there is one area where I disagree with certain aspects of the North American view of what makes a good director. Consultants insist that anyone who is a good 'manager' can be a good museum director. I disagree. My point of reference is the European model, which requires that the director first be a specialist in the museum field, with a university degree. Afterwards, if he wishes, he can take management training to hone his skills. Of course, management is a part of my job – a large part, in fact. I divide my time between three tasks: fundraising, artistic and scholarly management, and the general administration of the museum. But to be a good museum director, you have to be an expert first, because, as a director, the fundamental principles guiding your actions have much more to do with the museum's mission – that is, the preservation and dissemination of your collection – than with notions of profitability. Today, museum directors are under a great deal of pressure to position their institutions in the free market, but in doing so they must choose what risks are acceptable. They have to draw a line between what can be done and what cannot be done. Private donors and partners often have good ideas, but, given the nature of the museum's products, those*

ideas may not work in a museum. In your capacity as director, you have to be able to make decisions and impose those decisions.

Social challenges

Cultural diversity:

One thing we must always keep in mind is that, to a certain extent, museums represent a political statement on society and the state. In order to contribute to the world dialogue and foster a better understanding of cultural diversity, the world's four leading museums – the Louvre, the British Museum, the museums grouped under the Berlin Museum and the Hermitage – reached an agreement two years ago to coordinate their actions and reaffirm certain commitments. For the moment, our focus is Islamic art, in order to make it better known. Together, we are working on the cultural and political front in the hope of fostering a world dialogue that promotes respect for cultural diversity.

Values and future generations:

The museum has an ongoing responsibility to educate. This is a key component of our mission. We must teach and set an example. Through its exhibitions, educational workshops, conferences, digital collections, scholarly references, the richness of its collections and its state-of-the-art technology and access to computers, the museum can guide young people and transmit strong values that will influence their actions. The museum must also work to develop the public's interest in contemporary art. This is part of its educational mandate, and it is one of my priorities for the coming years. Contemporary art is poorly represented in our collections. It is therefore important that the Hermitage establish partnerships with other world museums in order to disseminate the most significant examples of this type of art.

Conclusion

The State Hermitage Museum is one of the world's oldest and most prestigious museums. In this chapter we have traced the evolution of the institution through an examination of some of the many challenges it has faced over the years. In particular we have examined the period of major upheaval brought on by the end of perestroika. During these particularly trying years, the Hermitage was forced to review its structure in order to adapt to the political and economic changes sweeping through Russia. At the height of the turmoil, the Museum appointed a new director, Mikhaïl Piotrovsky. We have highlighted here some of the principles and business processes adopted by the new director in order to manage the institution and deal with the crisis. Having successfully guided the Hermitage through the transition to the new reality of Russia, Piotrovsky now faces equally important challenges that require reflection and choices at the ethical, strategic, organizational, commercial and political levels. For the Hermitage (and for its leadership), the challenges of the 21st century are possibly even more formidable.

Acknowledgments

We would like to acknowledge that this chapter is based on case study # 9 40 2007 038, *Mikhail Piotrovsky et le Musée de l'Ermitage*, by Sylvie Cameron & Laurent Lapierre and published by the HEC Montréal Center for Case Studies. It was then subsequently published in the *International Journal of Arts and Cultural Management* 2007, volume 10, number 1 Fall 2007 pp. 65-77 as 'Mikhaïl Piotrovsky and the State Hermitage Museum'. We want to thank the authors for permission to reprint it here in a slightly altered form.

Questions

1. What challenges did Mikhaïl Piotrovsky face after Perestroika, and how would they have impacted on the Hermitage Museum?

2. Mikhaïl Piotrovsky engaged the help of the international community to protect the Hermitage. Can you discuss why he did this, how he did this, and what the advantages and disadvantages of this approach were?

3. The Hermitage has significance for the Russian people in many different ways. Can you discuss the actions of Mikhaïl Piotrovsky to save the Hermitage in the context of its meaning for the Russian people and whether his actions will have had any impact on this, both positively and negatively?

References

Bogdanov, A 2003, 'Technologies and the Hermitage: New Opportunities', *Museum International* (UNESCO, Paris), number 217, pp. 29-31.

'Bringing Modern Art to Palace Square' 2005, Interview with Thomas Krens in *Hermitage Magazine* (St. Petersburg), number 5 (Summer), pp. 41-5.

'The Director's Vision' 2005, Interview with Mikhaïl Piotrovsky in *Hermitage Magazine* (St. Petersburg), number 5 (Summer), pp. 51-5.

Gibson, S 1996, 'The State Hermitage Museum: A Modern Challenge', *Museum International* (UNESCO, Paris), number 190, pp. 46-50.

Gibson, S 2003a, 'The Hermitage and Institutional Change: A Leap into the Twenty-first Century.' *Museum International* (UNESCO, Paris), no 217, p. 20-26.

Gibson, S 2003b, *The Hermitage UNESCO Project*. St. Petersburg: UNESCO.

Shvidkovsky, D, Lukin, V, Norman, G, Yawein, O & N, 2005, 'The Greater Hermitage' *Hermitage Magazine* (St. Petersburg), number 5 (Summer), pp. 18-35.

Haltunen, M 2003, 'The Greater Hermitage: A Grand Future', *Museum International* (UNESCO, Paris), number 217, pp. 33-8.

Norman, G, *Hermitage Magazine*. 2004/05, State Hermitage Museum, St. Petersburg, Issue 4 (Winter), pp.34-8.

Lamarche, B 2005, 'Le MoMA et l'Ermitage en expansion', *Le Devoir* (Montréal), 24 May, p. B8.

Piotrovsky, M 2003, 'The Hermitage through the Centuries', *Museum International* (UNESCO, Paris), number 217, pp. 9-11.

Piotrovsky, BB and Suslov V A 1990, 'Introduction' In *Paintings in the Hermitage* by C Eisler. New York: Stewart, Tabori & Chang.

Rey, MP 2002, *Le dilemme russe.* Paris: Flammarion.

Rey, MP, Blum, A, Mespoulet, M, de Tinguy, A and Wild, G 2005, *Les Russes : de Gorbatchev à Poutine.* Paris: Armand Colin.

Soldatenko, A 2003, 'Hermitage Merchandising and International Marketing' *Museum International* (UNESCO, Paris), number 217, pp. 75-8.

Vilinbakhov, G 2003, 'The Hermitage: Diverse and Vast' *Museum International* (UNESCO, Paris), number 217, p. 200.

Vison, I 2003, Editorial. *Museum International* (UNESCO, Paris), number 217, pp. 6-7.

Chapter 2

The leadership style of Mira Trailović
An entrepreneurial spirit in a bureaucratic world

Milena Dragićević Šešić

Background

Introduction

This study explores the leadership style of theatre director, producer, and manager Mira Trailović (1924-1989). Her personal story is one of professional development within the field of theatre in Yugoslavia but it is also a story about the social and cultural development of Belgrade and Yugoslavia from 1956 to 1989 (the period of her most intensive professional activity), to which she contributed a great deal.

A major concern in this essay is to what extent Trailović's leadership capacities contributed to the development of *new organizational forms* in culture, of *new managerial methods* (adaptable quality management), and to *specific organizational cultures* (Dragićević Šešić & Dragojević 2005). In addition, there is consideration of the extent to which those leadership capacities contributed to the changing horizons of expectations within the cultural field, as well as their impact on opinion-makers and political leaders in Socialist Yugoslavia (specifically expectations regarding the aesthetic and ethical values of theatre performances).

This study is designed to elucidate what qualities distinguished Trailović and made her successful at a time when leaders were predominantly men who were drawn from the ranks of the Yugoslav Partisans. These 'men in charge', who came from a working class background, served the official state ideology while Trailović stood in opposition to everything they represented.

The methodology presented here comprises archival analysis, bibliographic research, interviews with key collaborators, and, the personal experiences of the author of this text. As a student I had an internship at the Belgrade International Theater Festival (BITEF) in 1973 and 1974 where I was able to work closely with Trailović. This experience was recorded in an internship 'diary' and takes the form of ethnographic research, which was in accordance with the university curricular demands at that time.

Context

After World War II, Yugoslavia entered a period of 'renewal and construction'. The country was liberated by its own resistance movement emanating from the Yugoslav Partisans (under the leadership of Josip Broz Tito). This differentiated Yugoslavia from other East European countries where 'freedom' and an ensuing communist social order were secured with the assistance of Soviet Red Army tanks. In Yugoslavia the enthusiasm surrounding the vision of a federal state of social and multi-ethnic justice was shared by the majority of the population, except for farmers, (who resisted entering *kolkhozes* until 1948 and ultimately succeeded in retaining their small land ownership[1]), and small portions of the urban bourgeois population, (which had longed for a lost democracy). This small segment of critical intelligentsia was isolated and silenced. Those who did raise their voices were imprisoned or exiled, which has been well-described in the autobiographical trilogy *The Years the Locusts Have Devoured* (1997-2000) by Borislav Pekić.

Perhaps it helps if we introduce the notion of a *ketman*[2] (Milosz 1987), which is used to explain the 'intellectual allure' of socialism and different collaborative practices with socialist regimes among intellectuals in post-war Central and Eastern Europe. In the case of Trailović we can use this concept to explore how it was possible for a non-party member of bourgeois origin to advance within the communist system and become a leader of the cultural awakening in Yugoslavia. Among other things she created the first platform for the gathering of Eastern and Western 'dissidents' and provocative artistic movements in the 1960s.[3] The peak

---

[1] This was Tito's only 'failure' and the reason why villages were not part of a developmental socialist vision. (Đukić-Dojčinović, 1997)

[2] Milosz described the practice of a *ketman* as paying lip service to authorities while concealing personal opposition. However, the case studies he described cannot apply to Trailović as she never joined the communist party and was never part of the socialist nomenclature (which was possible in Yugoslavia as opposed to Poland and other socialist states).

[3] For the first several editions of BITEF, financing to bring American troupes such as Living Theatre, Schechner, Schumann and Bread and Puppet did not come from the American embassy, as all of these troupes were part of the anti-war civil movements. BITEF also invited Grotowsky, Esrig, Krejča, Menzel and many others who had been part of dissident movements in Poland, Romania and the USSR. By coming to the festival, these artists had to overcome numerous obstacles raised in their own countries to prevent them from communicating with the rest of the world. BITEF was also a platform where theatres from East and West Berlin often met each other – and that was a significant part of Trailović's cultural diplomacy technique. See

of Trailović's career was reached when she was invited by Jack Lang, the French Minister of Culture, to be the artistic leader of the Théâtre des Nations in France. However, this international acknowledgement was considered a 'step too far' back home and led to an attempt to remove Trailović from Atelje 212, the Belgrade experimental theatre which she had founded.

To understand the context in which Trailović developed her cultural activity it is important to emphasize that in 1948 Yugoslavia was expelled from the Cominform[4] and as such, left the sphere of influence of the Soviet Union. In 1953 Yugoslavia began introducing self-management as a governing system in both enterprises and public institutions (Horvat, Markovic & Supek 1975). By the end of the 1950s Yugoslavia became one of the founding countries of the non-aligned movement (Kullaa 2011). Yugoslavia demonstrated its willingness to create a 'different socialism' – socialism with a human face, which focused on 'the worker and the dismantling of the power of the state' (Wilmer 2002, p. 88).

In Yugoslavia, cultural policy of the postwar period went through several phases: from *socialist realism and a repressive cultural model* (1945–1953) to a period of *democracy in culture* (1953–1974), when two parallel processes were identified – one related to state and ideological control and the other to a creative approach, which slowly gained a wider space for artistic freedom. This meant 'by the end of the 1960s and beginning of the 1970s, many new institutions and prestigious international festivals for different art forms had been established' (Compendium, Serbian profile, 2011, accessed 10 December 2011). The third phase, *decentralization and self-management* (1974–1989), reformed the entire cultural system. *Self-managing communities of interest* were introduced and 'free labor exchanges' facilitated closer links among cultural institutions and local economies through theatre communities, private galleries, etc. This process ended in the mid-1980s with the rise of strong nationalist movements which emerged amongst political and cultural institutions (a process which was, paradoxically, endorsed by the liberalization of the media which began after Tito's death). This new phase of cultural policy became known as the *culture of nationalism* (1990–2000).

Approaches

The story of Mira Trailović's cultural leadership begins in the early 1950s when, as a recently graduated theatre director (she was already employed while a student as a radio announcer in April 1945[5]), she started creating an informal circle of

---

more: http://www.bitef.rs/festival/?pg=simple&jez=en&smpl=festival, accessed on 10 January 2012.

[4] The Cominform (the Communist Information Bureau) was initiated by Stalin in 1947 as a grouping of key European communist parties.

[5] To understand the meaning of this simple fact it is important to know that although Belgrade was liberated, the war for the liberation of Yugoslavia was on-going (the German army had surrendered in Yugoslavia only on 15 May 1945) and radio broadcasting was considered a major propaganda tool. The entire radio staff was still in Partisan uniforms and all of those in

intellectuals. These intellectuals would normally not belong to the same arena: communist intellectuals, activists (who had both official and non-official power in society) and bourgeois intellectuals whose progressive articles and essays Trailović discovered in the back pages of various cultural reviews and newspapers. She was already planning to change the artistic scene and thus create different platforms and opportunities for creative expressions and ideas, for both herself and others.

Trailović began directing dual-format radio dramas in 1953 that were staged simultaneously in front of an audience, which in Yugoslavia, were unthinkable prior to her pioneering input. She included adaptations of the work of Henry James, Remarque, Rostand, Huxley, Tagore, Flaubert, Shaw, Williams, O' Neill, and also many Japanese, Chinese and domestic authors. For Atelje 212, she directed Goethe, Sartre, Ionesco, Camus, Weiss and Stoppard. However, her major successes were local staging of *Hair* (the first after Broadway), *Who's Afraid of Virginia Wolf*, and *Miracle in Šargan* by Ljubomir Simović. As a result she was invited to Paris for the Théâtre des Nations festival in 1977, as well as for many other international festivals and tours. *Miracle in Šargan* became one of the longest-running performances in Yugoslavia.

Trailović came upon the idea that Belgrade was in need of another type of theatre — a studio-theatre. She initiated numerous discussions in Belgrade cafes, knowing that she would have to find those with not only personal charisma and authority but also 'functional' authority, which would grant social access. At this time 'functional' authority was linked to participation in the wartime resistance on the side of the Yugoslav Partisans. That was the reason why she assembled a variety of people (establishment academics, dissident writers, etc.) who on first sight had nothing in common.

She succeeded in developing her theatre space as an organization that would place its mission in concordance with the international *zeitgeist*, while adhering to certain social norms and regulations.

These included:

- Atelje 212 would be created in 1956 as the first open theatre venue, using an empty room (that could fit 212 seats) in the offices of the daily newspaper *Borba*;
- Creating a repertory which would combine the international vanguard with contemporary Yugoslav dramatic writing;
- Transforming Atelje 212 in 1961 – in spite of her vision – into a theatre with a permanent company to accommodate the wishes of Bojan Stupica[6] in becoming the new director;

---

front of microphones were members of the Communist Youth or Communist Party. Trailović was an exception. (Pašić 2006, 38)

[6] Stupica was a famous Slovenian theatre director who had become the first artistic director of the Yugoslav Dramatic Theatre in Belgrade when it was established as the only official state-run

- Building a venue for Atelje 212 in 1962 and persuading Stupica (an architect by education) to realize the project himself;

- Engaging visual artists to create conceptual installations in the windows of Atelje 212 for each premiere (Dadić Dinulović, 2007);

- Creating the Belgrade International Theater Festival (BITEF) in 1967 together with Jovan Ćirilov;

- Discovering and opening hundreds of non-theatrical spaces for theatre performances (mostly for BITEF) together with Ćirilov, Todor Lalicki, Arsa Jovanović, and other members of the BITEF team (operational factories, stone mines, shops, department stores, underground passages, powder storage, film studios, parks, etc.); and

- Organizing theatre tours in the United States, Iran, Mexico (15 countries and 26 cities) and making Yugoslav theatre culture present in the world through participating in international festivals in Paris, Persepolis, and many other locations.

All of these achievements remain to this day, and retain the organizational culture and philosophy determined by Trailović and her co-founders. This represents an organizational philosophy of the theatre as a laboratory, a space of innovation for research and risky endeavors, but also the theatre as a space for gathering progressive arts and intellectual ideas.

> The 'laboratory' is an organization that places innovation at the centre of its programme, either in its local community or on an international scale. Such organizations are built on the principle of excellence in arts production ... organizations that are truly innovative experiment with forms and methods of artistic expression, sometimes destroying them or putting a question mark over their relevance. At the same time, they must seek and find suitable organisational forms within which they can operate in an appropriate manner (Dragićević Šešić & Dragojević 2005, p. 148).

In short, every program and every institution Trailović created and managed was a complex organism with several streams:

a) an esthetic, vanguard experimentation platform (Bekett, Ionesco, Boto Strauss, etc.);

b) a social research and political criticism platform (Bulgakov, Ćosić's *The Role of My Family in the World Revolution*); and

c) a popular representation of mentality through stimulating young domestic talent to create works which could be appreciated by large audiences (*Radovan III* by Dušan Kovačević).

Sometimes these three streams would unite in one performance (e.g. *Le Roi Ubu*), but in most cases they were present in a complex process of curating the theatre or festival repertory (for BITEF, besides the first two streams, the third was different:

---

theatre in 1947. He left for Zagreb (Croatia) in 1955 and returned to Belgrade by the invitation of Trailović, who viewed him as a strategic appointment for political and artistic reasons.

the representation of theatre traditions, like Bunraku, Buto, Kathakali, Karagjoz, Sicilian puppets, etc.). For Trailović, a key element of the 'laboratory' method was its functioning as an open platform for expression. As each of her endeavors quickly gained a reputation, an atmosphere of 'chaotic openness' was created in the organization which was exactly what was needed, in the period of a bureaucratic socialist institutional system in Yugoslavia.

Challenges

For those who can recall the *institutionalized* system of culture in socialist states, it can be understood how difficult it was to create something outside of bureaucratic restrictions. At that time the term 'private initiative' was as much of a pejorative as was 'private interest' and if an idea was labeled as such, it meant that it was immediately discredited. Those who were inside the institutions and who sat on the committees were supposed to present ideas and initiatives in front of party officers or city authorities. However, if you were only an individual artist or independent group of artists and intellectuals, you had to find a way to promote your ideas and achieve your goals between a rock and a hard place.

Trailović forged paths that led toward substantial social change (introducing the spirit of cosmopolitanism, citizenship, 'urbanity'[7] as a value, etc.). At the same time she was a 'PR machine', capable of 'spinning' and creating campaigns by herself in a world where those terms had not even been known and where similar activities were considered blasphemous for cultural organizations. Trailović compensated for a lack of authority by choosing to be surrounded by people who did have formal (mostly political) authority. She knew that she had to show how close she was to them, so, for example she would call them 'partners' in front of the collective). And she would try to make sure that they would be present at every première at her theatre. For example, to show that the festival had political importance and value, Mira invited the mayor of the city to make a speech to open the festival at BITEF.

The phrases 'lobbying' and 'advocacy' were not known at that time but she used many related techniques in promoting her entrepreneurial ideas. In this sense Atelje 212 became a mythical place for gathering the city's intellectual elite. Its geographic position between Radio Belgrade and Television Belgrade was in a street which everybody had evaluated as 'non-theatrical'[8] (a street without cultural infrastructure). Even the free coffee that was served in the lobby during

---

[7] Under socialism, urbanity was linked to a despised 'bourgeois' way of life, as the official discourse emphasized the working class as the 'actor of changes'. However, theatre dramaturgy was conceived mostly from international or domestic classics where key players had been those issued from bourgeois urban circles. For example, it was only through the repertory of Atelje 212 that the first plays of Aleksandar Popović, linked to the life of small craftsmen or clerks in suburbia, started to challenge the official discourse.

[8] Cultural life in Belgrade was concentrated in a very narrow zone which ended with the Politika publishing house and Radio Belgrade. Trailović chose a location for Atelje 212 just outside of this zone.

performance breaks was a part of a strategic process – it made the Atelje 212 audience feel like friends of the house (drinking coffee is a common ritual of friendship in the Balkans).[9]

By making the public identify her and her theatre with an important group of policy-makers, Trailović succeeded in obtaining the transfer of necessary political authority to herself during socialism. This was a time when the major policy decisions were made within the Communist Party governing structures. She clearly understood this parallel functioning of the system and was not wasting her time on those personalities who had only formal (nominal) power (for example ministers, or city administrators for culture). Trailović would communicate only to those who had, because of their party functions, real decision-making power.

Those functionaries (she chose the most educated and visionary among them) found their interests to be closely-aligned with this woman who was opening new doors for Yugoslavia in societies where they did not have much influence, particularly in the Western world. Her entrepreneurialism coincided with the political opening of the society and the desire to depict the Yugoslav self-management system to the rest of the world as free and democratic. Atelje 212 as a 'studio theatre'[10] and later BITEF were excellent platforms for this aim. As a result of Trailović's influence on political elites, Belgrade became a much more cosmopolitan city.

In 34 interviews with her collaborators (Pašić 2006), numerous qualities are attributed to Trailović and many metaphors are used to describe her. Trailović's leadership pattern was based on her specific individual characteristics (the trait theory of leadership) including her patterns of behavior, thoughts, and emotions. These traits adapted to different situations and in different environments and became known as the 'Mira style'. By applying the *leader attribute pattern approach*, we can identify what her abilities, skills, and expertise were — what allowed her the chance to have real personal authority in a cultural field before obtaining functional authority (or 'political' authority, which she never had).[11]

---

[9] Research on Belgrade theatre audiences shows the extreme loyalty of the Atelje 212 audience towards what they call 'our' theatre. This is the only theatre in Belgrade where a large audience share claims to see the same performances more than three times (up to an amazing 20 times for *Le Roi Ubu* and *Radovan the III*).

[10] For the second presentation after the opening of Atelje 212 in 1956, *Waiting for Godot* was performed after it had been prevented from premiering at Belgrade Dramatic Theatre earlier in 1954. Inviting this performance was in itself a political act – an act of confrontation. Belgrade Dramatic Theatre had been the leading theatre in the beginning of the 50s and it never recovered after this act of censorship (as the majority of the ensemble left following the political crisis).

[11] Political authority in the cultural sphere (a political position within the Communist Party) was extremely effective. It was sufficient that a person with political authority, often without personal authority (when any expertise was lacking) and without functional authority (not being a director or manager), expressed his or her negative opinion about a theatre or film project and then that institution would censor itself immediately.

I have grouped the characteristics of Trailović's managerial personality as explicitly expressed in published texts and the afore-mentioned interviews into four categories (Adizes 1999), all of which respond to different managerial and leadership domains (PAEI):

- *Production:* convincing, devoted (to the job), decisive, perfectionist, steady, with a sense of balance, credible.

- *Administration:* skillful in selecting collaborators, serious, persistent, cautious as a housewife, determined, good listener, respecting interlocutors, resourceful.

- *Entrepreneurialism:* energetic, pervasive, penetrating, ready for action, skilled, risk-taking, enthusiastic, ingenious.

- *Integration:* charming, kind, vivacious, amiable, pleasing, seductive, communicative, sociable, considerate of others but also self-centred, Machiavellian, eruptive, witty, maneuvering, unscrupulous, impatient, choleric, manipulator.

As often related in interviews, she was 'a person with governing skills'. However, those 'governing skills' are explained in an ambiguous way. With regards to the way she ran organizations, it was often said that she 'enjoyed governing' and managed the theatre or the festival by 'deliberately creating chaos' through 'pulling the rug out from underneath our feet'. Furthermore, it was said that 'she was keeping us – her employees – alert all the time'. This method of management, while not producing efficiency, kept the organization from adopting 'routines' and prevented 'organizational sclerosis' (Klaic 2008) while incubating alternate approaches and new, creative solutions.

Metaphors used to describe Trailović's personality both in the East and in the West (especially in France) have been not only picturesque but also extremely significant for her original managerial and leadership style. These include: a Don Quixote fighter, the Theatrical Lioness, the Lady from the Big World, the Woman of the World, the Andre Malraux of our culture, Big Mama, a Royal fleet, a phenomenon, a personality with a hundred faces, a person of wide horizons, a person of big moves (gestures), the woman who shines (*une femme qui rayonne*), a bulldozer in a fur coat, a volcano ('from volcanic magma the best crystals are created'), the Iron Lady, the Tigress with Velvet Claws, a woman with a masque, a 'monster' of a woman, a paradox, Noah's Ark …

Trailović presented herself differently, detesting a lot of the descriptives which the press used in writing about her. In 1977 she was listed as one of the 10 most popular public personalities in Yugoslavia – due to the fact that she became a media personality at a moment when media outlets were reluctant to write about politicians. Thus, athletes and personalities from the media and cultural sphere dominated public opinion political surveys. She did not like to be called witty, enthusiastic, persistent or skilled. She insisted that she was a theatre creator, whose main characteristics were responsibility and critical self-awareness. She used to say: 'Only a responsible person is working well, achieving excellence in results' (Pašić 2006, p. 19).

It is obvious from this analysis of the perceptions of her collaborators about the extent to which she had developed a charismatic or referent authority. However, Trailović was at the same time an authority with a wide range of expertise. Her cognitive abilities were numerous and joined with a set of socially-important motives and ambitions. Something that was neglected in discussions about Trailović was her rhetorical strategies and storytelling management capacities. These are the 'obligatory' leadership skills in an oral culture such as what existed in Serbia (until 1920 a majority of the population was illiterate, so the values and ways of thinking are still linked to this 'technology of communication' which stimulates mythical thinking [see Lorrimer 1994, p. 12-13]). Her extensive knowledge of world literature and contemporary dramaturgy enabled her to use citations and terms that made any issue 'mythical' or 'poetic'. Even today her friends still remember the Baudelaire verses she used to recite. Foreign theatre artists that she used to meet would be 'conquered' in a few minutes by an appropriate story she would choose 'just for them', showing deep respect and careful attention.

There were often difficult situations in which she had to apply all of those contradictory skills, where she had to be more of a 'diplomat' than a 'manager'. As in numerous cases in socialist countries, suspicion often arose that in a certain text there was a direct critique of political authority (read: Tito or the Communist Party). If Trailović realized this possibility in time she would react immediately, trying to prevent the gossip that would spread and reach authorities by creating counter-intuitive 'gossip' and 'promotional campaigns'. This meant not confronting accusations directly but rather underlying other positive values of the performance instead.

If a reaction arrived abruptly, or as in the case of *Hair* four years after its première,[12] she would withdraw without any comments or say something such as: 'After four years of performing, *Hair* is not what it was as the 'tribe', composed of amateurs, did not have the necessary discipline to sustain the show throughout this length of time, and therefore it should not remain in the repertory'. If the party journal (*Communist*) attacked her for introducing Western values she would never respond directly but rather find a way to give an interview in some alternative publication to explain her position. She would fight using her networks, appearing in public with friends from powerful political circles, and speaking with them about new projects and ideas. She would also personally greet important political and public figures coming to the theatre and do everything necessary to distribute tickets directly to them.

---

12 The students of the military academy came to a performance in 1973. It was a moment of political crisis – in both Croatia and Serbia leadership was removed and the cultural scene began to be criticized under the label 'black wave', which meant representing life in Yugoslavia in dark shades. The anti-militarism of *Hair* 'offended' students of the military academy and they wrote a letter accusing the theatre of promoting defeatism and presenting the importance of the Army in ambivalent terms.

Reinforcing her position among political circles, Trailović would succeed in widening the spaces of freedom every day by her work in the theatre (Ćirilov in Pašić 2006, p. 103). In delicate situations she would apply different defense instruments:

> Her mechanism of suppression was so powerful that it would deserve a clinical (research) study, as she could equally suppress small as well as the biggest issues, both private and public. (Jovanović 1989)

For example, when Atelje 212 introduced the plays of Aleksandar Popović (until 1968 only four of his plays had been performed), *Kape dole (Hats Down!)* had been staged just three times when the telephone rang with the advice not to run it anymore. In a self-managing system, a system without official censorship, such a decision had to be made by the theatre board. In this instance Trailović simply took it upon herself to state: *Tonight the performance is cancelled*. In the following month, it disappeared from the repertory.

In this instance, gossip had travelled around the city before reaching the theatre, insinuating that the two main roles were satirizing Tito and his wife. In addition, the title *Kape dole!* could be written as *KaPe dole!*, which, if pronounced a certain way, meant 'down with the Communist Party'. Immediately after this scandal, Trailović placed a new production in the repertory by the same author. This new play dealt with the 1968 revolution and focused on the role of those who strangled this uprising. Here, she had entered into the battle thinking that she would win, but in the self-management system it was not only the artistic staff that had voting power. The theatre board which included 'outside' members (delegates from the community and usually those that had been cultural workers close to the ruling party), voted together with the technicians, to stop working on the performance. It would seem that there were many 'failures' and a lot of censorship. This was not the case however, regardless of the fact that in each performance there were usually words which represented a provocation to the system (for example: *Proletarians of all countries, be serious!*).

To prevent her theatre employees from becoming depressed and losing courage, Trailović would do everything necessary to try to save the performance. If she was not successful, like in the case of *Hats Down!,* she would find another solution for 'keeping the team spirit up' by suppressing the memory of the difficult incident. In the case of *Hats Down!*, that meant undertaking a successful tour in the United States during the revolutionary year of 1968, ending with her selection of the most critical contemporary performances for BITEF.

Trailović even succeeded in temporarily increasing the space of freedom in the Soviet Union, where she arrived with her theatre program in May 1968 (after several previous invitations were cancelled). Mrs Furceva, the then Soviet Minister of Culture, asked Trailović to postpone the trip only a day before she was scheduled to leave Belgrade. Trailović responded by saying that the set design was already on its way (which was not true). When she arrived in Moscow, Trailović asked how many tickets had been sold, and the answer was all of them. But the Ministry took steps to insure that very few audience members were in attendance. The auditorium was half-empty at the first performance. Trailović then sent a message to the radio broadcast, *Voice of America* announcing her open invitation for everybody to come to the theatre to see *'Who's Afraid of Virginia Woolf?'*. A large number of people appeared and Trailović had to personally fight with the Soviet guards so that everybody who came without tickets, was able to get a seat.

Outcomes

After analyzing leadership styles developed within political theories, as well as those within managerial and organizational sciences, it seems to me that they are not sufficient for understanding artistic leadership. Instead, cultural management and cultural leadership theories must contribute their own definition of leadership styles[13] as well as organizational cultures and organizational philosophies. In many cases the managers of art institutions are artists themselves and therefore lead by different (mostly artistic) visions. They are generally not obsessed with the efficiency of a production or its cost-effectiveness, neither for having a 'strategic plan' (which might be more inhibiting then inspirational). Any future research on arts management should focus more on visions as strategic energizers for artistic collectives.

One of those theories that has defined profiles in (art) management emphasizes six leadership dimensions: charismatic/value-based, team-oriented, participative, humane-oriented, autonomous, and self-protective.[14] Regardless, these theories are more logical for leaders of art organizations than theories in which 'a job analysis of leadership reveals three components: planning, organizing, and persuading'. (Coffin 1944) These features would be components of any managerial job aimed at achieving efficiency but none of them rely on innovation, or lead an organization towards an uncertain future — a future which is presented as a leader's vision.

In this respect it is interesting to see how Trailović, 'the citizen of the world' (she would prefer this term, although 'woman of the world' with its ambiguous meaning in the Serbian language was used much more often), coming from the European margins, succeeded in creating several institutions with unique organizational cultures. She succeeded in creating many informal national and international theatrical, artistic, and intellectual networks, around BITEF[15] or the BITEF Theatre[16] and with even more circulating around Atelje 212.

---

[13]Autocratic or authoritarian style, participative or democratic, laissez-faire or free rein, narcissistic leadership, toxic leadership, etc. None of these are applicable in the case of Mira Trailović.

[14]http://www.andrews.edu/services/jacl/article_archive/2006_summer/6_br_globe_(2004) .pdf, accessed 15 November 2011.
[15] In 1999, BITEF was the first international theatre festival to be awarded the Special Prize *Premio Europa Per Il Teatro*, the European Theatre Prize. (A project launched by the European Commission in 1986 as a prize for personalities or companies that 'have contributed to the

In the local setting this network was her wide artistic circle that encompassed such personalities as the writer Danilo Kiš, the painter and filmmaker Mića Popović,[17] and the politician Milan Vukos, to cite only those who 'indirectly' contributed to the development of her artistic and managerial vision. They acted as her interlocutors and supporters in difficult moments of decision-making. From this wide circle she utilized the most needed personality at any given moment — either just for consultancy (about a new Sartre text to be put on the repertory, for example), for lobbying the authorities, or to mediate some internal conflict.

In creating institutions Trailović also relied on a team she personally selected – from writers and translators, to box office managers and coffee-makers and even temporary employees for BITEF such as troupe managers and drivers. Her team was made up of extraordinary individuals of very different capacities and interests. Many of them are, still to this day, leading other innovative institutions or programs, such as the Centre for Cultural Decontamination in Belgrade (Borka Pavićević), Yugoslav Drama Theatre (Jovan Ćirilov), OSF Support Program for countries of the Western Balkans (Beka Vučo), etc.

It is obvious that Trailović's overall success depended much on the teams she developed. These teams were based on the combination of different principles and creating conditions for complementary partnerships within a managerial team. The partnerships were always with the top people in their professions and based on the diverse visions she would see for and with them. BITEF as a platform offered the world as an attainable horizon — both geographically and metaphorically. During the 1990s the BITEF Theatre became a space of refuge for performing artists who wanted to experiment within their disciplines[18] in the most difficult times of war, the dissolution of the country, international embargoes, economic crises, etc.

This illustration about how a person becomes a charismatic leader within an administrative, bureaucratic socialist model shows the need for a complex personality with comprehensive and complementary convergent skills and abilities. Such a person should be fearless in front of political authorities (or at least should not show fear, thereby giving confidence to other team members). They should also have a capacity for 'manipulation' in relation to persons who have political and formal functional authority. Above all they should have expertise, motivation, energy and a high sense of responsibility for the artistic as

---

realisation of cultural events that promote understanding and the exchange of knowledge between peoples').

[16] BITEF Theatre is now a member of ENPARTS (European Network of Performing Arts).

[17] Popović was associated with the 'black wave' in Yugoslav cinema through his anti-traditional, oppositional and critical films.

[18] The BITEF Theatre was oriented toward non-verbal performance and other experimenting and was an open venue with regards to both its own productions and also guest productions. Under the artistic directorship of Ivana Vujić in the 1990s, BITEF Theatre created the festival *Airplane without Engine* for site-specific performances. Today, BITEF Theatre is still devoted to innovative forms, mostly in the domain of contemporary dance.

well as the larger cultural community, so that they can fight for certain ethical and aesthetic values which then work to liberate expression and creativity.

Conclusion

Mira Trailović's uniqueness as a leader was in enabling others to share her vision and inspiring people to look towards a better future. She was more of a transformational leader than a transactional one. In a socialist republic that kept 'utopia' under its tight ideological control, people were encouraged to only look at the here and now, to be active locally and to leave big ideas and projects to the 'real' leaders (the Communist Party as such). Trailović did not accept the *status quo* and chose to take on the role of a bold creator and manager. What authority she had was based on her personal qualities and she would state:

> *If your words can change the artistic value of the performance, its process and understanding – that is authority. This authority is not given by function or by anyone outside the theater (Pašić 2006, p. 117).*

She also had to struggle with herself in facing a 'founder's trap' (Adizes 1999) in which she was caught. In avoiding the expected humiliation of not being re-elected to her position leading Atelje 212, as her international success raised a lot of jealousy,[19] she made a decision to resign from the theatre. This left the option to her successors as to whether they would continue a similar complex path or choose one of the 'repertory lines' she had traced. This fate shows the difficulty of real leadership, given that for the next 25 years her successors chose to continue only the most popular aspect of the work of Atelje 212: domestic contemporary comedy. However, the present director, Kokan Mladenović, using the existing memory of and respect for Atelje 212 as a 'critical social' institution, has tried to return this critical social component to the theatre. In deference to this illustrious tradition he has named the last three seasons: *Revolution, EX/NEXT YU*, and *Utopia*.

Trailović's leadership capacities contributed to the development of *new organizational forms* in culture (experimental studio theatre, theatre as open venue, etc.), of new *managerial methods* (destabilization of teams to avoid stale routines), and to different and *specific organizational cultures* (entrepreneurial culture, laboratory organization, activist organization) not usually found in public institutions of socialist states. In her own way, without direct confrontation with authorities, Trailović fought against censorship and the artistic marginalization of the country, while at the same time succeeded in putting Yugoslavia on the map of international theatre.

---

[19] Among all the directors of different cultural institutions, Trailović was attacked the most and criticized repeatedly in the press. For example, in each issue of the satirical magazine, *Jež*, she was represented as a powerful woman with bourgeois styling, a snobbish creature surrounded by 'trendy' Western artists.

Her collaborator, the writer and dissident Borislav Mihailovic Mihiz, has written several words regarding their generation in his *Autobiography about Others*, words which are very relevant in this context:

> *Every generation, each human being, is prone to believe in the specificity of their historical destiny. My generation, unfortunately, exhibits far too much evidence of this. In the entire history of modern Europe, except for the peers of Chateaubriand, there was no other generation in which political history was imprinting the many stamps of its numerous tumultuous turns, inscribing her fate on our skin and our souls. Born after World War I, we had to race across the field of life following large successive European and local reverberations (Mihajlović Mihiz 1995).*

This is very true for Trailović. When it was required of her she could turn left, right, or reverse course, but even with all of the necessary compromises, she never abandoned her ethics or the aesthetics of her theatre. Consequently, her influence went far beyond the institutions she created. Her work was inspirational for other artists who, following her example, lobbied the City of Belgrade and realized the creation of international festivals in other art domains: BEMUS for music, FEST for film, April encounters for visual arts, and more. Throughout these years Serbian cultural policy changed — it became much more open and conducive to innovation and experimentation; it became more tolerant toward social and political critique. This is the lasting legacy of Mira Trailović.

Questions

1. Mira Trailović used many different strategies to ensure that the work she believed in was presented. Can you discuss these strategies and reflect on their relevance in a contemporary context?

2. Discuss the ethical and political issues influencing the way Mira Trailović functioned as a leader. What was their impact on her work, and do you think she could have done things differently? If so, how? If not, why not?

3. Discuss the key elements of Mira Trailović's leadership approach, and evaluate its strengths and weaknesses.

References

2007, 50 years of Atelje 212, Belgrade.

Adizes, I 1991, *Mastering Change: The Power of Mutual Trust and Respect in Personal Life, Family Life, Business and Society*, Adizes Institute Publishing, Santa Barbara, California.

Adizes, I 1999, *Managing Corporate Lifecycles: How and Why Corporations Grow and Die and What to Do About It* (Revised Ed.), Prentice Hall, New Jersey.

Adizes, I 2004, *Leading the Leaders: How to Enrich Your Style of Management and Handle People Whose Style is Different from Yours*, Adizes Institute Publishing, Santa Barbara, California.

Burns, J McG 2010, *Leadership*, Harper Collins, New York.

Coffin, T E 1944, *The Journal of Abnormal and Social Psychology*, volume 39(1), January 1944, pp. 63-83. doi: 10.1037/h0054371

Collins, J 2001a, *Good to Great, Harper Collins*, New York.

Collins, J 2001b, 'The triumph of humility and fierce resolve', *Harvard Business Review*, 79 (1), pp. 67-76.

Council of Europe & EricArts 2011, Compendium, Serbian profile, accessed 10 December 2011.

Dadić Dinulović, T 2007, Theory of Display and Representation: The Theater Window and Window as a Theater, MA thesis, University of Arts, Belgrade.

Dinulović, R 1999, 'Ambijentalni prostori Bitef festival/Ambiental Scenic Spaces of Bitef Festival', Annual of Faculty of Dramatic Arts, Belgrade.

Đukić-Dojčinović, V 1997, Pravo na razlike selo – grad/Right to the Difference: Village – City, Zadužbina Andrejević, Belgrade.

Dragićević Šešić, M & Dragojević, S 2005, *Art Management in Turbulent Times, Adaptable Quality Management*, Boekmanstichtung and ECF, Amsterdam.

Horvat, B, Marković, M & Supek, R 1975, *Self-Governing Socialism: A Reader*, International Arts and Sciences Press, New York.

House, RJ, Hanges, PJ, Javidan, M, Dorfman, PW & Gupta, V (eds.) 2004, *Culture, Leadership, and Organizations: The GLOBE Study of 62 Societies*, Sage Publications, Thousand Oaks, London.

Jovanović, A 1989, *A Diary: Making of a Theater: Story of Bitef Theater*, manuscript.

Klaić, D 2008, 'Surviving the Cultural Shock: Cultural Institutions Facing Globalization and Multiculturalism', Zbornik radova Fakulteta dramskih umetnosti/Annual of Faculty of Dramatic Arts, #13-14, pp. 255-263.

Kullaa, R 2011, *Non-Alignment and its Origin in Cold War Europe: Yugoslavia, Finland and the Soviet Challenge*, I.B. Tauris, London.

Looseley, D 1990, 'The World Theatre Festival, Nancy, 1963–88: A Critique and a Retrospective', *New Theatre Quarterly*, 6, pp. 141-153 doi:10.1017/S0266464X00004218

Lorrimer, R & Scannell, P 1994, *Mass Communications: Comparative Introduction*, Manchester University Press, Manchester.

Mihajlović – Mihiz, B 1995, Autobiografija o drugima/*Autobiography about Others*, BIGZ, Belgrade.

Milosz, Cz 1987, *Zarobljeni um, BIGZ, Belgrade* (2001, Captive mind, Penguin, London).

Northouse, PG 2009, *Leadership: Theory and Practice*, Sage Publications, California, USA.

Pašić, F 2006 *Mira Trailović, Gospođa iz velikog sveta/Mira Trailović, lady from the world*, Theater museum Serbia, Belgrade.

Pekić, B 1987-1990, *Godine koje su pojeli skakavci/The Years the Locusts Have Devoured*, BIGZ, Belgrade.

Tichy, NM & David, OU 1984, The Leadership Challenge – A Call for the Transformational Leader, *Sloan Management Review*, Fall 1984.

Wilmer, F 2002, *The Social Construction of Man, the State, and War: Identity, Conflict, and Violence in Former Yugoslavia*, Routledge, New York.

Weber, M 1947, 'The Nature of Charismatic Authority and its Routinization' translated by AR Anderson and Talcott Parsons, *Theory of Social and Economic Organization*.

Chapter 3

Vladimir Misharin

Charisma and innovation in the modern Russian arts scene

IRINA KHIZHINSKAYA AND MARIA NAIMARK

Background

Introduction

According to Shakespeare: 'The more I give, the more there is to give'

According to the Russian writer Abramov: 'I'd rather not live if not in good conscience'.

Openness and friendliness in business and personal relationships (life credo of Vladimir Misharin).[1]

On his desk there is always a bunch of sharpened pencils, pointing upwards like a metaphor of ever-onwards movement and development. According to his own words, answering challenges for him is like an addiction that drives his decisions and deals.

The subject of our case is a charismatic and entrepreneurial Russian arts leader Vladimir Misharin. Every five to seven years he leaves his current successful position/organization and takes on a new challenge almost from zero. He started his leadership career at the age of 20 — very early, especially for Russia and

---

[1] All citations, unless otherwise specified are from a series of interviews granted by Vladimir Misharin to the authors of this chapter between November 28 and December 1, 2011 at his office in Sochi. All translations from original Russian for this work are made by Maria Naimark.

especially in the arts sector. For over 20 years he has made a successful career from starting as a young pioneers' camp director to being chief of the major cultural operator for the Sochi-2014 Cultural Olympiad as well as a Member of the Working Group on Culture of the Presidential Council of the Russian Federation, dealing with the preparation and operation of the XXII Olympic Winter Games.

In the middle of his current career Misharin came across a work of Vladimir Tarasov, organizer and leader of the Tallinn School of Management – *Technology of Life: Book for Heroes*. This handbook, which is not just for managers, suggests appointing the date of your death and making a perspective plan for your life till then (Tarasov 2007). Vladimir has followed this advice and found out that life is too short, and its meaning and success are in moving forward. In this movement he has never missed his chance for professional development; discovering different sides of leadership in the different art organizations, and everything he has touched has become successful.

In this work we set out not just to acquaint the reader with the early years and career of Vladimir Misharin, with his further progression as an art-leader and with the challenges and achievements at his current position. We also try to discover what drives him forward, as well as to learn more about the 'who', 'where', 'why', 'when' and 'what' lessons from his rich experience that are helping with his continuing development. In short, we are trying to prove that Misharin is a leader not just by position, but by nature and behavior.

Young Pioneers Camp[2]

Vladimir Misharin was born in 1967 in Poliovskoi – a small town on the territory in the Sverdlovskaya region at the centre of the Ural Mountains. His parents worked shifts at a local factory, so often one of them slept during the day. His sister studied at a musical school and needed complete silence for her exercises, so the young boy always had to behave quietly in their little flat.

This led him to a neighborhood children's photo studio, where very soon he was entrusted to conduct independent classes, together with a fully-equipped classroom and the keys. Misharin was merely 12 at that time.

Soon he got bored in the photo studio, and went looking for a new challenge. Thus, at school he became responsible for the Pioneers office. First he got a desk there, and then the keys to the room where he arranged everything according to his taste and preferences. But when the school director gave a pot of flowers, which Misharin had brought there, away to another classroom, Misharin left his duties at the Pioneers' office, and very soon after had taken full control of the school broadcasting centre, complete with regular programming and all-school broadcasting.

---

[2] The Young Pioneer Organization of the Soviet Union was a mass youth scout like organization for children of age 10–15 in the USSR between 1922 and 1991.

Like most Soviet school children during the summer vacations, parents regularly sent him to the Young Pioneers' Camp. And, of course, he became a leader there. One time, his older sister took him along to another camp where she had to complete her traineeship as a musical college student. The poor girl could not cope with a gang of adolescents, and her younger brother immediately came to the rescue. He was a contemporary of those teenagers, but soon became their tutor. By graduation time, Misharin had become absolutely indispensable at that camp and, by his own words, firmly decided to become a geography teacher, who, with the pointer in hand, would lead children by countries and continents.

For better or for worse, after the first year at the Sverdlovsk (now Yekaterinburg) Pedagogy Institute, Vladimir was called up for national service in the army, like every other young man of that age. That was during a period when the moratorium on calling up students for the army had been suspended. But even in the army, Misharin managed without delay to get into the élite ranks in East Germany, and then to be appointed as the head of the political and cultural centre of the division, where, as a consequence of successfully taking on these responsibilities, he got his own living space and never had to sleep in barracks again.

After the army Misharin returned to the Institute to continue his education and visited his former (not any more Pioneers) Camp – he had always kept in contact with its director. Good fortune was awaiting Misharin there. As it is said, 'every cloud has a silver lining'. A disaster happened – a considerable number of children fell ill with an intestinal infection, and all senior staff left for an official inquiry. Thus the camp was left unattended. Misharin took on the responsibility of sending children to hospitals, of communicating with parents, and of keeping everything in order. At the age of 20, and for the next seven years, he became the director of the Country Children's Health Camp, 'Vostok', with 300 children and 100 employees. He combined this work from the start with full-time study, then with teaching at the same Institute, followed by work at the professional ballet company and finally with the Yekaterinburg Actors House.

Misharin insists that he has never ever felt as self-confident and happy as he was during the 'Camp' years. Maybe that was the courage and confidence of youth!

The major lesson he learned was that nothing was impossible if he really wanted it, and that he could achieve each of his goals. But the most important thing, he says, is that older people trusted him and the younger ones followed him, and if something isn't working or if you can't gain agreement, do not bang your head against a wall. There is always another solution, direction or way through – just be able to see it and use it.

Theatre

Theatre entered his life via a box of marionettes, a birthday present. He wrote plays, sold tickets, arranged spectators and performed. From then on, there was 'theatre' in everything he did. He was a show-man and magician in the house of culture of his native town, and gave shows and concerts in the Camp and the army.

But a significant shift happened during his study years in Yekaterinburg which is the third biggest theatre centre in Russia. His favorite genre was musical comedy theatre. He was there six nights a week, and on this theatre's closed day he was in a different theatre.

By that time school-teaching was no longer a dream, it had become a reality. Pedagogical self-esteem had been reached first at the Camp, and then at his own Institute, where he started teaching. But his heart required something new, facing new and different challenges. That was the beginning of the 1990s – a time of big changes in the entire country. New initiatives and new enterprises were flooding all spheres of activity. New independent theatres appeared like mushrooms after rain.

On this wave Yekaterinburg became a Russian modern dance capital, and Vladimir Misharin joined one of these companies as a volunteer. There he started working in audience development: systematizing the advertising, implementing repertoire run planning, etc. Very rapidly he became director of that company – which was called Ballet Plus. But all this finished when one of the funders – a big bank – went out of business. Misharin says:

> *The fact is that I very quickly reached a level of incompetence – I came in as a manager, but in just three months I was appointed managing director. I was not ready. Also I did not want this. I was already a successful director of the Camp by then... But here, I had to admit that I did not know how to work in a situation when our funder left the game. I had to terminate our relationship, because that was a different model. I had a position and salary (at the camp). I've never been so free, as at that time. I was the most free and independent person. I didn't work in the company for the salary, nor for ambition; I just worked for the interest. It was an exciting game.*

This challenging situation did not prevent him from applying for the vacant position of the Director of the Yekaterinburg Actors' House[3] and being appointed to it. By that time Misharin was already a part-time student of the Management Department at the Yekaterinburg Theatre Institute. He has kept studying and teaching formally and informally all his life, as well as making steep career turns every five to seven years.

---

[3] Ideally the Actors' House combines the purposes of the headquarters of a regional branch of the Theatre Union of Russia and the functions of a professional club for theatre workers. The Union, established in 1877, is the oldest one of this kind in Russia and has professional rather than trade-union purposes.

Challenges

Yekaterinburg-Moscow-Yekaterinburg

From 1994-2002, Vladimir Misharin was Director of the Yekaterinburg Actors' House of the Sverdlovsk Branch of the Theatre Union of the Russian Federation (TURF).

He had inherited this organization in quite a pitiful state; the building itself – an old merchant's house, one of the few remaining in the city – was occupied by doubtful businesses, while its own activities were close to zero. The main goals were – to rebuild its reputation as well as filling it with appropriate activities.

Consistent policy and the proper motivation of associates allowed him to achieve these outcomes:

1. Development of an image of the Actors' House and to make it widely known in public, business and cultural circles of Yekaterinburg, Sverdlovsk oblast, Russia and abroad as the 'House that delights the heart'.

2. Reactivation of the House cafe – 'Debut'.

3. Development and launch, from zero, of a unique fundraising project 'Christmas tree in the House of Tupikova'.[4]

His success was noticed in Moscow in the central office of the TURF, where he was invited to work in 2003 as Deputy to the Chairman of the Union focusing on organizational and creative issues. After one year in this position he:

1. developed and successfully introduced to the Ministry of Culture a Comprehensive Program of the Union 'Theatrical panorama of the Russian Federation', aimed at enhancing the state and social life;

2. developed and launched a new creative project – 'Chekhov's Seasons in Yalta' – which includes the restoration of the oldest theatre in Yalta (Crimea, Ukraine) which holds the eponymous annual theatre festival;

3. developed a concept and started from zero a unique non-profit partnership – 'Theatre Centre of the TURF' on Strastnoi[5]. It was the first theatre space in Moscow that did not occupy any particular company and had an innovative approach to its mission – to be a 'Performing space, open for creativity and cooperation'.

The aims of the Centre are:

- to provide the conditions for temporary creative groups that do not fit into traditional formats of professional activity,

- to achieve creative self-realization, and

---

[4] Tupikova is the last name of the historic owner of the house.
[5] Strastnoi boulevard, Moscow is the address of the TURF Central office and the Union major theatre center.

- to have the possibility to present their creative products in front of an audience.

The Centre required much work and attention, so very soon Misharin became its first director. During his first year he managed to launch the concept, build a team, and start projects – some of which are still in action today. As happened on previous occasions, once a concept started working well by itself, Misharin looked for a new challenge.

This time it turned out to be an invitation from the Federal Agency on Culture and Cinematography. There he took on the position of Head of the Performing Arts Department. This was a really senior position with huge responsibilities, wide visibility, and all federal theatres within his orbit. But in reality he could not overcome the bureaucratic system and implement his own up-to-date ideas. With good writing skills, by his own words, he became a 'typewriter' for the bureaucracy above him. Added to that, he never had his own home in Moscow, even though at that period he was married and had a son.

That made a good time to look for the next challenge. Misharin returned to his native Yekaterinburg to be elected for the next five years as the Chairman of the Sverdlovsk Regional Branch of the TURF. It was very unusual in the entire history of the Union for a candidate from a non-creative profession to win an election for such a position. Usually it works, as in the theatre relationship of artistic and managing directors – the chairmen are respected actors or directors, while it is their deputies who are mostly from the management field. That is probably why he was immediately involved in a lengthy court process to defend the building of the Actors' House, home for the Union branch, from being taken over by the government. He used all his knowledge, skills and diplomacy gained from his education, experience and observation and won that battle.

In the middle of his term, twice Misharin received an invitation to join the Ministry of Culture of the Perm' Krai – another big region in the west of Ural. But he refused the offer both times, arguing that he had a serious responsibility to those who had given him their vote for his present position. By the end of his term everything worked like 'clock-work' there; the key positions were occupied by Misharin's apprentices, so he did not need to worry about the business. Approaching the termination of his position, Misharin started looking for something completely new in another different environment.

From this Yekaterinburg-Moscow-Yekaterinburg quest, Vladimir Mishrin learned that what he does best is to develop a business successfully from zero. While it requires more risk and responsibility, it gives more space and opportunity to satisfy his 'success addiction' than does routine work following existing patterns.

In the middle of 2010, Misharin found on the map of Russia a place in which to exercise his talents. The Sochi City Administration was seeking someone to implement the merging of two major cultural institutions: the Sochi Philharmonic/Winter Theatre and the Hall of Organ and Chamber Music, starting from their foundation to develop a new institution – the Sochi Concert and

Philharmonic Association. Misharin applied for the role and was successful. Why Sochi, we asked? He responded:

> Because of the Olympics, because of the Black Sea, because of a warm climate for my wife, and because there was a 'big zero' to begin with.

Information about Sochi [6]

'Sun city', 'Magnolia region', and 'Pearl by the sea' – these are epithets and images which have been associated with Sochi. It is the only city in Russia to be located in the sub-tropics, and it has all the climatic and natural conditions for complete relaxation and recreation. Sochi is a resort of federal importance: it belongs to the Krasnodar region and extends as a narrow line for 145 km along the Black Sea coast at the foot of the Main Caucasus Range. The longest city in Europe – Greater Sochi had a population of 341,902 as at 01 January 2010[7] – includes four administrative districts with their unique features and lifestyle.

For over a hundred years Sochi has been the largest health resort area in Russia and has more than 200 health centres of all kinds. Its Krasnaya Polyana area has become an acknowledged skiing centre with all facilities for winter sports and holiday. Sochi is famous worldwide now, not just for its health and recreation complex, but for the fact that in 2014 it hosts the Winter Olympics. The city, as a result, is now gaining a new look.

Sochi offers a variety of entertainments to serve all tastes and cultural life and the resort city is diverse and full of events. While there are no local permanent theatre companies, there are festivals, art contests, and tours which take place regularly in Sochi. The major stages in the central Sochi area are the open-air concert hall 'Festivalny' and the Summer Theatre with its distinguishing architecture. They are[8] both used during the 'summer' season, while the Winter Theatre and the Organ and Chamber Music Hall are used all year round. Sochi's 'Kinotavr' Summer Festival, held in the open-air space in front of the Winter Theatre, presents for a wide audience the latest masterpieces of contemporary Russian cinematography.

Zimniy Theatre (Winter Theatre)

The Zimniy Theatre (Winter Theatre) is a distinctive cultural landmark of Sochi city just as the Bolshoi theatre is for Moscow or La Scala for Milan. The building, erected in a neo-classicist style, is surrounded by 88 columns and fits well into the peculiar look of the southern resort. The open foyer is decorated with a colonnade. The auditorium is lit with a huge chandelier decorated with brightly glittering crystal. The theatre was constructed in 1937 as a part of the general plan, which aimed to convert a provincial health resort – Sochi – into one of national

---

[6] Source: Official site of the Administration of the resort-city Sochi, www.sochiru.ru
[7] Source: Russian Federal Service of the State Statistics, www.gks.ru/bgd/regl/b10_109/Main.htm
[8] Summer Theatre has been under reconstruction for several years already.

significance. The building was taken under state protection immediately after construction as an architectural monument of national importance. The idea was to make it the best USSR Black-Sea stage, fit to receive the best of performing arts works from all over the country all year round.

Today for Russia, it remains a unique theatrical stage. The Winter Theatre is the place where Russian and International Art Festivals and Contests are held. Names such as Valery Gergiev, Dmitry Khvorostovsky and Yury Bashmet adorn the windows of the Winter Theatre all year round. The Winter Theatre has 970 seats. Its interior was completely renovated recently: the technical equipment, stage curtain, act drop and arm-chairs were replaced; the orchestra pit was enlarged; and new heating and air-conditioning were installed. The Winter Theatre now indeed offers year-round facilities.

Organ and Chamber Music Hall

Located centrally in the city of Sochi, this hall possesses a wonderful acoustic which allows organ, symphony, chamber-ensemble, choral and vocal music concerts all year round. In 2006 when the Sochi Organ and Chamber Music Hall celebrated its twentieth anniversary, the legendary Russian musician, Gary Grodberg, gave the first organ concert in Sochi. Apart from the regular concert activity, important city events, conferences and meetings are held here. The annual International Organ Music Festival is held in Sochi, and outstanding international organists take part in the festival.

Approach and challenges

Vladimir Misharin and Sochi Concert and the Philharmonic Association (SKFA)

> 'If I had known what would be the reality of Sochi today, I would never have moved there', Misharin admits.

The reality surprised and disappointed Misharin, and only his principle – 'once you start a job, you have to see it through'– persuaded him to remain to finish his work there.

What were those challenges as we understand them?

First of all, an approach to business in the entire region which is very old fashioned and, in most places, long out of date. A mentality and approach where the only business instrument is an administrative one, and the telephone call is the main management instrument. One example of this is that the regional heads until very recently saw the Winter Theatre as totally and completely under their control, where they could use it for their assemblies without any preliminary warning or agreement, and with no respect to the major scheduled activities of the space.

The other major factor is to do with external relations. The city had not noticed that times have changed since the Russian borders have been open and it is no longer the only and the best southern resort for Russians. Guests now very rarely come for a long 21-day sanatorium course; instead they come for just three to seven days and have a full-day range of services at the old hotels and sanatoriums, as well as in the newly built ones. The visitors do not have the time or the desire to move out of their resorts' territories. But the inhabitants are still convinced that the uniqueness of the place must hand them customers on a silver platter, so the 'market', which should have been a major driver of business, is ignored. Surprisingly, the entire buzz about the Sochi Olympics has not yet influenced the inhabitants' way of thinking.

While these are factors that concern the city, they are also reflected within the culture of the theatre, because the people who work in the theatre are themselves normal citizens of the city.

All these factors forced Misharin to rethink his initial strategy and to develop a new one on the fly. This was in parallel with his official task of implementing the re-organization.

As he says:

> *I had no time for takeoff. The decision on the re-organization of the Sochi Philharmonic needed to be implemented, and therefore there was little time for thinking...*

His first step was to position himself as a *presence* in the City of Sochi. This meant using as much public relations as possible, and demonstrating a high visibility at all official and professional levels accompanied by complete openness and transparency in everything he did. For instance, Misharin appeared next to the city's mayor at official meetings and receptions, and published his business diary and decisions as widely as he could on the internet.

At the same time he began to systematically accustom the regional and municipal heads and box office agents to understand and be familiar with 'modern' systems of business relations, based on written agreements and contracts. He has achieved some success in this direction:

- The regional and municipal heads now coordinate their plans of events in the Winter Theatre in advance and include an actual working plan of the venue. They also provide written applications to the SCFA in this regard. It is a great achievement even though Misharin is the one who composes these applications for the heads to sign.

- Misharin refuses to host any performances without a signed contract in the SCFA venues – even the annual and famous ones. At first he suggested that their box office agents put down on paper the terms and conditions, according to the established traditions. As the next step he suggested his own variant of this agreement. In the beginning there were objections, but finally the 'other side' realized that with appropriate preparation, this would be a 'win-win' way of cooperation.

In addition he and his new team have started conquering this territory from beneath as well – all of them have gone to teach at the Municipal Culture College in order to introduce their ideas and to attract adherents to this more contemporary way of thinking.

As for the SCFA itself, a re-organization was a good reason for a staff restructure. While at the time of re-organization the Hall of the Organ and Chamber Music had a relatively sustainable and consistent programming and operation, the Winter Theatre required much more attention; most of all in the areas of programming and audience development. Table 3.1 and figures 3.1 and 3.2 below, demonstrate the old and new organizational structures.

Table 3.1[9] Staff List of the Sochi Hall of Organ and Chamber Music, before re-organization (99 employees)

1. Administrative staff – 9
2. Artistic management – 4
3. Sochi municipal symphony orchestra – 46
4. Chamber choir – 14
5. Creative personnel – 10
6. Production-technical personnel – 16

Figure 3.1 Organizational chart of the Sochi Philharmonic, including Winter Theatre before re-organization (167 employees)

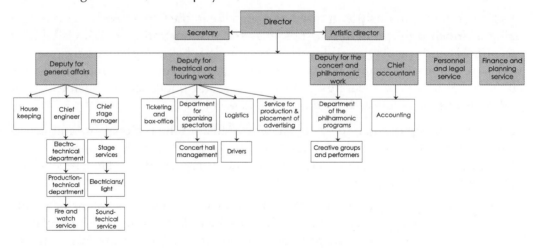

[9] Source: the SCFA archive.

Figure 3.2 Organizational chart of the Sochi Concert-Philharmonic Association (293 employees[10])

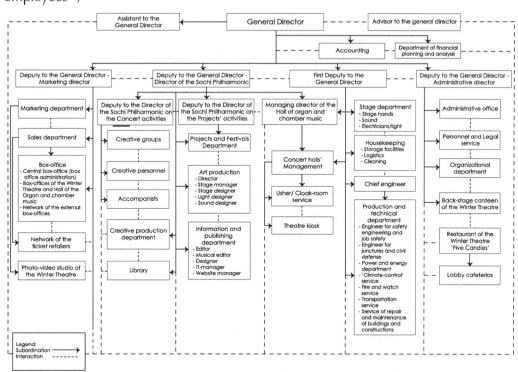

All internal links are revised now, with the major changes being made in the Administrative section. First of all there appeared a completely new marketing department in this section. SCFA has now the following distribution of employees: creative department – 120; administrative personnel – 80; stage department – 20; others (including ushers) – 73.

As a result, the SCFA (see Table 3.1, Figures 3.1 & 3.2, and Appendices II & III):

- at last has a computer ticketing system with a network of external box-offices,
- has developed a scheme of regular programs,
- has increased the number of activities of both its own and touring creative groups,
- has launched a strong marketing campaign, firstly targeted at the residents,
- arranged transport for spectators after the shows at the Winter Theatre to distant parts of Greater Sochi,
- increased the number of spectators and attendance rates, and

---

[10] Source: SCFA Personnel and Legal service.

- increased income (in comparison with the pre-reorganization period) by 358 percent.

Today the budget of the SCFA is evenly balanced; 50 percent of the income comes from the Municipality and 50 percent from its own activities. This was achieved due to the persistent and methodical use of traditional marketing tools aimed both at the box office agents and at audiences. These efforts, on one hand, led to the significant activation of work of the guest organizations, and on the other hand stimulated attendance which resulted in a 483 percent income growth of this kind of events. The increased income is mostly spent on the payment of five new high quality marketing department specialists and a Personal Assistant to the General Manager. After the first year's work in Sochi, Misharin has selected the new employees from among his Yekaterinburg pupils. There was no resentment from the other staff when he brought in new people from another place, as there was no marketing department before, and no one already working there wanted to take on these new responsibilities. But there was strong and continued resentment and resistance from some of the existing staff to the implementation of 'new' (for this place) technologies given their old-fashioned approach. For example, five of Misharin's predecessors were not able to launch a computerized ticketing system, yet it had been installed. When Misharin decided to start it, at the beginning of his work in Sochi, all ticketing office personnel (five people) applied for termination of their employment contracts simultaneously. For him, this was like blackmail and sabotage at the same time, but nevertheless he signed their termination applications and managed to find new people to fill these positions by the next day. In addition, the new income has been spent towards the development and running of new art programs produced by the SCFA, on creative groups and on the improvement of the general working conditions, both at the base and on tours.[11]

As noted above, Misharin concentrates much of his efforts at the Winter Theatre, where the priority is to establish for the Sochi residents, an expectation of artistic events in a comfortable environment. In relation to visitors, he says:

> …the ultimate priority of the SCFA is to attract visitors for whom the event would be the primary attraction, while the sea, a wonderful climate and other benefits of the resort would be a secondary factor (Misharin, quoted in Macharadze 2011, p. 13).

To be continued…

Conclusion

As the word itself implies, leadership is a direction that originates with an individual. […]

> One can learn and develop one's potential. This can be a life-long process, in which any opportunity to learn is seized upon, whether it be training

---

[11] One of the SCFA duties is to serve the population of the 145 km-long Greater Sochi.

programs, significant encounters, personal or professional experiences, readings, works of fiction, etc. In fact, for a person who is eager to learn and develop their potential, the possibilities for learning are endless and they take full advantage of them (Lapierre 2001, p. 153).

The case of Misharin illustrates Bass's theory of leadership that suggests three major ways to become a leader (Bass 1990): the trait theory, the great events theory, and the transformational or process leadership theory. Being born a leader, he keeps learning, has healthy and strong ambitions, sees and takes advantage of opportunities, agrees that leadership brings troubles and responsibilities but has the courage to take difficult decisions, and so on and so forth.

We believe that Vladimir Misharin is a rare example of the arts-leader in Russia. During his professional development he has always held high managerial positions, but he has never been just a 'boss' with an 'assigned leadership' style (Rowe 2007). He is always a 'leader', and this makes the 'followers' want to achieve high goals (c.f. emergent leadership), rather than simply bossing people around (Rowe 2007). Thus with assigned leadership achieved by position, Misharin demonstrates emergent leadership by influencing people to together aim for high achievements.

It is not easy to define the leadership style of Misharin. As any gifted and experienced leader, he combines all typical styles in his work in accordance with a particular case or need. However, he has a very particular background, which has affected all his further development as a leader. In the best sense 'pioneer camp' stays with him, and in him, even today. Being a leader-teacher and leader-mentor, he builds his relationships with the younger generation in a form of 'master-apprentice' and recruits from there, his future associates and team-members. The other side of the coin is that perhaps he protects and supports them too much, thereby not allowing them the chance to fail. This is understandable (but perhaps not excusable), because working mostly as a crisis manager he does not have time for failure. But doing and supervising too much himself, Misharin just does not have enough time and energy to make sense of everything properly, and in his haste, definitely misses some important business elements. Thus, for example, we were surprised when he (with his habit of putting everything down on paper) could not provide us with a written future or business plan for the SCFA. There are only major visionary goals … Equally, we were surprised to find that on the internet the SCFA is presented on the pages of the Municipal Administration and does not have its own web site. The explanation, quite reasonably, is that it must be well-done and he does not have enough time to think properly about it and to work with a designer[12]. But then why should he do this himself and not delegate this to another? But of course there are no perfect leaders and all this just gives some space for 'self-improvement' for Vladimir Misharin.

In one of his first interviews in Sochi, Misharin declared:

---

[12] Our dialog took place on December 1, 2011.

At each stage of my professional realization I pursued certain goals. Now I've made another step towards self-realization. Life is very short and I would like to have time to try different directions in arts management. I am very interested and have some ambition to prove myself once again about the possibilities of marketing and management technologies. [...]This step is professional development, rather than simply raising or moving sideward. [...] There is a misconception that management is not creative. This is not the case. [...] All the streams of creative production come together in an arts manager (Misharin, quoted in Semenova 2010).

Acknowledgement

We deeply appreciate Michael Quine (London) for his attention to this work and constructive suggestions.

Questions

1. How did Vladimir Misharin's early career as a youth leader influence his leadership approach in the arts? Provide examples.
2. Vladimir Misharin demonstrates attributes of a 'change' agent. Can you discuss this in the context of his various professional roles?
3. In his present role, Vladimir Misharin has had to confront several key issues to bring about a transformation in the way arts and culture are delivered in Sochi. Can you highlight what these are, and consider the success or otherwise of his method of addressing them?

References

Bass, B 1990, *Bass & Stogdill's Handbook of Leadership: Theory, Research, and Managerial Applications* (Third edition), The Free Press, New York.

Bass, B 1990, 'From transactional to transformational leadership: learning to share the vision'. *Organizational Dynamics*, vol. 18, no. 3, pp. 19-31.

Lapierre, L 2001, 'The Case for Non-Teaching', in Klein (edition), *Interactive Teaching and Learning across Disciplines and Cultures*, WACRA, Boston, pp. 153-157.

Macharadze, I 2011, 'Scena Peremen' ['Stage of Changes'], *Sochi Business-Journal*, vol. 55, no. 9, pp.12-13.

Rowe, WG 2007, *Cases in Leadership*, Sage Publications, Thousand Oaks, CA.

Semenova, N 2010, 'Direktor Sochinskoi filarmonii Vladimir Misharin: Teatr – Dorogoe Udovolstvie' [Director of the Sochi Philharmonic Vladimir Misharin: 'Theatre is and Expensive Pleasure'], *Zhivaya Kuban'*, September 9, http://www.livekuban.ru/node/202541

Tarasov, V 2007, *Tehnologiya Zhizni. Kniga dlya Geroev* [Technology of Life. Book for Heroes], Dobroe delo, Moscow.

Appendix I

Timeline: Vladimir Misharin (1967-)[13]

Date	Biographical detail
22 Feb 1967	Vladimir Misharin is born in Poliovskoi, Sverdlovskaya oblast, Soviet Union
1984	Graduated from the Poliovskoi school, entered the Sverdlovsk (now Yekaterinburg) Pedagogy Institute, Geography and Biology Department
1985 to 1987	Military service in the armed forces of the USSR
1987 to 1991	Studying full-time at the Sverdlovsk Pedagogy Institute
1987 to 1994	Director of the Country Children's Health Camp, 'Vostok', for 300 children
1992 to 1994	Literary advisor, manager, managing director of the Municipal choreographic company 'Ballet Plus' (Yekaterinburg)
1993 to 1996	Studying part-time at the Yekaterinburg Theatre Institute, Theatre Management Department.
1994	Training under the international USIA (USA) program on « Arts-management in the USA» (the USA cities)
1994 to 2002	Director of the Yekaterinburg Actors' House (2001-2002 – Deputy to the Chairman of the Sverdlovsk Branch of the Theatre Union of the Russian Federation (TURF))
1996 to 1998	Studying at the High School of the Men of Stage (Russian State Theatre Arts Academy), management department
1997 to 2002	Assistant professor at the Yekaterinburg Theatre Institute
1998 to 2002	Anchorman at the popular television series of the Yekaterinburg State TV and Radio 'Our good, old TV'
January 2003 to June 2004	Deputy to the Chairman of the TURF on organizational and creative issues (Moscow)
May 2003 to June 2004	Director of the Theatre Centre TURF 'Na Strastnom' (Moscow)
2003	Got married
2004	Birth of a son
2004	Member of the editorial board of the 'Stage' journal
April 2005	Short-term training at the Russian Academy of civil servants under the President of the Russian Federation (Moscow)
Dec 2004 to Dec 2005	Head of the Performing Arts Department of the Federal Agency for Culture and Cinematography (Moscow)

---

[13] More details at http://domaktera.ru/person/show/2

Date	Biographical detail
Dec 2005 to Dec 2010	Chairman of the Sverdlovsk Regional Branch of the TURF (elective position)
2006 to present	Vice President (voluntary), Charitable Theatre Fund 'Support Society'
2006 to 2009	Assistant professor at the Ural State University. Editor in chief 'Bulletin of the Sverdlovsk Branch TUFR'
2009 to 2010	Member of the Board of the Ministry of Culture and Tourism and of the Public Chamber of the Sverdlovsk region
June 2010 to present	General Director of the Sochi Concert and Philharmonic Association
2011 to present	Member of the Working Group on Culture of the Presidential Council of the Russian Federation on the preparation and operation of the XXII Olympic Winter Games 2014 in Sochi

Appendix II

SCFA Creative groups and long-term programs.

Creative groups

- Sochi Municipal Symphony Orchestra
- Chamber Choir
- Orchestra of Folk Instruments 'Russian Souvenir', named after Necheporenko
- Ensemble of Cossack song 'Lyubo'
- Song and instrumental ensemble 'Kudrina'
- Folk instruments quartet 'Sochi-Surprise'

Winter Theatre – The system projects

Date	Project
January	International festival of the students' humor teams 'KiViN'
February	Winter international music festival of Yury Bashmet
April	The inter-regional open festival-competition of army songs *'For faith! For Motherland! For love!'*
June	Open Russian Cinema Festival *'Kinotaur'* City festival *'Constellation of young talents'* Festival-panorama *'Sochi Theatre Olympus'*
July	The annual festival in honor of the upcoming Olympics *'Sochi-2014, Yes!'*
August	Open jazz festival *'Black Sea'*
September	The Russian Valerie Barsova competition of vocalists Sochi International Investment Forum International Yury Grigorovitch competition *'Young Ballet of the World'*
October	International Fashion festival of Lyudmila Ivanova *'Velvet Seasons in Sochi'*
November	International children and youth festival of the arts and sport *'Kinotauric'*
December	New Year holidays campaign

Hall of the Organ and Chamber Music – Major concert cycles

- *Musical Olympus* – with participation of the laureates of the all-Russian and international contests.
- *Piano Concert Cycle*
- *Masterpieces of the Russian Music*
- *Ludwig van Beethoven*

- *Viva Opera* – with participation of the soloists of the principle Russian opera theatres.

- *Musical Transit* – with participation of the foreign conductors and soloists.

- *Popular Musical Collection*

- *Musical subscriptions for children and youth* – from October until April in cooperation with the Municipal Committee of Education and Science.

Source: The SCFA web page of at http://kulturasochi.ru/concert?m=1

Appendix III

Indicators	Number of events			Number of spectators			Income (US$[1])		
	2010 (6 month)	2011 (6 month)	2011/ 2010, %	2010 (6 month)	2011 (6 month)	2011/ 2010, %	2010 (6 month)	2011 (6 month)	2011/ 2010, %
1. Major activities	293	377	129%	74,500	115,600	155%	232,070	830,900	358%
Concerts, given by SCFA groups	244	255	105%	52,000	52,400	101%	70,820	52,000	73.4%
*including charitable		68							
at the WT	18	47	261%	5,600	19,300	345%	12,730	1,000	7.85%
at the HCOM	89	57	64%	12,500	9,100	73%	34,620	26,060	75.3%
tours on the territory of the Big Sochi	137	151	110%	33,900	24,000	71%	23,460	22,930	97.7%
Activities of the guest organizations	49	122	249%	22,500	63,200	281%	161,200	778,930	483%
2. Entrepreneurial activities							74,160	8,360	11.3
3. Incl. renting of spaces							32,000	37,760	118
TOTAL:	293	377	129%	74,500	115,600		338,240	877,060	
% attendance at WT				47,000	54,200	115%			
% attendance at HCOM				41,300	53,800	130%			
Activities for children	82	104	127%	9,500	27,500	289%	24,560	208,000	847%

[1] We have converted the monetary indicators from the Russian rubles into US$ for the convenience of the international readers. Yet, in our opinion, absolute data here is only important for illustration of the growth rate.

% rate of activities for children	28.0%	27.6%	98.6%	12,800	23,800	187%	350	830	236%
Average cost of an event, in rubles							790	2,200	
Including:									
given by SCFA groups							290	200	
given by guest organizations							3,290	6,380	
Average price for 1 visit (US$)							US$5.83	US$7.20	

WT – Winter Theatre

HCOM – Hall of Chamber and Organ Music

Source: SCFA Department of finance planning and analysis.

Part II

Leadership in Different Organizational Contexts

Chapter 4

The Utah Shakespeare Festival
An evolving arts leadership partnership
William J Byrnes

Overview

In May of 2010 the Utah Shakespeare Festival (USF) announced it would be bringing two of its high profile actor/directors on board as co-artistic directors to work with its executive director. While not widely publicized, the Festival actually began a leadership transition between 2002 and 2005. The retirement of several long-serving members of a management team – a team that helped direct the Festival toward its Tony Award for Best Regional Theatre in 2000 – and the founder's transition to a fundraising leadership position, put in motion several scenarios that led to the 2010 announcement of a leadership team.

This case study will include a brief historical perspective that examines the unique team management and leadership structures of the first 45 years of USF. It will examine the new leadership structure (as of 2011) as a work-in-progress and will offer observations about the potential and pitfalls of shared leadership models.

Background

In 2011, the Utah Shakespeare Festival (USF), situated on the campus of Southern Utah University, completed its 50th anniversary season. The Festival produces a season rotating repertory theatre (three to four Shakespeare plays and classics and modern titles) from late June to October in the small town of Cedar City, Utah (pop. 28,000) situated near several of America's most celebrated national parks and monuments. (Cedar City is 159 miles north of Las Vegas, NV (255 kilometers) and is in the high desert at an elevation of 5,800 feet or 1,767 meters.)

Three of the Festival's plays are performed from late June to early September, in an open-air 887-seat theatre built in the late 1970s and modelled after the original 'Globe Theatre' in London. Three additional summer plays are performed in a traditional 776-seat proscenium theatre which opened in 1989. The season continues into the fall with one Shakespeare production and two other plays performed in the indoor theatre through the end of October. Visitors to the Festival often sightsee or camp in national parks such as Zion, Bryce Canyon or the Grand Canyon, in addition to attending performances and educational programming produced each year by USF. The unique combination of location and programming supports the needs of cultural tourists and dedicated theatre lovers from around the world.

By the end of its fifth decade the Festival had over 300 seasonal employees, 28 year-round full-time staff, and an operating budget of US$6.2 million, and sold more than 100,000 tickets annually.

Leadership models in regional theatres

The organizational structure often found in the top leadership positions in American regional theatres, recognizing that there are many variations on the theme, tend to cluster around the job titles of artistic director and managing director. Designations such as producing artistic director (TCG 2010 Membership Directory) have also found their way into the expanding lexicon of position titles.

In general, the artistic director and managing director are responsible for the artistic/theatrical and the business/financial portion of the organization respectively. For example, the artistic director typically selects or proposes the season, hires key directors, choreographers and designers, oversees casting, and may even act in and direct the season of shows. The managing director deals with fiscal management, budgets, support staff, marketing, fundraising, operations and facilities.

Depending on the evolution of the governance system of the organization, the artistic director and managing director may both report to the board as equals, or one or the other may have been empowered to have the final authority when it comes to 'running' the theatre company. In some organizations, the producing artistic director has the ultimate control of the company with the managing director reporting to them. However, it is not uncommon to find dual leadership structures in place in many regional theatre companies in America.

USF leadership structure

In the early days of the Festival, the Founder Fred C Adam's title was that of producing director. As the seasons progressed, the leadership team expanded to include associate artistic directors and a managing director. Cameron Harvey and Douglas Cook joined the production team in the 1960s. Cook designed the Globe-replica outdoor theatre, and Harvey was the resident theatre and lighting consultant on the new indoor theatre. Harvey and Cook were also deeply involved in monitoring the productions and they established the benchmarks and production values still in place to this day.

By the mid-1990s the leadership team consisted of Fred C Adams as Founder and Executive Producer, Cook and Harvey as Producing Artistic Directors, and R Scott Phillips as Managing Director. This group selected the productions for each season and oversaw the operation of the Festival. However, only Phillips and Adams were in residence in Cedar City. Cook and Harvey maintained full-time jobs and careers at other universities in America.

In the early 2000s, Cook and Harvey started phasing out of the operations and were eventually replaced by Kathleen Conlin, a director and dean at the University of Illinois, and J R Sullivan, a freelance director, as associate artistic directors. Cook became an *emeriti* of the Festival in 2002, and Harvey retired in 2005. The path to leaderships in the Festival for Conlin and Sullivan began with directing USF productions. For a number of years, Conlin held the additional responsibility of auditioning actors for the Festival. However, neither Sullivan nor Conlin were in residence in Cedar City.

The next big leadership transition took place when Adams stepped down from the executive producer position in 2005. He stayed on to assume the responsibilities as Director of the Center Project and Executive Producer Emeritus. Adams' charge was to raise funds for a new Shakespeare Theatre (estimated to cost US$26 million) to replace the current Adams Theatre. Adams continued to maintain an office in the Festival's administrative building with the other full-time staff, and works with the Festival's Development Director to raise money for the new theatre.

With Adams' lateral move, R Scott Phillips was appointed Interim Executive Director in 2006, and was named Executive Director in 2007. J R Sullivan moved on to assume Artistic Direction of The Pearl Theatre in New York City in 2009. Conlin transitioned out of the Associate Artistic Director/Casting Director role after the fall 2010 season. Both Sullivan and Conlin continued to direct plays at the Festival, and were part of the artistic staff for the 50th anniversary season.

The filling of a full-time artistic director position at USF carried with it careful consideration of the unique history of the Festival and its place in the Utah arts and culture ecology. Utah has a long history of support for and engagement in the arts. The Mormon pioneers who settled in Utah in 1847 brought with them a legacy of music and performance that was embedded in their religious upbringing. By 1852 the Deseret Dramatic Association was established in Salt Lake City, and performances were taking place in a newly constructed Social Hall (Engar).

The Festival built its reputation on the presentation of family-friendly productions that artfully skirted around the more vulgar side of Shakespeare's plays. The Festival also took a similar approach when it expanded its repertory in the Randall L Jones Theatre in 1989 by producing what Adams referred to as the 'Shakespeares of other lands' (Ruth, p. 49). Some plays are not to be found in the

USF repertory because the subject matter or language is deemed too offensive for the audience they serve. Throughout its history, USF has charted a path that has not veered too far from the expectations of its relatively conservative audience base. Therefore, the selection of an artistic director carried with it the necessary criteria of someone sensitive to the cultural and social context of USF and the trust-bond it had built with its audiences over the last 50 years.

The Festival announced, in May 2010, the hiring of two artistic directors for the 50th anniversary season. Long-time actors and directors Brian Vaughn and David Ivers would be Co-Artistic Directors of the Festival effective January 2011. Ivers and Vaughn had 15-plus year histories with the Festival, having performed in numerous plays since their days as interns in the 1990s. Both had also successfully directed plays at the Festival and were familiar with the seasonal operation. Ivers had built a career as an actor and director, most recently at the Denver Center Theater Company, and Vaughn likewise had established a strong presence in the regional theatre scene through his many years at the Milwaukee Repertory Theater in Wisconsin. Both men were well aware of the need to honor the Festival's long history of presenting theatre that fits within the unique social and cultural mix of its audiences.

In the case of USF, R Scott Phillips is the Executive Director of the organization, and Vaughn and Ivers report to him in their equal roles as Co-Artistic Directors. The division of duties and responsibilities was given considerable thought by Phillips and was part of the initial negotiation with the new leadership team. Work among the three was divided along the lines of programming and operations. Ivers and Vaughn assumed leadership of the artistic company and the Production and Education departments. Phillips would manage the overall finances, fundraising, marketing and facilities side of the Festival. Some areas, such as budget development, fundraising and managing the relationship with the Board of Governors, would fall under the leadership duties of all three.

Approach

USF leader profiles

Brian Vaughn brings an interest in programming and a keen awareness of the type of plays that will fit well into the Festival's repertory. He also brings a vision of the role good theatre can play in developing and expanding audience awareness of the larger issues we all face as human beings. He comes across as pleasant, outgoing, and incisive. His listening skills and ability to weigh options gives the impression of an individual that will be fair and attentive to employee and board member concerns. Vaughn is sensitive to the fact that there are many sides to an issue or to conflict in the workplace and therefore, he subscribes to the idea that careful consideration of decisions is a primary leadership behavior required when working with people. He firmly believes that the staff help shape the day-to-day culture of the Festival and his leadership role is to support and enable the people he works with to be successful. Vaughn also looks to and often speaks of the many types of leaders found in Shakespeare's plays for examples of good and bad leadership styles and management decision-making.

David Ivers offers a contrasting and complementary leadership and management style when compared to Vaughn and Phillips. Ivers is dynamic, expressive and action-oriented. When opportunities present themselves, he is disposed to take action rather than sit back. He is not impulsive, but he finds inaction in the face of opportunity frustrating beyond measure. As a compliment to Vaughn's interest in the programming side of the Festival, Ivers enjoys diving into budgets and studying the 'stories' being told in the spreadsheets. He finds organizational infrastructure both fascinating and revealing. The decisions reflected in how budget resources have been allocated speak directly to him about leadership priorities. He has a broad awareness of where the Festival has been and many ideas on where it could go. He is also very self-aware of his tendency to take centre stage when it comes to the conversation about the Festival.

R Scott Phillips' first experience with the Festival was as a sixteen-year-old audience member in 1971 (Ruth, p. 12). He became enamored with the organization and sought employment with the Festival after college. His career with the Festival began in the late 1970s in marketing and public relations, and eventually moved up to the Managing Director position in 1991. Phillips's winning smile and gregarious personality have helped him shape a career in the theatre that is widely recognized, especially among Shakespeare theatre managers and leaders. Having worked with Festival founder Fred C Adams for over 30 years, Phillips knows the Festival inside and out. His transition to the role of Executive Director was supported by Adams, and while Phillips has assumed much of the role Adams played in running the theatre, he has made the job his own.

Phillips speaks of his leadership style in the context of developing a consensus with those he works with. He recognizes that final decisions are his, but his preference is to gather input from others before making his choice. He also is very much of the mindset that he would not ask others to do anything he would not do himself. He prides himself on building positive working relationships with diverse groups of people. His decision to bring Vaughn and Ivers on as a team was driven by what he saw as the leadership attributes of both of them, along with their ability to work with each other. Phillips had observed Vaughn and Ivers' working styles over the years and noted that the two had a real synergy.

Phillips also had the challenging task of succeeding a founder who is much revered and honored in Utah and in the theatre community. These types of leadership transitions can be the undoing of an arts organization. For many, the Festival is Fred C Adams and Adams is the Festival. However, in this situation, Adams fulfilled his role of Executive Producer Emeritus and Director of the Center project without stealing Phillips's limelight.

Both Ivers and Vaughn came to their leadership positions from the model that emulates Fred C Adams' background, i.e. that of the active artist-manager, rather than as arts managers. The ability to be able to act as well as direct allows these leaders to stay close to the business they manage and lead. Whatever differences and similarities exist among Phillips, Ivers and Vaughn, their common interest is the plays and the process of bringing the season to life for the actors, designers, artisans and audiences. The inherent risks of failure that are embedded in the creation and presentation of live theatre seems to fuel their collective passion to make the Festival the best they can make it to be.

Taking these leadership personality profiles into account, let us now examine how these three leaders fit into the larger dialog of leadership and management theory and practice.

The challenges

Goals of the leadership team

Early in the leadership transition process, Philips, Ivers, and Vaughn held a mini-retreat. Out of this January 2011 meeting came the following list of ten leadership goals.

Table 4.1 USF leadership goals

USF leadership goals	
1. Support, protect and inspire staff 2. Develop and complete a five-year strategic plan 3. New strategies for season planning and product selection 4. Realign earned and unearned/contributed income (goal 30%) 5. Stronger board involvement	6. Office relocation & why (resolution of issues) 7. Job title and job descriptions 8. New Shakespeare Theatre project Enforcement of Act and Regulations 9. Increase national and international profile of USF 10. Increase volunteer base

By establishing these goals and then articulating them to the staff and board, enabled Ivers and Vaughn to create momentum and interest in their leadership aspirations immediately.

Leadership in action

The leadership goals they articulated mirror widely accepted techniques found in many books offering models and practices for leaders to adopt and emulate. For example, Kouzes and Posner's *Leadership Challenge* offer 'five practices of exemplary leadership': model the way, inspire a shared vision, challenge the process, enable others to act, and encourage the heart (Kouzes, Posner, p. 14). Ivers, Vaughn and Phillip's ten leadership goals relate directly to *Modeling the Way* by directly sharing and discussing them with all the staff and board. The USF leadership goals also demonstrate the connection to the other four practices: two – inspiring a shared vision (goals 1, 2, 3, 5 and 9), three – challenge the process (goals 3, 4, 6 and 7), four – enable others to act (goals 1, 2 and 7), and five – encourage the heart (goals 1, 5 and 10).

A deeper analysis of these ten leadership goals also demonstrates a strong connection to the 'ten commitments of leadership' (Kouzes, Posner 207, p. 26). For example, Ivers and Vaughn regularly employ the vocabulary of the ten commitments of leadership as they communicate in board and staff meetings (i.e. clarifying values, setting examples through alignment actions, envisioning a future, enlisting others, seizing opportunities, experimenting and taking risks, fostering collaboration, strengthening others by developing competence, showing appreciation, celebrating and a spirit of community) (Kouzes, Posner 2007, p. 26).

Examples can also be found of Ivers and Vaughn engaging in the practices of Level 5 Leadership as outlined in Jim Collins monograph *Good to Great and the Social Sectors* (Collins 2005). They exhibit level one leadership as highly capable individual(s) through their talent, knowledge, skills and good work habits as directors and actors. On level two, they are contributing team members who work effectively with others. At level three, they exhibit competent managerial skill by way of directing productions, which after all is about 'organizing people and resources toward the effective and efficient pursuit of predetermined objectives' (Collins 2005, p. 12). Their level four efforts to be effective leader(s) are consistent with Collins' description of someone who 'catalyzes commitment to and vigorous pursuit of a clear and compelling vision…' (Collins 2005, p. 12). Level four activity is revealed in their planning initiatives, including a commitment to produce the full cannon of Shakespeare's plays in the next ten years. Lastly, their level five executive leader behavior matches with Collins' description of someone who builds 'greatness through a paradoxical blend of personality and humility'. Both Ivers and Vaughn are able to be leaders, but they also consistently articulate the fact the Festival cannot succeed without the support and full engagement of the staff, artists and the Board.

Another facet to the paradox Collins references at Level 5 Leadership is the clear understanding Ivers and Vaughn have about the continuum of leadership and managing. The evidence of their leadership and management performance mirrors Henry Mintzberg's perspective about management being 'a practice learned primarily through experience, and rooted in context' (Mintzberg 2011, p. 9). For example, neither Vaughn nor Ivers have had formal training in arts or business management, but both point to the context and observation of effective leadership, management and communication styles of mentors they had at the Milwaukee Rep and Denver Center Theatre Company. They further acknowledge that they have learned valuable lessons from observing and being managed and led at times by people who were not effective in their jobs.

One of the challenges these Co-Artistic Directors face is that USF is really two companies operating under one roof. For the portion of the year that the Festival is in production, it runs like a typical theatre company with over 300 people all attempting to effectively fulfil their roles in a collaborative work environment. In fact, by being a repertory theatre company, the need to attain high levels of cooperation and coordination is reinforced everyday beyond the actual public performances. However, when the Festival is not in production, energy levels drop and a routine sets in that seems to sap the creative energy of the organization. Maintaining a consistent level of cooperation, collaboration, and enthusiasm year round will prove to be a big challenge, and a tremendous opportunity, for the new leadership team.

As we ponder the successful elements in place for the new leadership team, we must also reflect on the pitfalls and potential for falling short of the ten goals articulated by Phillips, Ivers and Vaughn. There can be inherent problems in any shared leadership situation, and this case study will conclude with an exploration of possible solutions.

Pressure points

The process of leadership and management is seldom linear and tidy. The number of behavioral variables that can be introduced in the workplace, which is a complex social environment, can be intimidating. There is a reason that the ability to focus and establish priorities is leadership behavior that is highly prized in any organization. In this case, the Ten Leadership Goals help narrow the list of options to provide the focus necessary to go forward. Let's look at three potential pressure points that could have an impact on the new leadership team.

Communication

Ivers and Vaughn have a substantial history of working together, but not in the type of leadership structure they now find themselves. Ivers and Vaughn are still evolving their working relationship in this new situation and the fact is there are fundamental differences in how they approach their work. Phillips also introduces a new element to the Ivers and Vaughn working relationship. Both are familiar with Phillips in his former role as Managing Director, but they are still adjusting to his leadership and decision-making style in his capacity as Executive Director.

The three will need to be vigilant about the pitfalls and problems related to that most basic of work place functions – daily communication. The tendency for any one of them to dominate a conversation could be a potential point of friction. The risk of marginalizing the contribution of the other members of the team is possible. While all three exhibit a high need for achievement, Ivers comes across as the most confident and seems least reticent to share his opinion. Vaughn tends to lay back and formulate his thoughts before contributing to the conversation. Phillips seems deferential in his general dealings with people and with Ivers and Vaughn. While there is an inherent communication competition among the three, none appears to suffer from any of the fatal flaws that can undo a leader's effectiveness (e.g. insensitivity, abrasiveness, arrogance, or low levels of adaptability) (Hersey, Blanchard and Johnson 2008, p. 78-79).

An obvious strategy for heading off potential communication-related personality conflicts would be for the three of them to openly, intentionally and constantly share information about each other's management style and tendencies. Simply agreeing to make it a practice to openly communicate how they see the other's leadership and decision-making behavior impacting their respective leadership domains could help diffuse conflict. While sharing these differing management styles seems perfectly reasonable, the tendency most people have to internalize conflict could undo the positive dynamic exhibited by these three leaders.

Another useful tool they could employ would be to apply the theatre directing skills they have already mastered. For example, they know that as actors and directors, the key to successfully mastering a character, or building an effective performing ensemble, depends in large part on how well you understand what motivates a character's actions and what moves the story along. Just as actors and production staff must support each other on the stage, these three will need to go out of their way to share information about what is driving their choices as leaders and managers.

Staffing

There are distinct personality and temperament differences among the three that could undo their leadership efforts when it comes to the second internal problem area, staffing. Each exhibits differing tolerance levels for confronting conflict in the workplace. It will be of interest to see how they agree on remediation and staff replacement decisions, given the long-term goal they share to optimize the mix of the Festival staff. Implicit in this goal is the fact that some of the existing staff may not be able to meet the current and future needs of the organization.

All three profess the importance of the contribution of the staff to the success of the Festival. However, based on my observation of the Festival over the last seven years it has not exhibited a strong culture of staff development, and this could present a challenge to the new leadership team. One by-product of the weak staff development culture has been a trust deficit with the Festival leadership. The trust level in an organization is an important barometer of the follower's willingness to go with the leaders as they chart a new course. The building of what Stephen M R Covey refers to as the 'trust accounts' takes time and strategic leadership effort (Covey & Merrill, p. 130-132). Ivers and Vaughn recognize this trust-building process will take time.

Interviews with the new leadership team revealed a consistent recognition that changes will need to be made in the organization's personnel management systems if they are to be successful in building a stronger sense of trust among the Festival employees. The number one goal they all agreed on was the need to 'support, protect, and inspire (the) staff'. Goal 7, 'Job Titles and Job Descriptions,' is also designed to directly confront the alignment of people and positions with accountability. All three articulated trust-development plans that closely align with Covey's '4 Cores of Credibility' in *The Speed of Trust* (Covey, Merrill 2006, p. 43-44). These four cores are: a focus on integrity and honesty; a transparent intent; having the capabilities as leaders to produce positive results; and, lastly, the results themselves as an outcome demonstrating the delivery on the promise (Covey, Merrill 2006, p. 54-56).

Capacity

As is the case with many arts and culture organizations, the programming and activities that have become the baseline for daily operations at the Festival often exceed the financial and human capacity of the organization. Incremental programming additions, often developed with the best of intentions, reach a point where the smallest reduction of funding support or a diminution of staffing support jeopardizes sustainability. As the new leadership team looks to the future capacity of USF, goals 2, 3, 4 and 5 come into focus as priorities that could make or break the organization. These four goals centre on strategic planning, season selection, revenue and contributions, and stronger Board involvement. These four goals are interlocking in the sense that building organizational capacity will be hindered if one or more are not realized at or near their full potential.

Outcomes

As the new leadership team engages in developing a five-year strategic plan, the reality of supporting the demands of the day-to-day operation of the Festival has already manifested itself. Both Vaughn and Ivers acknowledged the demands of their acting and directing superseded any actual work on developing the strategic planning process for the Festival during the summer of 2011. If progress is to be made on the developing a strategic plan and the other leadership goals, the new leadership team will need to reassess the number of commitments they make to support the productions. However, this may be easier said than done. Part of the financial plan that allowed the funding to support their new positions as Co-Artistic Directors, was that actor and director salary savings would be re-allocated to cover the costs of Ivers and Vaughn's positions. Therefore, Vaughn and Ivers must continue to act and direct to, in a sense, balance the budget.

While there is no easy answer to this dilemma, both recognize they will have to partition their time and activities related to planning in another part of the calendar year. From May, when company members arrive and rehearsals start, until the season closes in October, quality time to engage in long-range strategic activities is simply not realistic. While all three possess a tireless commitment to making the Festival a high quality operation, they also realize that there is still only going to be 168 hours in a week. Therefore, they will have little choice but to attain a 'piercing clarity' about how to produce the best long-term results, and then (exercise) the relentless discipline to say, 'No thank you to opportunities that fail' what Collins calls 'the hedgehog test' (Collins 2005, p. 17).

The other goals they have established for season planning, revenue enhancement and stronger board involvement are all very demanding strategies that will require detailed planning and execution to fulfil. No doubt they will have to establish priorities within their priorities when it comes to their ten goals, or risk appearing to be less than successful implementing their strategic leadership. The

Festival hedgehog activity that will probably yield the most return for building capacity will be programming (which could bring them a larger audience base) and aligning income and donations.

Conclusion

This case study has tried to place the evolving leadership structures of the Utah Shakespeare Festival in the context of its 50-year history. Over time, we have seen how USF has moved from a founder-led and managed organization, to a multiple leader management structure. With the retirement of the founder, USF moved to a single leader with the title of Executive Director in 2006. As USF approached its 50th anniversary season in 2011 it appointed resident Co-Artistic Directors to work with the Executive Director.

As the leadership team formed, they developed 10 leadership goals to help define tasks for themselves and aspirations for the organization. These goals were analyzed using multiple leadership models found in management literature. The aspirations of the new USF management team were found to be grounded in best leadership practices cited by the several sources. In addition, each of the new team was profiled regarding their management and leadership styles.

Lastly, three challenges the new leadership team will face over the next few years were outlined. Internal organization issues facing the team include the potential for communication disconnects, the lack of a strong organizational culture of staff development, and the pressing demands of meeting the goals aspired to, in the face of financial and human capacity constraints.

The leadership vision, passion and luck required to sustain what has become an arts institution is in the hands of what seems to be a cohesive and dynamic leadership team. It will be interesting to observe the evolution of this leadership partnership as it attempts to meet the demands of a very challenging future.

Questions

1. Discuss the key attributes of the Utah Shakespeare Festival, including its leadership and governance, and review its challenges in terms of its location, program and audience.
2. The Board of the Utah Shakespeare Festival decided to appoint its new leadership from within the organization. Consider the advantages and disadvantages of this approach.
3. How does this triumvirate leadership model work in practice? Consider this model's strengths and weaknesses in the context of the Utah Shakespeare Festival.

References

Collins, J 2005, *Good to Great and the Social Sectors*, Jim Collins, Boulder, CO.

Covey, Stephen M R 2006, *The Speed of Trust*, Free Press, NY.

Engar, AW 2011, Theatre in Utah, www.media.utah.edu/UHE/t/THEATERS.html.

Hersey, P, Blanchard, K & Johnson, D 2008, *Management of Organizational Behavior*, 9th Edition, Pearson Education, Upper Saddle River, NJ.

Kouzes, J & Posner, B 2007, *The Leadership Challenge*, John Wiley & Sons, San Francisco, CA.

Mintzberg, Henry 2011, *Managing*, Berrett-Koehler Publishers, San Francisco, CA.

Paul, R 2011, *Celebrate 50 Years Utah Shakespeare Festival*, Utah Shakespeare Festival, Cedar City, UT.

Theatre Communications Group website: http://www.tcg.org/tools/profiles/member_profiles/main.cfm?CFID=1769105&CFTOKEN=12299531.

Chapter 5

Leadership in Australian arts companies
One size does not fit all

Kate MacNeill and Ann Tonks

Background

No one management structure exists across all sectors of artistic activity; nor is there a common model of leadership. In fact there are many different management structures in the arts and a wide variety of leadership practices. In this chapter we present two levels of analysis of management structure and leadership. We treat the management structure as the means by which formal accountabilities are determined, whereas leadership is used to describe the way in which key individuals contribute to achieving organizational success. Initially we examine the management structures of a range of major arts organizations in Australia. These include theatre, dance and opera companies and symphony orchestras, together with the state and national galleries. Interwoven with the management structures are the particularities of leadership practices, and we give attention to the factors that appear to influence their adoption in different situations across a range of art forms.

After this overview of existing management models we concentrate on one model of leadership commonly found in Australian performing arts companies, namely co-leadership. Two distinct strands are evident within the structure of most arts companies: the artistic activities and the management functions, each with their respective leader. Co-leadership describes a situation where these two leaders work closely in partnership, a specific variation on shared leadership. We draw on interviews that were conducted with the artistic leaders and managerial leaders of companies within the Australian Major Performing Arts Group, to illuminate the ways that these two leaders conduct the shared task of company management.[1]

While we do not have this same level of rich data on which to draw for our discussion of the state and national galleries, we have chosen to include them in our more general discussion of management structures so as to demonstrate the often quite different nature of management structures and leadership models in the performing arts sector as compared to museums and galleries.

Approach

Success of an arts company depends on, at least, two key factors: the quality of the artistic output and the financial stability of the company. The harmonization of the artistic and corporate sustainability of the company is a key challenge for the management team (Cray, Inglis & Freeman 2007; see Reid & Karambaya 2009 for a discussion of the possible conflicts that may arise). This view was also presented by a number of our interviewees, with examples being:

> Practically speaking, there really isn't an artistic decision that can be made without a conversation about the administrative, financial side and for some, there is no financial decision you could possibly make without impacting the artistic output of the company. [General Manager]

> And then I'd go, 'You said I didn't have to think about the money. How are you going to make it work?' So we'd sort of challenge each other but then we also really supported each other as well. [Artistic Director]

> So this has been the biggest compromise till now, finding the right amount of money in order to achieve what we want to achieve. [Artistic Director]

In our research, interviewees were emphatic that privileging the artistic project was integral to the company's success. However, the privileging of artistic output can present challenges in terms of appropriate management structures and leadership models. It is most common for companies, regardless of art form, to have an administrative leader with specific organizational responsibilities and an artistic leader more closely connected to the artistic project of the company, although the structure and hierarchy of these varies (Stein & Bathurst 2008). This bifurcation of the organization and its personification in an artistic director and a general manager is seen by some as giving rise to inevitable conflict, especially if

---

[1] The Australian Major Performing Arts Group's membership consists of: Adelaide Symphony Orchestra, Australian Brandenburg Orchestra, Australian Chamber Orchestra, Bangarra Dance Theatre, Bell Shakespeare Company, Belvoir St Theatre, Black Swan State Theatre Company, Circus Oz, Malthouse Theatre, Melbourne Symphony Orchestra, Melbourne Theatre Company, Musica Viva Australia, Opera Australia, Opera Queensland, Orchestra Victoria, Queensland Ballet, Queensland Symphony Orchestra, Queensland Theatre Company, State Opera of South Australia, State Theatre Company of South Australia, Sydney Dance Company, Sydney Symphony Orchestra, Sydney Theatre Company, Tasmanian Symphony Orchestra, The Australian Ballet, West Australian Ballet, West Australian Opera, and West Australian Symphony Orchestra.

the artistic director is not the head of the company (Gronn 1999). However, the concept of a company functioning with two quite separate spheres of activity is in itself misleading. In fact, in a successful company a shared commitment to the art will draw all aspects of the activities together. The leadership practices employed by those in key positions will be crucial. In other words the successful synthesis of art and business may rely as much on the leadership models as it does on the formal management structure.

Challenges

In this section we examine the different ways in which management structures in arts organizations in Australia appear to accommodate this necessary synthesis of art and business. At the same time we explore a range of factors that influence the management structures that exist at any point of time and the extent to which these structures encourage a model of co-leadership between the artistic leader and the general manager.

Management structures and leadership models

In Australia we can observe a wide range of management structures across the major arts organizations. The state and national art galleries, for instance, all have a single director who oversees an executive team with responsibilities for the curatorial program and also the operations, marketing and development areas. The director is almost without exception someone who has an established record as an expert in visual art and often with an academic specialization in art history. This has been the case for many decades and seems unlikely to change with Australian research showing that curators within a gallery and directors of other museums and galleries were considered to be the most likely candidates for a director's job (Suchy 2004, p. 235). Symphony orchestras, on the other hand, at first appear to adopt a model of sole leadership with a high profile chief conductor often being seen as synonymous with the public profile of an orchestra. However, in reality the company structure places ultimate management responsibility with a chief executive officer who is, in many instances, also a member of the Board. While the management structure will clearly identify the responsibility of the Chief Executive Officer for all aspects of the company's activities, some organizational charts show a direct line of accountability to the Board by the Chief Conductor who is invariably appointed by the Board.

The two largest performing arts companies in Australia, the Australian Ballet and Opera Australia, each have a different management structure. The Australian Ballet very clearly establishes equality between the two key managers. The Artistic Director and the Executive Director are joint CEOs and both answer directly to the board. In one sense this makes the Australian Ballet a very clear cut model of co-leadership with equal status of both managerial leader and of the creative leader. Opera Australia on the other hand has established a structure that more closely resembles that of an orchestra with a Chief Executive Officer and an artistic director who is accountable to the CEO and to the Board.

Australia's state-based theatre companies all appear to share a similar structure with an artistic director taking on artistic leadership of the organization as well as being its public face, and a general manager working behind the scenes to oversee the organizational leadership. However the formal management structures vary considerably. While the majority of theatre companies nominate the artistic leader as CEO, for example Melbourne Theatre Company, some explicitly show the artistic leader and the managerial leader as being equal in the hierarchy on an organizational chart – both reporting independently to the Board (for example Belvoir St Theatre), and a minority nominate the general manager as the company CEO. This is the case with the State Theatre Company of South Australia.

Figure 5.1 illustrates four variations of management structures and leadership models across performing arts companies and galleries. The management structure refers to the hierarchy conveyed by the organizational chart and accountabilities to the company board. Leadership refers to the practices of the primary company leaders and the degree to which they act as co-leaders or as solo leaders.

Figure 5.1 Management/leadership interaction

Dual management/ Co-leadership	**Solo management/ Co-leadership**
Joint CEOs	Single CEO
A relationship of parity, trust, shared vision and communication between the co-leaders	A relationship of parity, trust, shared vision and communication between the co-leaders
Examples: Australian Ballet, Bell Shakespeare, Circus Oz, Belvoir St Theatre	**Examples:** Melbourne Theatre Company, Black Swan State Theatre Company, Sydney Dance Company, Opera Australia
Solo management/ Dual leadership	**Solo management/ Solo leadership**
Single CEO	Single CEO
Two leaders operate separately with separate fields of vision	No other sole senior leader - rather departmental heads on similar status
Examples: Melbourne Symphony Orchestra, Sydney Symphony Orchestra	**Examples:** National Gallery of Australia, Art Gallery of New South Wales

In the left hand top quadrant we show a pure co-leadership structure, one in which the two leaders are joint CEOs, both report to the Board and function on a day to day level as co-leaders. The right hand top quadrant shows a single CEO who reports to a board, yet a co-leadership arrangement operates in practice due to the close interdependent relationship between an artistic leader and a general manager. The left hand bottom quadrant shows an organizational structure with a single leader who is the manager but where there is also a publicly acknowledged artistic leader. The result is not co-leadership but rather separate strands of leadership within the company. In the bottom right hand quadrant we show a sole management and sole leadership structure, where a single CEO is employed by the Board, and a number of divisional heads answer directly to the chief executive officer.

A single snapshot of these management structures at any point in time might give a misleading impression; organizations are dynamic entities and the adoption of a management structure is not a once and for all decision. Structures evolve and can reflect the preferences of governments and/or funders at different times. In the remainder of this section we discuss a range of factors that appear to have influenced the management structures that we have observed.

Founding documents

Many of the galleries are established under an Act of Parliament. The National Gallery of Australia is constituted under the National Gallery Act. The National Gallery of Victoria is constituted by an act of the state parliament as is the Art Gallery of New South Wales. These acts establish a board of governance, which in turn delegates its powers to the sole director/CEO, in other words a standard corporate organizational structure. The Museum and Art Gallery of the Northern Territory has no separate corporate form and remains within a territory government department. As guardians of priceless artworks (assets representing a significant portion of the national cultural estate), it is understandable that the management structure of state and national art galleries is determined by the government.

When we look at the management structures of the theatre companies, the few where a sole CEO is present have management structures which were also determined by an act of parliament and follow the practice of galleries in most closely resembling a standard corporate organizational structure. For example, the State Theatre of South Australia is established under an act of the South Australian Parliament and has as sole CEO, its General Manager.

Artistic production

The state and national galleries are not primarily creators of art; nor do they directly employ artists. In contrast, in 2010 40 percent of the Australian Ballet's personnel were directly involved in the artistic aspects of the company's activities, either as dancers or ballet mistresses/masters, with additional designers, choreographers and musicians employed in each season. The Artistic Director and

Executive Director share overall responsibility for the company's artistic and financial outcomes, demonstrating a clear commitment to the interwoven nature of the dual priorities of artistic excellence and sound company management. This is further evidenced in the close co-leadership practices of the two leaders. Once again a theatre company will contain two distinct strands of activities with the administrative operations and the work of actors and artists on the stage. While the theatre companies do not generally have ensemble members, in the course of any year there are likely to be as many actors and artists engaged in productions as there are administrative staff employed by the company.[2] The interviews we conducted with leaders in the major Australian theatre companies, discussed more fully below, supported the existence of co-leadership models in practice, even where the management structure identifies a sole CEO.

The impetus for shared or co-leadership between an artistic leader and a managerial leader would appear to be greater in organizations where an actual art production occurs. However, the presence of artists and artistic production does not always lead to co-leadership models.

A part-time artistic leader

Symphony orchestras and opera companies in Australia tend to share a similar structure. On the one hand performers comprise a substantial proportion of the company's employees (around 70 percent in the case of the Melbourne Symphony Orchestra in 2010) which might suggest that the artistic leadership would be given prominence in the management structure. However, unlike theatre companies, symphonies and operas tend to be managed by a sole CEO who is not the artistic leader. One likely explanation is that the artistic leader, in a number of the orchestras, operates on a part-time, fly in fly out, basis. This significantly limits the opportunities for a leadership role in the company as a whole. In the case of both the Melbourne Symphony Orchestra and the Sydney Symphony, the Managing Director is a member of the Board. The Chief Conductor is likely to be an internationally renowned artist yet does not have the same managerial status as the Managing Director. Nonetheless, the Chief Conductor will often answer directly to the Board, providing the possibility of a co-leadership practice. However, in reality this is seldom observed and the closer leadership relationship is between the CEO and a Director of Artistic Planning, a full-time employee of the company. As noted, we believe that a major factor in the management structure and leadership model is that the Chief Conductor is not a full-time member of the company and will often have commitments to other orchestras. Opera Australia might previously have been described in a similar manner when a UK-based conductor continued a schedule of international engagements while being musical director of the company. However, with the appointment of an

---

[2] The Sydney Theatre Company did at one stage have an ensemble known as 'The Actors Company' but its ensemble activities are now confined to the educational and development activities of the company.

Australian-based Artistic Director in 2009, a model of co-leadership appears to have emerged.

Change in internal or external environment

While there is a significant body of literature available on leadership and orchestras, much of this focuses on the leadership status of the conductor in relation to the musicians within the symphony orchestra itself rather than the wider company (see Ropo & Sauer 2003; Ropo & Sauer 2007; Solia-Wadman & Köping 2009). In practice there has been a gradual decline in the physical presence of the Chief Conductor within the orchestra companies more widely. There are several reasons for this. In a study of US orchestras, Robert Jones identifies the emergence of air travel as enabling conductors to hold two or more positions and the increasing corporatization of orchestras; both factors are likely to dilute the influence of a conductor over any one orchestra (Jones 1991, p. 9). In Australia, while the Chief Conductor may also hold the position of Artistic Director or Artistic Advisor and ostensibly oversee the orchestra, in general they are not as directly involved in the overall leadership of the organization as are artistic leaders in the other institutions we examined.

On the other hand there are a number of music companies, including orchestras, that have adopted different structures. These companies tend to have full-time artistic leaders, some of whom are founding members of the company. In these cases we are more likely to see a co-leadership model practiced. For some years Orchestra Victoria adopted a co-leadership structure with the full-time Artistic Director/Chief Conductor and the Managing Director sharing the organization's management – and both reporting to the Board. In the Australian Brandenburg Orchestra, the Managing Director is the CEO, but the full time Artistic Director, who founded the company, is on the Board, leading to an integrated co-leadership model in the day-to-day operations of the Company.

Major structural change and/or shift in funding base

Since the mid-1990s, the Australian symphony orchestra sector has undergone major structural change. This resulted from a Commonwealth Government decision that the Australian Broadcasting Corporation should divest itself of its state-based orchestras, and that these should be incorporated as separate entities. As part of this process very deliberate decisions were made about management structures. In this sense the symphony orchestra may fall into the same category as galleries, in that they were perceived to represent a public asset, and the recent history of close government oversight may explain the preference for a sole CEO with a management focus. Reid & Karambaya (2009) have also suggested that the power and focus of a growing organization necessarily changes from the artistic leader, who is the initial focus as the public face of the company, to the administrative leader, who is able to draw in funding as the organization grows, and engage with a wider range of potential stakeholders and sponsors. This would most certainly have been a consideration as divestment from the

Australian Broadcasting Corporation presented major challenges in the area of fund-raising and sponsorship.

Outcomes

As noted at the outset, leadership practices cannot be looked at in isolation. Management structures can encourage certain styles of leadership and signal to potential managers that they will be expected to conduct themselves in certain ways. Yukl describes the way in which 'internal and external constraints interact with each other and with the leader's personality and skills to influence the leader's behavior' (Yukl 2010, p. 378). In the case of an arts organization there are particular characteristics associated with the main leadership positions. Often there is an expectation that the artistic director in an arts organization is the charismatic leader and the general manager is the servant to the art, and hence to the wishes of the artistic director. However, as we demonstrate through this case study, this particular hierarchy is not so evident in the day-to-day leadership practices within many arts organizations. What we found in a number of companies, regardless of formal management structure and accountabilities, is a practice of co-leadership.

Co-leadership in practice

While co-leadership might seem uniquely suited to arts organizations it is not the sole preserve of the arts industry. Complementary or shared leadership models are practiced in corporate settings where senior managers take responsibility for distinct activities along the lines of managing either the external or internal operations. In this context, co-leadership has also been credited with ensuring that 'the whole is much greater than the sum of the parts' (Miles & Watkins 2007, p. 92). Miles and Watkins give the example of a common combination of a chief executive officer and chief operating officer, and name successful pairings at Goldman Sachs, Coca Cola and Microsoft (pp. 92–95). Critical factors in determining the success of co-leadership are considered to be communication and shared vision. In the arts companies the shared vision was most clearly associated with a joint commitment to the pre-eminent status of the 'art'. Communication in successful co-leadership models was evidenced through frequent and often informal communication, practiced daily.

While forms of co-leadership are adopted in other settings, arguably it is a unique model of co-leadership that is practiced in an arts organization. In this section we draw on the observations of artistic directors and general managers engaged in this form of leadership to illuminate the conditions for successful co-leadership. These quotes were obtained through research conducted by the authors over the period 2008 to 2012 which addressed the characteristics of co-leadership within performing arts companies in Australia and elsewhere. To date we have undertaken over 40 interviews with artistic leaders and managerial leaders of 27 of the 28 companies that make up the membership of the Australian Major Performing Arts Group, and seven interviews with leaders in the US and four interviews with leaders in the UK.[3] In this section we utilize comments drawn from the interviewees from the Australian companies, all of whom receive significant funding from the Australia Council and from their respective state governments.

The art comes first

The majority of companies where co-leadership was practiced maintained a formal structure with the artistic director as CEO. A number of general managers were emphatic in their support for the artistic director to be the Chief Executive Officer of the company. This was in order to signal the pre-eminent position of art in the organization's mission. In this capacity the Artistic Director would also have the decision as to whom would be appointed to the general manager's role (with Board approval). The reason for this is in part practical, in that if the artistic director is constrained by an uncomfortable relationship with the general manager, then the company as a whole is hampered.

> *If you're destroying the output of the artistic director, therefore you're undermining your very existence. [General Manager]*

> *I like someone from the artistic side to do a little foot stamp and say: remember what we're supposed to be doing here? We're not an organization that's here to make money. We're not an organization that's here to write policies. We're here to make great theatre. So from that point of view ... I think that artistic organizations should be run by artistic people. [General Manager]*

As result it is often presumed that an incoming artistic director will seek to appoint their own general manager. In this scenario the role of the Board is to appoint an artistic director who will in turn have an enormous influence in the selection of the general manager. The role of the board in this situation was described by one artistic director as follows:

> *It's absolutely crucial that the Board ensures that each new artistic director has his/her own general manager. ... I would recommend to any Board of any organization that the most important thing that a theatre company does is to employ an artistic director. So it's absolutely crucial that they have in mind that the artistic director will pair themselves with a person that they want to work with. [Artistic Director]*

It was also considered to be deeply symbolic that the clear leader of the organization be the artistic director so as to emphasize the fundamental identity of the company as an arts organization.

> *But I think even on a symbolic level the important thing about the CEO position sitting with the artistic director is that it's symbolic. It says that at*

---

[3] The wider research project received financial support from the Faculty of Arts, University of Melbourne. This ongoing project seeks to determine the ways in which co-leadership within an arts organization is consistent with the broader management and leadership literature.

> *the topmost level of governance, whether it's speaking outside company or within the Board, it's saying: this is what the company's here for. This is the primary impulse. [General Manager]*

Although the view that the artistic director should be the Chief Executive Officer was widely held, not all company structures formalized this arrangement. In some cases the artistic director answered to a chief executive officer, although the public face of the company was still very much the artistic director. This structure is likely to be found in organizations where the artistic leader has a part-time role in the organizations such as orchestras and opera companies or to have arisen from the Board's unhappy experience with a previous artistic director, in which case it is not uncommon for a board to restructure the organization and place a manager in this key leadership role. In which case, this could be seen as a reflection on the prior staff members rather than the present.

Just as context may influence the management structure, it will also influence the style of a leader. An artistic director may adopt different styles of leadership for different activities – as will the general manager. For example both may exhibit different styles when dealing with artists or board members, sponsors or staff members. The company requires both a charismatic artistic leader and someone capable of managing the human, financial and physical resources of the company. Because this can rarely be one person and because both aspects of the company are integrally linked, for both to function as co-leaders of the company they must be able to recognize a co-dependence and shared vision.

A need for artistic vision and charisma

In our research, interviewees often referred to the charismatic presence of the artistic leaders as a critical aspect of attracting audiences and fundraising. While the general manager may be engineering the encounters and closing the deals, the public profile of the company must always be closely aligned to its artistic endeavors. As others have noted, even if the artistic leader appears to be lower in the organizational hierarchy, he or she may still take a high public profile as the necessary charismatic public face of the organization (Caust 2010; Khodyakov 2007). For example a distinguished and internationally acclaimed chief conductor will attract critical attention and possibly philanthropic support, and provide the orchestra with a necessary figurehead.

Many general managers considered the integrity and vision of the artistic leadership as crucial to the success of the company:

> *...you have to allow the artistic director to dream and come up with the craziest maddest ideas possible, but then be able to ... pull them back or coach them into seeing a different point of view if it's necessary. [General Manager]*

> *...who's a highly inspiring, very inspired, brilliant ..., who's able to hold the flag which everyone rallies around, [...] which provides that sense of artistic dynamism and restlessness. [General Manager]*

In many cases the notion of a tension between the artistic goals of the company and its financial sustainability was seen more as a challenge, a productive tension, almost an integral part of the conditions under which the artistic outcomes were achieved.

Servant leader to support the artistic director

In this chapter we have focused on leadership models rather than styles. Nonetheless it is clear that each individual leader will deploy a range of leadership styles. Many general managers likened their role to that of servant to the artistic leader. Greenleaf uses the concept of servant leadership to describe a relationship to the company overall (Greenleaf *et al.* 1996). A number of our interviewees used the concept to describe their relationship more directly to the artistic director's creative project. However, given the prominence that this has in the shared vision of the co-leaders we might see this as being equivalent to serving the needs of the company as a whole. The concept of leadership from behind was mentioned by one interviewee – indicating the ability to create space and to be:

> *...willing to let somebody else get the obvious rewards of doing things in terms of both the art and the company, [while you are] doing all the sort of hard edged, analytical, financial ... stuff. [General Manager]*

In other words, the role of the general manager is viewed as facilitative, one that enables the company or the 'creatives' to get on with their primary role of creating – serving the art:

> *... the primary job of management is actually to facilitate artistic vision. [General Manager]*

A view shared by a number of artistic directors:

> *Really the fundamental job of the general manager is to enable the art to be made. [Artistic Director]*

> *[The general manager] said a wonderful thing when we had our first meeting once [they'd] been appointed, [they] said "my role is to facilitate your vision". [Artistic Director]*

While the shared vision for the company might be encapsulated in the artistic vision, both leaders appear well aware that the success of the company relies on their joint contributions. In other words, the artistic director, in the best co-leadership arrangements, acknowledges the essential contribution made by the general manager.

Co-leadership: Awareness of interdependence

The necessity of the general manager role and the dependence on that person by the artistic director, was reinforced when artistic directors described themselves as lacking in certain skills:

> *...the company wouldn't run with just me as the CEO – it would be – fall apart into a chaotic shemozzle fairly quickly... [Artistic Director]*

Similarly, general managers were very clear about their specific skill sets and contribution:

> *[The Artistic Director] is just not interested in budgets and dealing with sponsors and strategy and policy development and all those sorts of areas. ...I get excited about trends and looking back at the information and churning figures through to see where we might be heading. [General Manager]*

At the same time there was a notion that the Artistic Director's role was an intuitive role, one of necessity unmediated:

> *It's just arts coming out of my head whereas the general manager's role is much more complex. [Artistic Director]*

> *In terms of the artistic vision and what the company can create, that very much comes from [the Artistic Director] and his knowledge of all things theatrical. Mine is about the pragmatic, how do actually get there, what do have to do to get there? [General Manager]*

> *I don't know what the General Managers will say to you, but I feel that their sense of facilitating what the person who is the Artistic Director needs is part of their essential skill set. So they adjust the nature of the contribution that they are making, according to the person that they are facilitating to be the Artistic Director. [Artistic Director]*

Conclusion

From this examination of a number of management arrangements we can identify factors that may influence whether co-leadership is observed in practice. One element appears to be a full-time commitment from the artistic director to the company. This may be crucial in leading to a relationship of trust and open communication between the two leaders, so necessary for successful co-leadership. It appears that the more the management structure is defined by government, for example through an act of parliament, the more likely the company is to have a standard corporate structure with a single CEO. Nonetheless, we have still seen a co-leadership model practiced in some of these organizations. This is particularly so when there is an artistic leader closely engaged with the company's artistic personnel on an ongoing basis.

We do not want to give the impression that there is one correct management structure for an arts organization. Similarly there is no one leadership model that will work in all structures and all circumstances. While one might conclude that the art form itself might determine the management structure, this was not always the case. The most obvious example of a sole CEO structure and leadership model was however observed in the museum and gallery sector. Although, as we noted, this was also the sector most closely aligned to government, often established under an Act of Parliament and with a role for government in the appointment of board members. We also noted that the gallery sector differs in that it does not directly employ artists whereas the performing arts companies are closely connected to the actual art making.

The performing arts companies which most often have the practice of co-leadership are those in which there is a high level of collaboration in the art form practice such as theatre and dance. The theatre and dance companies we examined had a very clear management structure, with separate leaders of the artistic activities and managerial activities of the company, even in cases where there was a sole CEO. The level of commitment of the leaders to that particular organization, and their openness and availability to the co-leader are also factors which influence the likelihood of co-leadership operating effectively in practice. The performing arts companies which most often adopt the practice of co-leadership are those in which there is a high level of collaboration in the art form itself, such as theatre and dance. The theatre and dance companies we examined also had very clear management structures, with separate leaders of the artistic activities and the managerial activities of the company, even in cases where there was a sole CEO. The level of commitment of the leaders to that particular organization, and their openness and availability to the co-leader, are factors which appeared to influence the likelihood of co-leadership operating effectively in practice. We also saw that even where the two leaders are not depicted in the organizational chart as being of equal status, a form of co-leadership can emerge through proximity, through openness and sociability, and, perhaps most importantly, through a shared commitment to the artistic output of the company.

Questions

1. Discuss the similarities and differences of co-leadership, dual leadership, shared leadership, distributed leadership and multiple leadership models in the context of the arts.

2. Why are dual or co-leadership models of arts leadership more common in dance and theatre? How do these models work in ideal circumstances?

3. What are the challenges inherent if the artistic leader is the positional leader of an arts organization and/or, vice versa, if the administrative leader is the positional leader of an arts organization?

References

Caust, J 2010, 'Does the art end when the management begins? The challenges of making 'art' for both artists and arts managers', *Asia Pacific Journal of Arts and Cultural Management*, vol. 7, no. 2, pp. 570–584.

Cray, D, Inglis L & Freeman, S 2007, 'Managing the arts: Leadership and decision making under dual rationalities', *Journal of Art Management, Law and Society*, vol. 36, no. 4, pp. 295–313.

Greenleaf, R K *et al.* 1996, *On Becoming a Servant-leader*, Josey-Bass Publishers, San Francisco.

Gronn, P 1999, 'Substituting for leadership: The neglected role of the leadership couple', *Leadership Quarterly*, vol. 10, no. 1, pp. 41–62.

Jones, R 1991, *Human Resource Management of the Arts: A Descriptive Analysis of the Professional Orchestra Manager's Operational Role in the Major American Symphony*, UMI Dissertation Services, Ann Arbor.

Khodyakov, D 2007, 'From a time beater to a music director: The paradox of conductor's power', *American Sociological Association*, Annual Meeting 2007. [available at: http://www.allacademic.com/meta/p182211_index.html]

Miles, S A & Watkins M D April 2007, 'The leadership team. Complementary strengths or conflicting agendas', *Harvard Business Review*, pp. 90–98.

Reid, W & Karambaya, R 2009, 'Impact of dual executive leadership dynamics in creative organizations', *Human Relations*, vol. 62, no. 7, pp. 1073–1110.

Rojo, A & Sauer, E 2007, 'The success of Finnish conductors: Grand narratives and small stories about global leadership', *International Journal of Arts Management*, vol. 9, no. 3, pp. 4–15.

Rojo, A & Sauer, E 2003, 'Partnerships of orchestras: Towards shared leadership', *International Journal of Arts Management*, vol. 5, no. 2, pp. 44–55.

Solia-Wadman, M & Köping, A 2009, 'Aesthetic relations in place of the lone hero in arts leadership: Examples from film making and orchestral performance', *International Journal of Arts Management*, vol. 12, no. 1, pp. 31–43.

Stein, T & Bathurst, J 2008, *Performing Arts Management: A Handbook of Professional Practices*, Allworth Press, New York.

Suchy, S 2004, *Leading with Passion: Change Management in the 21st-century Museum*, AltaMira Press, Walnut Creek, California

Yukl, G 2010, *Leadership in Organizations*, Pearson, Upper Saddle River, NJ; London.

Chapter 6

Strategic leadership in China's music industry

A case study of the Shanghai Audio Visual Press

JOHN FANGJUN LI AND GUY MORROW

Background

Introduction

The history of China's music industry can be traced back 5,000 years. It could be said that ancient music and dance are one of the earliest music industrial forms (Li 2010). 'The Music of Zhuxiang Clan' in particular is the most ancient form of music and dance in terms of the history of Chinese music (Qin 2002). It is the earliest recorded event and activity within the music industry in China[1] when it appeared approximately five thousand years ago. This original form of music practice has endured to the present (Li 2010).

During the early 1900s, China's recorded music industry began, then evolved and developed during the 20th century and into the early 21st century. This industry became a significant and typical part of the music sector more broadly. China's recorded music industry achieved two peak periods during its development: the first period occurred during the 1930s and the 1940s while the second period occurred during the 1990s through to the 2000s. This chapter will focus on the second period. Since the early 21st century to the present, the digital music

---

[1] China here refers to mainland China and does not include Taiwan, Macau or Hong Kong.

industry has become an example of a typical integrated industry[2] (ibid). It is evident that the music industry became one of the most essential sectors within the cultural and creative industries in the 20th and 21st centuries.

This chapter concerns strategic leadership within China's recorded music industry. Although leadership involves both the influence of leaders on other people in an organization and the role of strategic leadership in an organization, this chapter mainly focuses on the latter. Strategic leadership encompasses four tasks: establishing direction, creating a vision, clarifying a big picture, and setting strategies (Ricketts 2009). Thus, this chapter will discuss the influence and role of strategic leadership within China's recorded music industry during the second half of the 1990s by presenting a case study describing the development of the Shanghai Audio Visual Press (SAVP).

This chapter attempts to answer one key research question and two sub-questions. The key research question is:

> *What influence did strategic leadership have on the development of the SAVP and on the broader development of Shanghai and China's recording music business and industry during the 1990s?*

In order to better answer the key question, it is necessary to answer two related sub-questions:

> *What was the broader industrial context in which the SAVP was located and how did this influence its development during the 1990s?*

> *How did the leaders of the SAVP deal with the changes, difficulties, and challenges that the external context brought during this period?*

Approach

Literature review and theoretical model

This section offers a theoretical model through first conducting a literature review that outlines relevant concepts. To begin, it is necessary to define a meaning of the term 'strategic leadership'. The meaning of this term involves three core aspects: strategy, leadership, and strategic leadership. The following text specifically addresses these aspects.

Leadership not only involves the influence of leaders on other people in an organization or an event, it also concerns the leader's strategic management activities (Ricketts 2009). Thus, 'strategy' can be understood as 'strategic management'. Hunger and Wheelen (2006) point out that those strategic decisions affect the long-term future of the entire organization. Hunger and Wheelen (2006) also identify three characteristics of strategic decisions:

---

[2] This refers to the integration of the music industry with other information and cultural industries such as the computing technology industry, the telecommunications industry, the media industry and the cultural industry.

a. rare-strategic decisions (those that are unusual and typically have no precedent to follow);

b. consequential-strategic decisions (those that commit substantial resources and demand a great deal of commitment); and

c. directive-strategic decisions (those that set precedents for lesser decisions and future actions throughout the organization).

Thus strategic decisions are big decisions. These decisions affect an entire organization or a large part of it, such as a whole division or a major function.

Dess *et al.* (2007) intensively investigate strategic leadership and management. They argue that strategic leadership and management of an organization entails three ongoing processes: analysis, decisions, and actions. Moreover, they also contend that the essence of strategic leadership and management is the study of why some firms outperform others. 'Analysis' refers here to strategic goals such as vision, mission, and strategic objectives along with the analysis of the internal and external context or environment of the organization. 'Decisions' refer to the judgment according to the analysis. 'Actions' refer to specific measures employed to implement strategic decisions.

Strategy is also related to the competitive ability of a firm. Hitt *et al.* (2008) assert that a firm's ability to achieve strategic competitiveness and earn above-average returns is compromised when strategic leaders fail to respond appropriately and quickly to changes in the complex competitive environment; thus strategic leaders must learn how to deal with diverse and complex competitive situations (2008, p. 376).

It is necessary to define leadership before strategic leadership is explored. There is no standard definition of leadership. Taormina (2010) suggests that leadership is a quality that involves 'skill'. He defines this as the capacity to skillfully direct the activity, performance or operations of others towards a common goal (2010, p. 41). Northhouse (2007) identifies some components that are central to the majority of these definitions, such as 'leadership is a process', 'leadership involves influence', 'leadership occurs in a group context', and 'leadership involves goal attainment'. Leadership literature generally addresses the influence of leaders on other people in an organization or an event, whereas strategic leadership focuses on the leaders' strategic management activities (Ricketts 2009). Hitt *et al.* (2008) define strategic leadership as,

> ...the ability to anticipate, envision, maintain flexibility, and empower others to create strategic change as necessary (2008, p. 5).

They also propose that it is,

> ...multifunctional in nature. Strategic leadership involves managing through others, managing an entire enterprise rather than a functional subunit (ibid).

Ricketts (2009) notes that strategic leadership has four aspects: establishing direction, creating a vision, clarifying a big picture, and setting strategies. This indicates the importance of strategic leadership in business and industrial activities. Strategic leadership is also defined as the ability of an experienced, senior leader who has the wisdom and vision to create and execute plans and make consequential decisions in a volatile, uncertain, complex and ambiguous strategic environment (Col & Guillot 2003).

This case study of the SAVP will consider in particular the theories of strategic leadership outlined by Dess *et al.* (2007) and Ricketts (2009). This case study follows the three processes – analysis, decisions and actions – the leadership of the SAVP during the second half of the 1990s. This case study will also consider a theory of leadership by Ricketts (2009) where the importance of analyzing the context and situation in which an organization operates is noted.

Research methods: Case studies and historical studies

Historical studies often utilize archived files, material evidence, and observation (in particular, participant observation) and can be conducted and applied in case studies. Historical studies will be used in this chapter to investigate the context of the development of the SAVP and as well as China's music industry. Although this case study will mainly focus on leadership within the SAVP, it will also analyze the evolution and development of both the SAVP and China's recorded music industry from a historical perspective. Therefore the historical study is essential to the case study as it will be used to support it.

Although this chapter mainly uses case studies and historical studies, other research methods will also be used. These methods involve participant observation and secondary data to support the case study. Yin (2003) notes that:

> The case study's unique strength is its ability to deal with a full variety of evidence – documents, artifacts, interviews, and observations. Moreover, in some situations, such as participant-observation, informal manipulation can occur (2003, p. 8).

One of the authors, John Fangjun Li, worked at the SAVP as a music marketing manager and as a music producer/editor from 1994 to 1999. During this period Li observed the development of the SAVP and of China's music industry during the second half of the 1990s. In particular, Li had many opportunities to communicate with the Presidents Hu Zhanying and Zang Yanbin of the SAVP, regarding key strategic action and the external market environment in relation to their leadership of the organization.

Case study: Strategic leadership at the SAVP

It is necessary to outline the historical context in which the SAVP developed, in order to further understand the development logic of the SAVP in relation to the leadership strategies employed at this firm during the 1990s. The SAVP experienced two important developmental phases: the first was the period ranging from the 1980s through to the early 1990s. The second period was the 1990s and the early 2000s.

The SAVP originated in the audio-visual department of the Shanghai Music Book Store in 1983. During the 1980s and the first half of the 1990s, the SAVP mainly produced educational audio-visual products rather than musical audio-visual ones. The second half of the 1990s was the most essential developmental period for the SAVP. During this period, the firm rapidly developed and became the largest music company in China in terms of the annual sale of audio-visual productions. Along with the rapid development of the SAVP, other leading recorded music companies in Shanghai, such as the Shanghai Audio Visual Company and the Shanghai China Record Corporation also achieved much, demonstrating China's overall growth in this field. The SAVP played a leading role within Shanghai and China's recording industry during this period.

This case study involves an analysis of the context and situation analysis as well as the analysis of decisions and actions from the perspective of the organization's strategic leadership and management. The specific context and situation in this case involves the context, circumstance, condition, history and change that influenced the strategic leadership of the SAVP during the second half of the 1990s. This focus of this leadership is on the two executive officers – Mr Hu and Mr Zang. During the second half of the 1990s, the former, as the president of the SAVP, had overall responsibility for managing strategic development direction, human resources, and finance (mainly referring to the revenue and cost elements of this company's income statement); while the latter, as the vice president of the SAVP was mainly responsible for strategic marketing management (specifically referring to audio visual product development, artistic development, marketing management, and promotion in media). As SAVP was a state-owned enterprise, Hu and Zang were appointed to their positions by the Press and Publication Bureau of Shanghai. However before they were appointed as joint executive officers of the SAVP, they communicated with each other over a period of time. They found through this process, that they shared views about management thinking and their personalities were compatible. Thus in this sense, they actually chose each other.

The challenges

Strategic analysis: The context and situation

This section concerns the external context and situation. The analysis focuses on the strategic measures initiated by the leaders of the SAVP during the 1990s, and in particular the second half of this decade. It considers this from both a national and local perspective. Hu and Zang observed changes to the external context of China's recorded music industry and made appropriate strategic decisions in response to these changes. Leaders need to involve specific observations and develop appropriate strategies to address changes that occur within the external context (Kotter 1990; Ricketts 2009; Northouse 2007). During the second half of the 1990s, Hu and Zang led in this way.

It was important for them to analyze the external environment of the SAVP in order to develop some strategies for this firm. Such strategies were needed to generate the developmental direction and orientation of the company during the mid-1990s. Beijing, Shanghai, and Guangzhou dominated most of China's recorded music industry (Zhang and Wang 2009), so that is where they focused their research. Their comparative analysis of these environments then directly influenced the developmental orientation and direction of the SAVP from the mid-1990s.

During the first half of the 1990s, 'contracting' singers was the most important music business activity in China's recording industry. This influenced the development of China's music industry and in particular the recording industry during this period. Guangzhou was the first city to commence the activity of signing popular singers. Yang Yuying was the earliest singer to be signed to Guangzhou New Time Audio Visual Corporation (GNTATC) in 1990 (Wang 2009). Yang's three albums in 1991 passed one million cassette tapes in sales, creating a sales record (Wang 2009, p. 91). The success of Yang and GNTATC led to a rush of signing singers in China during 1993 and 1994. A great number of singers were signed to record labels in Guangzhou and Beijing as well as in Shanghai. The period 1993 to 1994 is considered to be 'the Signing Times' in China (*ibid*: 92), as well as the peak period for China's recorded music industry in the first half of the 1990s.

In order to work out an appropriate development orientation and direction, Hu and Zang compared Beijing and Guangzhou's recording industries in terms of commercial potential in the mid-1990s. Compared to both Beijing and Shanghai, it was evident that Guangzhou's recording industry was more successful during the first half of the 1990s. The main reason for this was that Guangzhou's record firms imitated the music business model of Hong Kong and Taiwan's record companies; in particular they applied the model of signing popular singers and promoting them. However, Beijing's recording industry focused on music composition, music production and popular music (such as Beijing Rock), and pursued personality and artistry more than commercial outcomes. These were the reasons therefore that Beijing's recording industry was not as commercially successful. However compared to Guangzhou and Beijing, Shanghai's recording industry was relatively weak during this period.

The structure of China's recorded music industry underwent a fundamental change in 1995. While Beijing's recorded music industry continued to keep its original development speed, Shanghai's recorded music industry rapidly improved during the second half of the 1990s. Guangzhou's recorded music industry dramatically declined after 1995. The main reason for this was the failure of the business model of just signing singers and then marketing them. The emergence of a large number of music pirates was another major cause. The combination of these factors made it difficult for Guangzhou's recording firms to make a profit. This forced a large number of musicians and popular singers to leave Guangzhou to head north to cities such as Shanghai and, in particular, Beijing.

At this point in time, Hu and Zang decided to analyze the context of Shanghai's recorded music industry so that they could make appropriate decisions concerning the development of their company. During the mid-1990s, there were three large music record companies. These were the SAVP, the Shanghai Company of China Record Corporation (CRSC), and the Shanghai Audio Visual Company. The CRSC was the largest. Hu and Zang particularly studied the CRSC in order to have a better understanding of their approach. It was evident that the CRSC was the leading record company in China since the establishment of the new China because its predecessor was Shanghai Baidai (EMI). In the early 1990s, the SAVP did not control much recorded music, but the CRSC had a current catalogue of recorded music. The CRCS did not develop popular music recordings but it did control recordings of Western classical music and Chinese national music. This gap in the market made the leaders of the SAVP think popular music recording was a good way to quickly improve the market position of the SAVP.

It was necessary for the leaders of the SAVP to examine the system of signing popular singers by Guangzhou's record companies in order to work out some appropriate strategies for the development of their company in the second half of the 1990s. Hu and Zang realized that the main reason for the market failure in Guangzhou was because the system of signing singers was not sophisticated in China. They realized many Chinese people did not respect intellectual property rights and businesses did not understand how to protect them. Moreover the marketing management system had severe problems, given that some Guangzhou salesmen, who were employed in the recording industry, also sold pirated copies at the same time.

Consequently it had become unsuccessful commercially to sign singers after 1995. It was essential to reduce the upfront cost as much as possible and so market distribution became more important. Thus a strategic decision of establishing a strong market distribution channel was made by the leaders of the SAVP. In this way they could attract a greater number of music programs for audio visual production from the external music production and record companies both nationally and internationally. This model was identified by them as the key for success.

Major strategic decisions and actions

In addition to reacting to the context and situation in which an organization is located, strategic leadership also involves strategic decisions and actions. An analysis of the national and Shanghai context as well as the characteristics of China's recorded music industry was necessary for the strategic leadership of the SAVP. This context and situation analysis enabled the leadership of the SAVP to identify some major ways in which to improve the SAVP. These decisions mainly focused on record distribution, the computing management system, the music program introduction and popular music production. The establishment of a method of record distribution was the key decision and action.

Record distribution as the leader

Hu and Zang recognized that the market channel was the key factor in developing the music record business during this period. They had carefully analyzed the nature and characteristics of China's recorded music industry and the market channel was identified by them as being the most essential factor/link within the recorded music industry. In other words, they argued that as record distribution played a key role within the whole chain of the record music industry, they concluded that the 'Channel is the King' and 'Distribution is the Leader'.

Consequently, they made and implemented their strategic decisions and actions according to this core idea. Their first decision and action was to change the organizational structure of the firm (see the Figure 6.1). The purpose of this change was to adapt the firm's structure to suit the requirements of the external context and situation. This change also benefited their method of record distribution. The new organizational structure demonstrated that record distribution would play a central role. The department of distribution was renamed 'The Distribution Centre' from being called 'The Distribution Department' emphasizing its central role in the firm's business. While other departments still kept their original names, such as promotion, production, logistics, duplication, material supply as well as finance, they were all now dependent on what happened at this distribution centre. The promotional department made decisions regarding record promotion according to record distribution. The departments of duplication and logistics also made decisions on the basis of record distribution. They all strove to realize the target of 'zero stock' in order to reduce loss caused by carrying an excessive inventory.

The Distribution Centre operated like a sub-company of the SAVP and there were sub-groups under it. The Centre was also expanded in order to extend the market channel and became four departments from previously being a single department. These were then called North, South, East, and Shanghai. In addition, the number of sales persons was increased from one to four.

In order to stimulate and motivate the sales people at the Centre, Hu and Zang started a new bonus system. The head of the Centre and the four regional managers were promoted. The bonuses they received were higher than the bonuses that the heads of the other departments received. In addition all sales people got higher bonuses based on the sales commissions they earned each month and each year. Thus the external sales network was expanded to 100 effective wholesalers in China after the implementation of this strategic measure in 1996.

Figure 6.1 Organizational structure

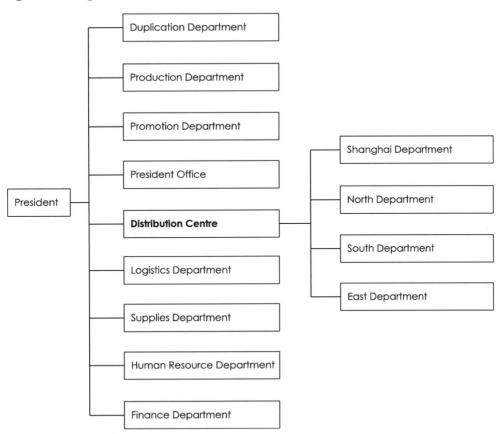

Computer information management system

The establishment of a computerized information management system was the primary strategy for increasing the capability and effect of distribution. During the mid-1990s, the leaders of the SAVP found that their work effectiveness was low and that some key departments had difficulty understanding sales and general finance issues. In order to improve the efficiency of the firm and in particular the effectiveness of record distribution, the computerized information management system was established. The establishment of this system was essential for realizing the developmental strategy of making 'record distribution the leader'. In fact, while this strategic measure greatly improved efficiency at the SAVP, it also achieved the objective of attracting a great number of music programs and record companies to release their music programs through the strong market channel developed by the SAVP.

This advanced, comprehensive, computerized information system was also designed to manage the general business of this firm. This system linked the works of all departments and it was able to show the progress of all works in the firm. The system specifically showed all kinds of dynamic data relating to record distribution, such as the profile of all wholesalers, debts (since the payment after the delivery was a rule in China's audio visual industry), sales volume (dollars amount, number of records, individual and regional sale volume, etc.). All the data could be shown by time, customer by customer, region by region, etc.

The firm developed greatly because of this and became more productive. The SAVP was the first record company in China to establish this type of management system and this approach influenced the development of the rest of China's recorded music industry. The establishment of this system greatly facilitated some top foreign record companies (such as EMI, Warner, Sony, BMG, Taiwan Rock Record, and so on) to release their recordings into China's market through the SAVP.

Outcomes

The network of music programs and popular music artists

Recorded music productions depend heavily on their distribution channels. A strong distribution channel directly affects the sale of recorded music. It also directly influences the source of recorded music programs. One of the main purposes of the strategy of having 'record distribution be the leader' was to attract many excellent music production studios and music recording firms to send their music programs to the SAVP.

For the first time some major Western music record and media companies collaborated with the SAVP. This included EMI, Time Warner, SONY, BMG, and VIACOM. The SAVP bought the copyright of their audio visual productions from these Western firms and released them in mainland China, but not in Taiwan, Hong Kong, and Macau. Artists such as Michael Jackson, Michael Bolton, Mariah Carey, Celine Dion, Kenny G, Wang Lihong, Mao Ning, etc who were with SONY and BMG, released their music through the SAVP. Chinese popular stars such as Wu Sikai, Cai Qin, Lin Yinlian, Zhang Xinzhe, Chen Shuhua, Meng Tingwei, who were signed to EMI, released their music through this firm as well. Meanwhile, the SAVP also released some Western television programs such as BMG Century Selection (with BMG) and Nickelodeon's children's television plays (with VIACOM). These productions all gained successful market outcomes.

A few leading Taiwanese, Hong Kongers, Japanese and Korean music and entertainment firms were also attracted by the distribution channel of the SAVP. Taiwan Rock Record Company was the leading record company in the Mandarin popular music market. Zhang Xinzhe, Zhou Huajian, Xiao Chong, Chen Shuhua, Su Huilun, Huang Yingying, Luo Dayou, Zhang Chu, Dou Wei, He Yong, Chen Long, Black Panthers Band, and Tangchao Band worked with this company to release their records through the SAVP in order to gain greater market success. Some prominent Japanese and Korean music companies also collaborated with the SAVP, such as SM Entertainment (such as HOT) and A & R Division of the Yamaha Music Foundation (such as Chage and Aska). Thus the SAVP also led the way for Japanese and Korean music in China during the second half of the 1990s.

The market distribution of the SAVP attracted many Chinese large media entities as well as some well-known individual musicians who released their recordings through the distribution channel of the SAVP. These companies included China Central Television ('CCTV') ('Six Hundred Children VCD'), Beijing Taihe Rye Music Company (Lao Lang, Gao Xiaosong, Ye Pei, Pu Shu), Guangzhou Tian Di Ren ('Heaven, Earth and Human') Music Studio (Wang Ziming), Beijing Dadi ('the Earth') Music Studio (Ding Wei, Lao Lang), Beijing Hongxing ('Red Star'), and Music Production Studio (Zheng Jun). Some individual prominent popular stars such as Liu Huan and Han Hong also released their records through the SAVP. These records and visual productions obtained a good market response.

Hu and Zang's strategic leadership while primarily concentrated on the market channel for music records, also involved artistic development during the second half of the 1990s. The priority in artistic development at the SAVP was cultivating new popular artists. Sometimes this involved a specific focus, such as the style orientation of the song or the music. Other issues were also addressed such as those related to the selections of songs (including songs written by the artists themselves), song writers (including composers and lyricists), music arrangement, recording (studios, recording engineer), and so on. These artistic decisions were usually related to current market trends. They always required internal music producers, marketing managers and external contracted music recording studios/firms to look for and identify potential popular music artists. Wang Ziming, Lao Lang and Gao Xiaosong are some successful examples from this development. They signed agreements with the SAVP, or their subsidiary music production companies, such as the Heaven, Earth, and Human Music Company or the Beijing Taihe Rye Music Company. The sales of these artists' debut albums (Wang's 'Shang Xin Yu'/'Sad Rain'; Lao's 'Tong Zuo De Ni'/' Your Deskmate'; Gao's 'Qing Chun Wu Hui'/'Regretless Youth') all exceeded 30,000 copies within the first year, making them instant national successes, demonstrating the success of the artistic and production choices made for them. In addition, the SAVP completed some essential music projects that greatly developed China's recorded music industry. The SAVP produced and released three major music audio visual series such as the 'Chinese Singer Series', the 'Chinese Drama Series' and the 'Chinese Original Music Series'. They all gained a successful market outcome.

Conclusion

This case study indicates that contextual changes greatly influenced the strategic leadership of the SAVP and of China's music business and industry more generally. This case study also implies that effective strategic leadership in organizations is achieved by establishing direction, creating a vision, clarifying a big picture, and setting strategies. This case study indicates the significance of three major processes of strategic leadership and management: analysis, decisions and actions. This case study also makes a contribution by providing a conceptual framework that integrates strategic leadership with strategic focus.

Strategic leadership both in the recorded music industry and in other sectors of the music industry requires analysis and study of the context. This strategic analysis includes the national, local and historical situations as well as an analysis of both past failures and the current situation. Thus a good strategic leader needs to learn how to understand the whole music system; this involves both its horizontal and vertical perspectives. In particular, they need to realize each different link in this industry and identify its core industrial link(s). Leaders need to learn what the advantages, disadvantages, strengths and weakness of their firm are and learn how to identify an appropriate way to develop their firms. Therefore it is necessary for a successful strategic leader to deal with all the challenges, changes and difficulties that are presented (Wanasika 2009: 14).

During the 21st century, the music industry has become one of the most significant integrated industries globally (Li 2010). This requires leaders in the music industry to learn how to identify complex industrial links and relationships within this large system. China is becoming one of the largest digital music markets in the World. According to the 2011 Report on Online Digital Music (2011) by the Ministry of Culture of China, online music sales reached 23 billion Yuan (US$3.65 billion) while mobile music reached 20.2 billion Yuan (US$3.2 billion) in income turnover. The digital music industry is an integrated industry, and as such, has brought many opportunities and challenges for leaders both in China and the world. In particular, globalization and constant change has caused intensive industrial convergence to occur. Thus successful leadership involves needing to constantly learn in order to rapidly adapt to external environmental changes.

Questions

1. What approach did the leaders of the Shanghai Audio Visual Press use to determine the future direction of their organization? Describe the strengths and weaknesses of this approach.

2. How would you describe the leadership of the Shanghai Audio Visual Press in terms of style, approach and outcomes?

3. The Shanghai Audio Visual Press is described as a state-owned enterprise. What does this mean, and how different are such organizations from privately-owned organizations? How does this organizational model influence its leadership?

References

Col, W & Guillot, M 2003, 'Strategic Leadership: Defining the Challenge', retrieved on December 26, 2011 from: http://www.airpower.au.af.mil/airchronicles/apj/apj03/win03/guillot.html#Guillot.

Dess, G, Lumpkin, GT, Eisner, A 2007, *Strategic Management: Text and Cases,* McGraw, Hill Irwin.

Hitt, M A, Ireland R D, Hoskisson R E 2008, *Strategic Management: Competitiveness and Globalization, Concepts and Cases,* South-Western College Pub, Boston Massachusetts.

Hunger, D, Wheelen T L 2006, *Essentials of Strategic Management,* Prentice Hall, Upper Saddle River, New Jersey, the Fourth Edition.

Kotter, J P 1990, *A force for change: How leadership differs from management,* Free Press, New York.

Li, F 2010, 'A Study of the Research Activity of China's Music Industry Since the Reform and Opening-Up and Some Other Related Issues', *Huangzhong,* Wuhan China, The issue 3, pp. 12-23.

Northouse, P 2007, *Leadership Theory and Practice,* Sage Publications, Thousand Oaks, CA.

Qin, X 2002, *The History of Chinese Music,* The Literature and Art Publishing House, Beijing, China.

Ricketts, K G 2009, 'Leadership vs. Management', retrieved on December 26, 2011 from: http://www.ca.uky.edu/agc/pubs/elk1/elk1103/elk1103.pdf.

Taormina, R 2010, 'The Art of Leadership: An Evolutionary Prospective', *International Journal of Arts Management,* Montreal, vol. 13, no. 1.

Wang, S 2009, *Chinese Contemporary City Popular Music,* Shanghai Education Publishing House, Shanghai, pp. 91-92.

Wanasika, I 2009, In Search of Global Leadership, retrieved on December 26, 2011 from www.aabri.com/manuscript/08011.pdf.

Yin, Robert K 2003a, *Case Study Research, Design and Methods* (3rd edn., vol. 5), Thousand Oaks: Sage.

Zhang, L and Wang J 2009, *A Study of The Sino-Foreign Audio-Visual Industry and Relevant Policies,* Chinese Book Publishing House, Beijing, pp. 31-32.

Chapter 7

Dual executive leadership in the arts

Rémi Brousseau, Pierre Rousseau and Le Théâtre Denise-Pelletier

WENDY REID

Overview

Dual executive leadership (DEL) is a common feature in the performing arts. It is also found in a wide number of other sectors involving professional specialists (newspapers, design and architecture, legal, engineering, accounting firms and lawyers, as well as religious congregations, film and academic institutions) (Alvarez & Svejenova 2005; Fjellvaer 2010). The arts provide a particular setting for studying this leadership form since the two individuals are usually appointed independently of each other, with separate contracts. Institutional logics can be strongly polarized in the arts (Lampel, Lant & Shamsie 2000). The potential for negative conflict is greater than in other settings. This case provides insight into an effective DEL relationship in an arts organization.

Background[1]

We are warmly welcomed by Rémi Brousseau, executive director and Pierre Rousseau, artistic director for Le Théâtre Denise-Pelletier in May 2009. They are

---

[1] This case was originally researched and written in French by Raymonde Gazaille and Wendy Reid. Interviews were undertaken with Rémi Brousseau, Pierre Rousseau, Michel Blais, the chair of the board of directors, and Manon Huot, the administrative director of the organization during May 2009. It is listed with the Case Centre at HEC Montréal and is used regularly in the cultural management program at HEC Montréal. Translation of the case and citations was undertaken by the author.

planning their first season in their newly renovated theatre. It was originally a vaudeville house, then a cinema, and it required extensive and creative solutions to enhance the experience for artists, production teams and the audience. The duo had just finished a year of itinerant productions using several theatres around Montréal. During the process, there were risks and stresses for the organization and the duo. Tired but pleased, they reflected on the history of leadership in the organization, their own relationship, and the challenges they had experienced over the last years.

While they were very lucky to find temporary office space and a small theatre for their experimental work in an old fire-hall with another theatre company in Montréal, presenting their usual season for 2008-09 in a larger hall was not easily resolved. They thought of a large cinema in the city centre. However, their audience is largely comprised of school groups in buses, and after numerous hopeful conversations with the cinema management, the planned school bus parking location was no longer available in busy downtown Montréal. They concluded that they would be better off to find several different performance spaces around Montréal to suit their schedule.

Normally Rousseau, the artistic director (AD) would develop one or two new productions for the season, to satisfy his artistic ambitions and the needs of his audience. But adapting new productions to several theatres made this practice very expensive and too risky. So he was forced to borrow older productions from other producers or reviving productions from past repertoire. As well, there was concern that their audience would not follow, since they were not visible in one place throughout the year. He commented:

> The challenge was very painful for me ... Every year, I had found it difficult to find the right classical work or two that was already produced (for the third production of the season) to interest the student public. But this year I had to fill a whole season with someone else's work!

And Brousseau, the executive director (ED), had to revise the budget extensively. Venturing into unknown territory was quite stressful. However, the transition season occurred without serious problems and the audience remained loyal. It was a great relief. But they still had to finish the renovations and produce their first season in the newly renovated hall. Such insecurity about the future would have been overwhelming for many duos and their relationship. But Rousseau and Brousseau's ability to communicate and understand other perspectives was particularly helpful during this period of their relationship.

History

Founded in 1964, the company was first called Nouvelle Compagnie Théâtrale (NCT). Resident in another theatre, they performed French classics to student audiences. In 1974, they moved to the 'Granada' movie theatre in the east end of the city, and continued their commitment to the founding mandate. Over time, the company added new work by Québec authors. But in the early 1990s, the company was led by two artistic directors who explored repertoire different from the original mandate – Guy Nadon (1989-1991) and Brigitte Haentjens (1991-1994). Pierre Rousseau followed as artistic director in 1995. Rousseau explains the current vision:

> The students need to have access to balanced programming that will express different styles and types of theatre across time: the classical repertoire allows us to see our culture through a historical perspective and to understand the voyage of that culture through time. In contrast, the contemporary repertoire sheds light on our lives through the eyes of current writers. As for Québec theatre, this repertoire provides insight into how our own culture fits into the larger world and confronts us with that vision.

In 1997, the company was renamed in homage to one of Québec's great female actors – Denise Pelletier – Le Théâtre Denise-Pelletier (TDP).

The current duo

Pierre Rousseau, artistic director

After being trained in the acting program at the National Theatre School of Canada in Montréal, Rousseau performed in the privately owned Québec touring company of the Corriveau family for seven years. But after that, he landed a position with a theatre for young audiences: Théâtre du Quartier.

> It was in the pre-union era where we did everything – acting, writing, directing, and then every other week, we were responsible for cleaning up, and selling the tickets! We each had to be very flexible and to develop many skills.

Rousseau was soon recognized as a dedicated theatre person with a talent for strategy. He was invited to sit on a number of association boards in the sector. He also directed plays and was eventually promoted to artistic director of a youth theatre, in Sherbrooke outside of Montréal. But he continued his freelance acting career in Montréal as well as teaching at the National Theatre School. He eventually accepted a position as head of theatre at the Montréal Arts Council.

> This allowed me to combine all my experience and abilities to analyze grant applications, as well as to have the opportunity to attend over 200 shows a year. The experience also provided insights into the next generation in Montréal as well as the English theatre scene. My perspective on 'institutions'[2] changed.

While there, he developed a policy for youth theatre. But wanting to avoid too much bureaucracy, he moved to the professional theatre association (Conseil Québecois du Théâtre, or CQT) as executive director. During his tenure, he was

---

[2] In Québec, theatres are grouped together according to their mission and artistic focus. There are creation companies led by a writer or director and their mandate is to develop and produce new work only. There are theatres for young audiences, and there are also theatre companies who present a range of repertoire with larger budgets and their own theatre facility. The latter are classed as 'institutions'.

involved in numerous policy development projects, including youth theatre again, cultural policy, and the founding of the Québec Arts Council. He had a significant impact on theatre at the time. But in 1995, the NCT board approached him to be artistic director.

They were seeking a champion for the theatre's original mandate of youth theatre.

Rémi Brousseau

Rémi Brousseau trained as an actor at the Consevatoire d'art dramatique à Québec, but he comments:

> *They don't fire you, but they encourage you to think of your future. I understood very quickly what that meant! I decided to register at Université de Laval in Québec City for the following academic year.*

But one of the teachers at the Conservatoire needed an assistant stage manager that fall. Brousseau was then invited to fill in a sick leave at a small local theatre company. His career as a stage manager evolved. He ended up at Le Théâtre Trident, the 'institutional' theatre company in the capital city of Québec, eventually as production manager for a couple of years.

He continued his career in Montréal, at the Théâtre de Nouveau Monde and the Théâtre Rideau Vert. He was curious, however, about administration.

> *When I was a stage manager, I was keen to broaden my field of vision ... I found it frustrating in production, because I had the impression that certain problems were systemic, and that there might be a solution at the administrative level. I was interested in being an administrative director.*

So he returned to Québec City as administrative director of Le Théâtre Trident for five years. Here, he honed his capacity for problem solving. At the end of 1992, he felt the need for new insights and stimulation, so he took a sabbatical. Partially funded by the City of Québec, he studied theatre production in England. At the end of the year away, he returned to Montréal as a dance company administrative director where he learned about international touring.

> *I learned to manage in the most practical manner possible ... contrary to what everyone thinks, when you manage, you do not have power, but rather, you engage the power... and you do not do what you personally want, but rather the best that you can under the circumstances.*

After two years in dance, he wanted to return to theatre. He had a first interview with the NCT.

> *It had been three years since I had been in a theatre, and when I entered the theatre at NCT, it was as if I had just left one theatre company on a Friday night and I was entering another one on Monday morning. I adore making theatre happen ... I felt at home. For me, the most exciting moment of the year is the announcement of the program for the next year. You invite people to come to your home ... The administration is connected to it all – you are part of the whole thing.*

The duo's arrival at NCT

Unusually, Pierre Rousseau and Rémi Brousseau arrived at NCT within one month of each other – February and March 1995. At the time, the theatre community was up in arms about the well-publicized and emotional departure of Brigitte Haentjens from the company. She and NCT's executive director and board were in a major conflict about her choice of repertoire. With her departure, the board sent a letter to the editors of the local newspapers, explaining that they wished to return to the company's initial mandate of classical theatre for young people. They wished to find a well-qualified team of people to do this. But the situation was highly charged. The board hoped for a calm and intelligent approach.

The challenges

For five years, the company had experienced difficulties. The two previous artistic leaders, Guy Nadon and Brigitte Haentjens, changed the founding mandate. While their work was of very high quality and innovative, it became less and less accessible to a student audience. As the decision-makers for most ticket sales, teachers were most interested in classical theatre. The box office was declining dangerously. Early in the process, the board judged the administrative director as not fiscally responsible. So after this person's departure, the board sought someone else to partner Nadon. But Nadon left in solidarity with the departing administrative director. The board hired Jacques Vézina, a well-respected manager in theatre and engaged Brigitte Haentjens as artistic director. The company had a significant deficit of CDN$500,000 which was one-third of the annual budget. According to the current board president, Michel Blais, the pair worked well together in their first year, but it became increasingly apparent that Ms. Haentjens' artistic vision would move the theatre even further away from its educational orientation. Conflict erupted again at the executive level. The board was also divided, so they set up a working committee to ponder the question of repertoire and the mission of the organization.

Jacques Vézina resigned, and it was in the interviews to replace him that Rémi Brousseau was first considered. The board chose another candidate, who, according to Brousseau, was probably less curious about the deficit. The president at the time explained it simply as a mortgaged loan. However, the new ED left quickly because of irreconcilable differences with Ms. Haentjens. Government funders signaled to the board their serious concern.

The board took the drastic step of informing Ms Haentjens that her contract would not be renewed after the end of June 1995. Ms Haentjens chose to leave immediately and very publically, along with a few board members. So in January 1995, the NCT had neither an AD nor an ED. The new president made a telephone call to Rémi Brousseau.

> He asked me whether the position was still interesting for me. And at that point, I interviewed the president. I questioned him closely about what was

happening. He gave a candid overview of the situation, and I decided to accept. Everyone told me that I was crazy!

To recruit a new AD, the board selected a committee including the current president of the board, two well-respected theatre professionals, and the new ED, Rémi Brousseau. The board was very concerned about two objectives: the partnership at the top and a respect for the original mandate of the company. After contacting a number of well-known directors and actors, the committee decided to reorient their search to change from the immediate past. They wanted a director and actor, but someone who understood and was associated with theatre for young people. They wanted someone who would support the founding vision of the organization. Brousseau called Rousseau who reflects on his reaction to the call:

I thought that he was calling me to be part of the selection committee because I was the executive director of the CQT. He explained that instead the committee wanted to meet me for the position of artistic director. All I could say was that I wanted to think this over during the weekend. On Monday morning I called him back giving him the names of five directors that should be on the list, but I gathered by his reaction that none of them wanted to be interviewed. I realized why they were calling me since it was clear they wanted a very different profile. They didn't want a high-profile star artist, but rather someone who would put out the fire and who would take the mandate of the organization seriously.

The current president, Michel Blais, explained that the board did not question the dual leadership structure. They wanted a relationship at the head of the company that would negotiate and balance the decisions for the company. Blais says:

For us, it was clear that they had to agree in order to function well.

The approach

The current duo's dynamics

The two leaders report equally to the board of directors and each has a contract renewable every three years, more recently off-set by a year. However, there is no independent document that outlines their respective roles and responsibilities in detail. Their initial contracts contain minimum job specs and these same contracts have been renewed every three years without change. The two are both members of the board, although non-voting. One has the role of treasurer and the other is the secretary.

Most permanent employees report to the ED, but anyone relating to the stage reports to the AD. There are 10 permanent employees, most of who have been with the organization for about 10 years. The administrative director, Manon Huot, has been in place for 20 years and experienced the full history of the earlier drama.

Both leaders consider themselves appropriately involved in the hiring process.

It isn't a highly formal and regimented process (Brousseau).

When we hire someone, we are always in agreement ... and when someone becomes difficult, we deal with the person together (Rousseau).

The relationship

The duo was quite perplexed about the structure of the 2008-09 season. Normally, they would develop two new productions, but this time, they needed three marketable productions from previous seasons or other producers. They had to work on unfamiliar stages.

Rousseau explained:

We weren't sure whether the schools and the public would follow us. But we were lucky – the whole thing worked out, but I have to say, only once in my life, not twice ...!

Both feel that their relationship thrives because they each understand and have lived the other's reality. As a result, for a difficult decision, each is able to understand the other's point of view and is able to live with jointly made decisions. Rousseau explains:

The fact that this works so well is because Rémi knows what is involved in a theatre production and I know what is in a budget.

They feel that they share a similar approach to work. He describes Brousseau:

What I like about Rémi is that he is very cautious, and so am I... In the theatre, you can manage all the expenses, but it is the revenues that can get beyond control.

They typically hold back, rather than confront.

Pierre and I do not feel that we are in conflict when we need to make a decision. We make decisions together ... This is not our company. We try to make the best decision for the company, not for our own personal interest.

Brousseau has a warm personality and he works hard. He is careful when confronted with a difficult situation. He appears to complement Rousseau who is a passionate man of action. But Brousseau explains: 'We don't lead the company with our emotions.' Rousseau elaborates:

We lead the company but we know that we are here for a time. When I leave, the person who replaces me will find a situation that may not be completely ideal, but it will be a good situation compared to what we inherited on our arrival. This is very important to me since we manage an organization that will continue. I don't want to create a CDN$500 000 deficit. And I think that Rémi wants the same thing. We are completely oriented to the mandate and all our decisions are made as a result of it. We have to understand the constraints of the educational system. The ultimate purpose is to provide young people with an introduction to theatre that will stay with them through their lives and they will be motivated to attend theatre later in life.

For Brousseau, success comes from an understanding of the company's mandate. He explains:

> In the Théâtre Denise-Pelletier the situation is very different from other theatre companies, because the mandate is very clear. This is not our company. It isn't my company and it doesn't belong to Pierre, either. In an 'institution', the individuals come and go, but the theatre remains. After us, there will be others.

The two relate to each other closely in their professional life, but do not socialize much outside of the theatre. Once a year, they meet in a restaurant with their families for Brousseau's birthday. Everyone in the organization recognizes their collaborative style. Michel Blais, the president, has never seen them argue:

> Everything is undertaken naturally with good humor and good understanding.

Manon Huot confirmed this collaboration:

> They complement each other. I have never seen either of them angry or in disagreement. They have their individual points of view, but they always seem to find a way to agree in the end.

She confirmed the good humor and understanding. She explained that Brousseau's rigour and thoroughness was key for the renovation project. Without his patience during study, after study, and in making repeated grant proposals, they would never have successfully concluded the project. The president felt the communication between the two leaders and with the board was important. He observed that numerous events had tested the relationship: the difficulties from the previous leadership situation, the financial challenge at their arrival, three teachers' strikes, and the recent renovation. These experiences created a bond that has continued.

> The difficulties that they had to confront were formative and were a common experience in which they had to work together. The renovation has been a challenge for both of them, both financially and artistically. They are capable of working together very well.

Manon Huot confirms:

> The 2008-09 season was an amazing team challenge when Pierre decided not to develop any new productions. It was a big decision to move from one theatre to the next – on tour for the whole season. They worked hard together on that one and there wasn't any major issue that fell between the cracks.

The future

They have announced their 2009-10 season, and have already sold 10,000 tickets in a week. This is encouraging news. But they remain cautious about the new season and the final stages of the renovation. Their audience has followed them on tour, but will they return to the new theatre? and will the theatre be renovated on time?

According to Brousseau, one of the secrets is being adaptable to enable decision-making.

> *Pierre and I are a team and we have this ability to adapt ... we find a solution that may or may not be the best solution for the situation, but it is the one that we have agreed on and we go ahead together with that.*

From Rousseau's point of view, he is hopeful. He is looking forward to the innovations for technical production in the new theatre as well as a new production which is '20 000 Leagues under the Sea', an adaptation of Jules Verne's novel. It will be a great test for the new theatre.

> *The actors will finally feel the audience close to them. The acoustics will be improved. It is going to be extraordinary. Now anything is possible!*

Rousseau is talking about extending the season, renting the theatre out to other producers in the summer, and putting new creators into his season mix. He finds it very satisfying to work with young professionals and to help bring their ideas alive.

The president is keen to use this new phase in the company's development to reassess the board, its role, and way of working with the two leaders. Despite these buoyant perspectives, the future is still unsure and the two will have to adapt to new ways of working in the new theatre.

A view in 2011

I toured the new theatre with Pierre Rousseau in spring 2011. He was justifiably proud. When the theatre opened, it was still under construction, and a lobby door needed replacement at the last minute on opening night. A few elements were yet to be completed, but the project came in on budget and has won a number of Montréal and Québec architectural awards for renewal and adaptation of a heritage building. The operating costs appear to be under control and the theatre community is enthusiastic.

Outcomes

Learning from the case and theory

The case provides helpful material to reflect on three topics of dual executive leadership: relational capabilities at the executive level, leadership as two people, and the influence of organizational history on the relationship and the board. The relationship in this case appears to be very effective with a positive impact on the organization. The two work well together and seem to have complementary personalities and backgrounds. The organization's immediate history was turbulent and difficult. The board made its decisions about the leadership structure and candidates as a result of that history. But the duo also has an awareness of past problems: the need to respect the original mandate and to maintain a balanced budget. These issues focused the two leaders as they made decisions through some challenging times of their own.

Relational capabilities at the executive level

In the study of the relationship, I found that there were four elements that were pertinent: the training and experience of each, personalities, trust and conflict management.

1. ***Individual backgrounds – training and experience:*** The pair that assumed leadership of TDP in 1995 was well-suited for their jobs. Each had broad experience within and around theatrical organizations. They were also experienced in small and large organizations. Both were trained in theatre, but neither had a high profile career as an actor or director. And each had spent time outside the immediate organizational experience of a theatre company – Brousseau worked in dance and travelled to England, and Rousseau had worked with the Conseil des Arts de Montréal and with the sector association as the executive director. They had both sat on boards of directors and had experienced an executive leadership role in another theatre company. All of this experience provided them with a larger sense of their role at TDP across the divide of the paradoxes of the sector (Lampel, Lant & Shamsie 2000) and each was able to understand the perspective of the other person.

2. ***Personalities and particular talents:*** The personalities of the two leaders are complementary. The board included the ED on the selection committee for the AD, and they seemed to choose Rousseau for the relationship. The duo was instructed to 'get along'. This emphasis on the relationship appears very unusual in the sector (Reid & Karambayya 2009). Despite the fact that the two had never worked together previously, they very quickly established a positive and respectful relationship. They certainly communicated well together, and did not anger easily. They were considerate of each other and others in the organization. They reflected a collaborative working style and even seemed able to finish each other's sentences. They were thoughtful and cared about quality in all aspects of the organization.

   Choosing someone for their relational capabilities is difficult when added to many other criteria for selection. In this case one of the duo members was included in the selection process and he would have focused on the relationship. Checking with references for collaboration and conflict management skills and an ability to trust could be useful personality indicators to assess.

3. ***Trust in professional relationships:*** In this case, there appeared to be a very high trust within the relationship. Rousseau was willing to make significant compromises to produce the itinerant season and to support the renovation project. Research on trust distinguishes between intimate and professional relationships (McAllister 1995). Emotional or affect-based trust suggests couples are willing to support each other even in circumstances not in their individual interest. Cognitive trust, on the other hand, requires regular proof by one partner to trust the other; it

works in a context of self-interest. In this case, the two appeared to demonstrate a level of affect-based trust.

Research also suggests that an individual can partially trust another person (Kramer & Lewicke 2010). For instance, one could trust someone to do a fine job of analyzing a situation, but not be relied on to arrive for meetings on time. Cognitive trust and partial trust suggest the need to spend time working together and for regular communication. Trust has been shown to be conducive to generating and maintaining positive conflict (Simons & Peterson 2000). While trust was not a term used in the interviews in this case, the give and take of the duo's relationship and the respect expressed for each other's skills and capabilities demonstrate a mature understanding of the relationship dynamics.

4. *Conflict and its management:* There appears to be very little conflict within the duo of this case. While there were indications that Brousseau and Rousseau were slow to anger and never confronted each other in an argument; there were no doubt differences for a time as they worked through their solutions for the company.

There are three types of conflict identified in the literature (Jehn 1997a, 1997b). It is useful to understand them in the context of DEL. First is task conflict, which involves a focus on what is to be done. The dynamic is positive and enables creative solutions. The second is process conflict, which concerns who does what and how. It can remain positive and similar to task conflict, or it can evolve into negative and emotional conflict, especially if opposition concerns territory and personal power. The third type is emotional or values-based conflict. This type of conflict is least likely to have rational resolution, erodes trust in any relationship, and can be dispersed into the rest of the organization. This is the conflict that many think of when they mention the word, yet conflict can be productive and useful.

In another study of dual executive leadership involving eight performing arts cases across Canada, we found that conflict can be disseminated beyond the duo into the larger organization. When it is negative, conflict can have a detrimental effect on well-being of the organization, affecting decision-making, morale, and organizational political climate and culture (Reid & Karambayya 2009). Leadership scholars argue the necessity of a single leader to present a clearly articulated vision and strategy of the organization. Conflict would undermine a leader's coherence. However, the research on DEL shows that when conflict is retained and managed within the duo, the organization can still function well. This appears to be the case at TDP.

In fact, DEL is considered most useful where there is inherent conflict, where the objectives can be paradoxical (Lampel, Lant & Shamsie 2000) and the culture is pluralistic with numerous institutional logics (Hining & Reay 2009). Duos will develop many strategies to manage the opposing logics within their relationship (Fjellvaer 2010). They support the organization's ability to collaborate across co-dependent professional (artistic) and managerial perspectives, even though these perspectives create internal tension. Funding bodies and market forces have grown in North America through the 20th century, and have generated pressure to add the managerial role to ensure that professional/artistic roles are accountable for resource allocation to organizational mandates (Peterson 1986). Unresolved negative conflict is always a potential threat and it can undermine the leadership vision and its influence in the organization. This was certainly the case in the era at NCT prior to the arrival of Rousseau and Brousseau. The organization's existence was seriously threatened and government funders were adding to the pressure indicating how damaging such conflict can be to an organization.

Leadership as two people

The leadership by two people also considers four elements: how the jobs are defined through contracts and job descriptions, decision-making, hiring, and the culture in the organization as a result of the duo's leadership.

5. *Contracts, job descriptions and division of labour:* Many would argue that a successful leadership relationship needs clearly coordinated job descriptions. However, in this case, there are no detailed job descriptions and the minimal descriptions that exist do not seem to define the relationship clearly. While the two individuals at TDP have established their roles and support them with their respective expertise, they overlap extensively and without problem. Everyone interviewed felt that the duo was a joint affair and that together they provided an inspired and coherent sense of leadership for the organization.

    However, it is interesting to note that Rousseau and Brousseau do not socialize outside of their jobs. They have built a very solid relationship based on responding to many challenges and a long time working together. They appear to have developed trust within this professional relationship to support a well-synchronized and collaborative relationship. Other successful relationships in cases studied elsewhere have demonstrated the same behavior (Reid & Karambayya 2009). Ironically, this evidence seems to contradict the frequent comments in the sector about how this is a marriage. While the relationship needs professional intimacy, these are often not personally related duos.

    The duo's approach to leadership and relationship was clearly appreciated by the board president, Michel Blais, and the administrative director, Manon Huot, both of whom had lived through the deficit and conflict-ridden period at TDP prior to Rémi and Pierre. The contrast was remarkable for them and for the organization as a whole.

6. *Decision-making:* The duo had acquired some relational resources over time by living together through some very difficult situations. They

inherited a deficit. Three teachers' strikes affected the audience attendance and the theatre's bottom line significantly. They planned the future renovations together. They invented and resolved the issues of an 'itinerant' production season and at the same time coped with the surprises inherent in renovating their theatre. Their relationship was long-standing and they knew how to function, making decisions together by thoughtful consideration of each other's perspective and expertise. When arriving at the particularly demanding double pressure of an itinerant season and renovations, they were well-equipped with experience in decision-making.

7. *Hiring:* They report hiring people together. Brousseau seems to lead and claims to hire most people. However, both provide approval for each addition to the organization. They jointly evaluate and fire difficult individuals. There is no significant employee turnover; people seem to find it an attractive place to work. Many have been with the organization for a long time.

8. *Culture of the organization:* The culture of the organization has evolved with respect for the duo. It is a small organization, so the dynamics of the leadership relationship influence everyone. Both the board president and the administrative director claim that they had never seen the two argue. Clearly, if there are differences, Rousseau and Brousseau are quite successful at resolving the issues between them.

Organizational history and context

The organizational history plays a significant role to define the duo's dynamics. There is frequently a shadow effect from conflict prior to the current duo, the duo's history, and the type of organization.

1. *Shadow effect of past conflict:* The history of the organization in the mid-1990s had a significant impact on the choice of replacements for the departing executives and the instructions to the new leaders. The board's controversial actions had forced them into the public spot-light and presumably they were not comfortable. Board members worked through the conflict (many left) and made a public declaration of their strategy to return to the original mission of the organization.

   This history cast a 'shadow' on events that followed and motivated decisions and relationship dynamics. The board chose to avoid high profile and potentially difficult people and both Brousseau and Rousseau accepted the board's definition of their role at that time. Despite their long tenure with the organization, they indicate that they are professionals passing through and are in service to the organization. They do not individually personify the organization. They have taken on the responsibility to ensure continued respect for the founding mission of the organization and to maintain a financial balance. Their relationship also appears to be guided by those very dramatic events in the past.

While their personalities work well together, they were also instructed to 'get along'. The board was clear that the organization would not tolerate negative conflict. The case does not provide much information about the early days of their relationship, but it is possible that this board-imposed framework guided them as they learned to work together. In other studies of arts organizations, immediate previous history appears to have a strong influence on the early stage of a duo's relationship (Reid & Karambayya 2011). Typically, executive duos in the performing arts are not self-selected; they are chosen independently by the board. So there is a greater potential of conflict emerging between the two and this early stage is important for enabling the development of cognitive trust at a minimum. In this case, the duo did participate in the choice of each other since Brousseau was part of the selection committee, but the shadow of the dramatic previous history of the organization also appeared to play a role in their relationship. Their comments about their role in an 'institution' and about wishing to leave the organization in good shape for successors reflect this pre-occupation.

2.   *Recent history and context:* The prior internal history of the organization is not the only contextual influence on the duo. They were also forced to work through some rigorous external circumstances that were imposed on them. Resource dependence is, of course, a very demanding environmental pressure and this duo's experience was not unusual in this regard (Pfeffer & Salancik 1978).

3.   *Type of organization:* The organization in this case is defined as an 'institution', as the protagonists explain. Their strategies and vision are contained within this larger purpose as defined from the early days of the organization. The market plays an important role in messaging back to the organization whether the mandate is being respected, since ticket sales have been seen to drop significantly if a certain repertoire is not produced from one season to the next. This organizational positioning appears to have played a major role in the choice of the current duo. Perhaps the board's eventual choice of a less visible and charismatic artistic sensibility has been key for the success of the duo and the organization. In other types of organizations, it is interesting to ponder the potential for conflict and trust, particularly creation-based performing companies where the artistic leader is the centre and sometimes founder of the organization. The contingencies for successful DELs have not been fully explored.

Conclusion

Dual executive leadership is a common structure at the executive level in performing arts organizations. Many argue that it is inefficient and difficult for the organization (Locke 2003) but others have recently argued that this kind of collaboration should be extended elsewhere in the cultural field, like museums (Antrobus 2009). This case provides useful insights into the dynamics of this kind of leadership, how it can be successful and what the limitations may be. My own experience and research indicates that both positive and negative examples are present in the sector. Hopefully, by understanding the elements that underpin a positive situation, more students and managers will usefully apply the lessons from this case to their own lives and organizational experience to enhance DELs throughout the sector.

Questions

1. Describe the relationship of the executive duo of Rémi Brousseau and Pierre Rousseau, and evaluate its strengths and weaknesses.
2. What are the effects of the duo's relationship on the management and leadership of the organization?
3. What has been the role of the board of directors regarding the leadership of the organization?

References

Alvarez, JL & Svejenova, S 2005, *Sharing Executive Power*, Cambridge University Press, New York.

Antrobus, C 2009, *Two heads are better than one: What art galleries and museums can learn from the joint leadership model in theatre*, NESTA Innovation Fellow in the Clore Leadership Programme, London.

Fjellvaer, H 2010, 'Dual and unitary leadership: Managing ambiguity in pluralistic organizations' *Doctoral dissertation*, Norwegian School of Economics and Business Administration.

Heenan, DA & Bennis, W 1999, *Co-Leaders: The Power of Great Partnerships*, John Wiley & Sons, New York.

Jehn, KA 1997a, 'Affective and cognitive conflict in work groups: Increasing performance in value-based intra-group conflict', in C De Dreu & E Van de Vliert (eds.), *Using Conflict in Organizations*, Sage Publications, Thousand Oaks.

Jehn, KA 1997b, 'A qualitative analysis of conflict types and dimension in organizational groups'. *Administrative Science Quarterly*, 42: pp. 530-557.

Kramer, RM & Lewicke, R J 2010, 'Repairing and enhancing trust: Approaches to reducing organizational trust deficits', *The Academy of Management Annals*, 4(1): pp. 245-277.

Lampel, J, Lant, T & Shamsie, J 2000, 'Balancing act: Learning from organizing practices in cultural industries', *Organization Science*, 11(3): pp. 263-269.

Locke, EA 2003, 'Leadership: Starting at the top', in CL Pearce & JA Conger (eds.), *Shared Leadership: Reframing the hows and whys of leadership*, Sage, Thousand Oaks CA.

McAllister, DJ 1995, 'Affect and cognition-based trust as foundations for interpersonal cooperation in organizations' *Academy of Management Journal*, 38(1): pp. 24-59.

Peterson, RA 1986, 'From impresario to arts administrator: Formal accountability in nonprofit cultural organizations', in PJ DiMaggio (ed.), *Nonprofit Enterprise in the*

Arts: Studies in Mission and Constraint, Oxford University Press, New York and Oxford.

Pfeffer, J & Salancik, G 1978, *The External Control of Organizations: A Resource Dependence Perspective*, Harper & Row, New York.

Reay, T & Hining, CR 2009, 'Managing the rivalry of competing institutional logics' *Organization Studies* 30(6): pp. 629-652.

Reid, W & Karambayya, R 2009, 'Impact of dual executive leadership dynamics in creative organizations' *Human Relations 62*(7): pp. 1073-1112.

Reid, W & Karambayya, R 2011, 'Trust and conflict at the executive level: Dynamics in dual executive leadership' *Unpublished manuscript*, Montréal.

Simons, TL & Peterson, RS 2000, 'Task conflict and relationship conflict in top management teams: The pivotal role of intragroup trust' *Journal of Applied Psychology*, 85(1): pp. 102-111.

Part III

Leadership and Organizational Change

Chapter 8

Leadership and change management

The case of the Norwegian National Museum of Art

DONATELLA DE PAOLI

Background

Museums, like other traditional art institutions, undergo periods of change. When it was decided that four previously independent museums should be integrated into one to become the National Museum of Art in Oslo, the intent was to prepare for an architecturally planned new museum in Oslo. This decision was both part of a larger museum reform to rationalize the sector and part of a period in Norwegian history where the wealth acquired through natural resources was to be invested in several high-profile centrally located new art buildings. There was an instrumental and political mandate driving the change, more than the internal needs of the museums. The National Museum of Art is a case that shows how difficult it is to implement change in art institutions, and how the process can be undermined when the issue of leadership and change is not taken well care of. This is the story of a change process that went wild, causing resistance internally from employees and criticism externally from the general public and the media. The management, the changing leaders and the board all were blamed, yet nothing improved while administration expenses increased. It attracted a lot of negative press coverage. Finally, a book was written about the whole change process called 'Everybody talks about the museum' (Sandberg 2008).

> *The modern museum arose out of knowledge ideals and became important in the development of the Nations during the 18th century in Europe and elsewhere. Today expectations and demands of the museums are changing. Museums are used as instruments for city branding and development, they*

are part of the tourism industry and some have accordingly downplayed their professional art principles and are to a greater extent then managed according to business models (Lotte, Sandberg 2008).

Art institutions in general undergo periods of change. There are many different environmental pressures behind the need for change, from budget cuts, rationalization, policy changes, new audiences, to including art in a wider economical and societal purpose. The need and pressure to change art institutions pose severe challenges for art leaders.

The questions raised here are about what kind of leadership styles are useful in times of change and what kind of organizational issues should particularly be taken care of. This case shows that merging previously independent art organizations, each with distinct art traditions and history, strong identity and their own directors, is a difficult endeavor.

Description of case study methodology

As recommended for the single-case method (Yin 1994), evidence from different sources was used here, covering the period from 2003 to 2010. Documents of different sources were analyzed, such as more than 300 newspaper articles (selected among many more), internal work documents, a report about the work environment and organizing (Salomon *et al.* 2008) and also internal documents. Interviews with central employees in the top level group and employees run over a time span of several years, as this case has also been described in depth in a book about the organizing of art organizations (Elstad & De Paoli 2008). The description and analysis of the case will be based on the different data sources throughout the years 2003-2010. The overall research design is inductive, being based itself on one case; the National Museum of Art in Norway. The rich and enormous amount of articles in the press, as well as the book written about the change process (Sandberg 2008), will be a useful background and serve to fill in the material gathered in the interviews. The case is special in this respect, as there are few other organizations in Norway with as much press coverage about internal organizational and leadership conflicts.

Review of previous studies of museums in the process of change

There are other studies examining museums in the process of change. In a study of the Glenbow Museum in Canada, the President Robert R Janes made an analysis of how organizational change and adaptation occur with great difficulty in museums (1999). Janes also wrote the book '*Museums and the paradox of change*' (1997). In this case, the change process started with developing a common understanding amongst staff and board members about such issues as organizational values, principles and missions. Following this, a strategic plan was developed, concerned with measures and standards of performance. The importance of staff involvement was seen as very important, with the claim that a participative leadership was required. Glenbow adopted a new form of organization that encouraged staff involvement in decisions at all levels, both to improve the quality of decisions and to increase staff commitment. The approach was more based on trust than control, and on diversity rather than uniformity (Janes 2010). The experience from this museum shows that a participative leadership approach is highly functional and relevant for the change of museums. In a study of large state museums in Moscow and St Petersburg (Chekova 2004), the organizational structure of museums was described and analyzed. The issue was to what extent the new structures brought solutions to the problems experienced by most Russian museums in a time of change.

It would appear that art institutions are difficult to change, but museums appear to be some of the most difficult art organizations to change because they are often symbols of national history and strong institutional artistic influences. A high degree of institutionalization leads to the conservation of values, traditions and competence, as well as static organizations which are difficult to change (Power & DiMaggio 1991). Art organizations tend to act as passive actors, more concerned in obtaining legitimacy in society than changing to serve new societal groups and renew their mission. However, when the issue of leadership is given high priority and the right leaders are appointed, change may succeed. The case of the National Museum of Science and Technology in Italy (Bagdadli & Paolino 2006) revealed that the appointment of an active and dynamic director made the change succeed, as improvements in services and towards audiences were implemented, as well as efficiency improvements. This case study demonstrated that museums are not inevitably passive elements according to institutional theory (DiMaggio & Powell 1991), but that directors can play a considerable role in the change process. The extensive data analysis showed that the director played an active role in managerial renewal of the museum, revealing an alignment of his statements and effective organizational moves. Apparently, the kind of leader and leadership style used is important for the change of museums.

Approach

Description of main events and decisions

The National Museum of Art in Norway is a politically constructed unit through the fusion of previously four separate museums: the National Gallery, the Museum of Arts and Crafts, the Museum of Contemporary Art, and the Museum of Architecture; the last one gaining its own museum building in 2005. Since July 2005 the touring Museum of Visual Arts was also included. The restructure of the Norwegian sector of museums is one of the biggest reform processes by the Norwegian Ministry of Culture, but also a highly discussed and controversial one in the museum world. Below is a chronological account of these major events during the years 1999-2010.

Events in the creation of Norway's National Museum of Art 2003-2010

1999 The ABM Museum Reform

The Norwegian Ministry of Culture decides on a 'Museum Reform', pushing towards integrating smaller museums into fewer units all over Norway.

2003 New director (1) appointed: Sune Nordgren at the newly founded National Museum of Art

The National Museum of Art is established in Oslo by integrating four previous separate museums into one. The board, with the help of head hunters, found a person with considerable previous experience in leading art museums, both in Sweden with Malmö Konsthall and in Great Britain with the Baltic Centre of Art in Newcastle. He has previously shown great entrepreneurial and leadership abilities and there were positive expectations of him.

2004 Centralized integration of the four museums with one leadership group

Sune Nordgren decides to integrate the four museums into one by firing the previous four directors and forming a central leadership group with newly appointed leaders in five new departments: 1) collections and exhibitions, 2) audience development and communication, 3) services of the museum, 4) security, and 5) administration. The previous importance and representation of the functional art areas in each museum is minimized as the administrative functions get more departments and managers.

2005 New exhibitions of permanent collection and 'Kiss-the-Frog' installation

The permanent exhibition is changed, the work of the Norwegian famous artist Munch is distributed through the museum and an architecturally designed froglike exhibit with contemporary art installations is launched, attracting 125,000 visitors over three months. These are all successful events in attracting a big audience, but are controversial and negative in the eyes of the cultural élites and art curators. This sees the beginning of continuous negative press coverage.

2005 Bad internal climate, cooperation and communication in the museum

After an open meeting for employees, an internal investigation of the internal working climate is commissioned; 28 employees are interviewed and the results are negative. The employees report considerable work pressure, lack of influence, and lack of communication.

2006 The director Sune Nordgren resigns voluntarily after criticism

2007 New director (2) is appointed: Allis Helleland

After a long period of seeking a new director, the board decides to hire a highly controversial director, with extensive leadership experience, from a similar art institution in Denmark.

2008 Massive protests from the unions occur in response to the leadership style of Allis Helleland

A group of employees send a letter to the board where they criticize the leadership style and competence of the director. A leading group of academics and cultural personalities send a letter to the cultural minister, where they ask him to intervene and reinstall the National Museum as a 'scientifically founded' institution. The employees' representative group and the 'ombud' also receive several complains from employees feeling harassed and victimized by the director. The unions and the employees try to stop planned changes within the organization.

2008 The director Allis Helleland is forced to leave after criticism

Despite the massive criticism and sacking of Allis Helleland, she nevertheless receives a six year pay-out covering the period she was originally contracted for in her appointment.

2008 The board director and board is changed

The director of the board, Christian Bjelland, is criticized and politicians demand his departure. A totally new board and board director is installed with the primary task of hiring a new director for the Museum.

2009 New director (3) is appointed: Audun Eckhoff

After previous Swedish and Danish directors, a Norwegian director is now appointed with relevant arts education and previous experience leading the Bergen Art Museum. He knows the Norwegian field well and has a good international network. Because of his previous experience as a journalist, the media is handled well and the announcement of his appointment is positively received.

2010 Functional traditional art units and departments reinstalled and a new top management group established

Eckhoff radiates stability and communicates the need for letting the art curators and art work be at the centre of the museum.

In addition, if there is any reason why the employee cannot perform the activity safely (for example, changes to the environment, such as rain that makes the ladder rungs slippery) they are required to advise the employer of the matter.

Generally, fusion processes are demanding and rarely fulfill the expectations that are expected in regard to synergy and efficiency. There were many challenges with integrating several independent museums into one. This included creating a new governing structure, implementing a new organizational structure (see organization chart), hiring a new top management group, and finding new ways of allocating tasks. The relocation of administrative and professional staff, while expositions remained in traditional facilities, also fuelled the growing tension and conflict of interest between the different art fields represented by each museum.

An important decision, when separate entities are to be assembled, is how closely the previously separated units should be integrated and how fast. In this case, the integration process went very quickly after the first director was appointed in 2003. He implemented a new organization chart for the whole museum, with high visibility and representation of the administrative staff, which were meant to represent the many functions of the curators and art professionals. The administrative functions ended up getting several new departments, while the professional art curators and professionals were all concentrated in just one department with only one director. While these art functions in numbers represented a large group of employees and were critical for the core value of the museum, they were totally underrepresented in the new organizational structure. In comparison, the accounting department with their 5 employees got one department and one director. The new organizational chart is shown after the fusion in Figure 8.1.

Figure 8.1 Organization chart of National Museum of Art in Norway in 2003

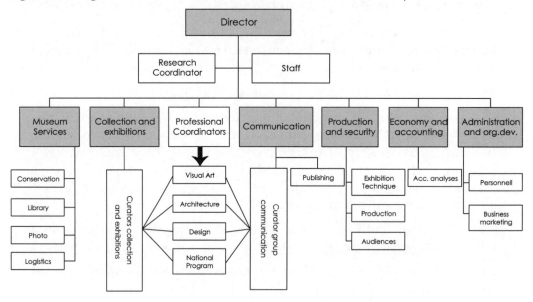

Challenges

Leadership styles of the three directors and subsequent reactions

The term leadership is understood in many different ways and researchers usually define leadership according to their individual perspectives and the aspects of the phenomena of most interest to them. Leadership has been defined in terms of traits, behaviors, influence, interaction patterns, role relationships, and occupation of an administrative position. Gary Yukl, who has provided one of the most extensive and thorough review of leadership theory (2010), posits:

> *Most definitions of leadership reflect the assumption that it involves a process whereby intentional influence is exerted over other people to guide, structure, and facilitate activities and relationships in a group or organization (Yukl 2010, p. 21).*

In one of the first international research articles on arts leadership, Lapierre discusses what art leadership is (2001). He makes a point of art leadership being rooted in the creation of art, as the mission of the arts organization is rooted in art. Leadership is directed towards the achievement of an artistic goal and is the responsibility of the artists, writes Lapierre, regardless of their position within the organization (2001, p. 5). Management is in the service of and subordinate to this goal. Lapierre makes a distinction between leadership rooted in the artistic staff and management rooted in the administrative staff. He says:

> *... within arts organizations, the artists assume the leadership of the company, while the managers (general managers, administrative managers and so on) ensure its management (Lapierre 2001,p. 6).*

This artistic perspective on art leadership got challenged when the National Museum of Art in Norway installed an organizational structure giving administrative functions the higher priority. Therefore, the issue is not primarily about whether the head director has the right arts background, but whether arts leadership is being executed or not. Arts leadership, as defined by Lapierre, is presented as a distinct leadership approach although it is not included in Yukl's review (2010).

General theory on leadership (Yukl 2010) highlights the different types of leadership encountered historically since the concept of leadership was invented. Based upon the extensive and thorough review of Yukl, the most prevalent leadership styles are presented and described shortly here. For a more in-depth understanding of the different leadership perspectives, there is extensive research and theorizing within each field.

Art leadership style

This perspective on leadership derives from arts management (Lapierre 2001) and position leadership in the arts as primarily concerned with artistic values, mission and expression. Art leadership is about art professionals having the top position in organizations, putting art content above administrative matters. The shared leadership model is an expression of this leadership perspective. The management of the arts is seen as a responsibility of the administrative staff functions, being in the service of and subordinate to art. Arts leadership is consequently about giving the artists the autonomy and power to create high quality art performances, which is the ultimate end of all art organizations according to this perspective. This perspective is based on the professions having ultimate power in organizations and can therefore also be relevant for other professional fields such as universities, healthcare, law, engineering, research, etc.

Activity oriented leadership style

The early descriptive research on managerial work was concerned primarily with providing a description of activity patterns. This perspective on leadership is developed further by Mintzberg (1973) that used observation rather than surveys to learn more about the content of managerial activities. He developed a taxonomy of managerial roles where activities can be explained in terms of at least one role, although many activities involve more than one role. The leadership style derived from this research is concerned with what kind of tasks, activities and roles the leader takes on.

Participative leadership style

Participative leadership involves the use of various decision procedures that allow other people some influence over the leader's decisions (Heller and Yukl 1969). Other terms commonly used to refer to aspects of participative leadership include consultation, joint decision-making, power sharing, decentralization, empowerment and democratic management.

Autocratic leadership style

This is a directive, authoritative and hierarchical leadership style with roots back to older times of emperors and kings. Some of the early theoreticians as Barnard (1952) and Weber (1947) paid attention to this classical leadership style. It is usually seen as the opposite of the participative leadership style as the leader does not involve anyone in the decision-making. Although being outdated in leadership research, it is highly prevalent in practice, not least within the arts where the artist as 'genius' and 'guru' still prevails.

Contingent leadership style

A contingent leadership style is based on the view that leader traits or behaviors are related to indicators of leadership effectiveness in different situations. Aspects of the situation that enhance or nullify the effects of a leader's traits or behavior are called situational moderator variables. Situational leadership theory (Hersey and Blanchard 1977) amongst other theories belonging to this perspective, proposed a contingency theory that specifies the appropriate type of leadership behavior for different levels of subordinate 'maturity' in relation to the work.

Charismatic leadership style

Weber (1947) used the term charismatic leadership to describe a form of influence based not on tradition or formal authority, but rather on follower perceptions that the leader is endowed with exceptional qualities. In the past two decades, several social scientists formulated newer versions of the theory to describe charismatic leadership in organizations according to Gary Yukl. Evidence of charismatic leadership is provided by the leader-follower relationship. A charismatic leader has profound and unusual effects on followers. Followers perceive that the leader's beliefs are correct, they willingly obey the leader, they feel affection toward the leader, they are emotionally involved in the mission of the group or organization, they have high performance goals, and they believe that they can contribute to the success of the mission (House 1977).

Transformational leadership style

The theories on transformational leadership were strongly influenced by McGregor Burns (1978) who wrote a best-selling book on political leadership. Transformational leadership appeals to the moral values of followers in an attempt to raise their consciousness about ethical issues and to mobilize their energy and resources to reform institutions. With transformational leadership, the followers feel trust, admiration, loyalty and respect towards the leader, and they are motivated to do more than they originally expected to do.

Leadership of change style

Change by many is seen as the most important and difficult leadership responsibility. For some theorists it is the essence of leadership as effective leadership is needed to revitalize an organization and facilitate adaptation to a changing environment. A leadership style oriented towards change takes into consideration the different stages in the change process and deals consciously with reactions to change. One of the earliest process theories was Lewin's model which included three phases; unfreezing, changing, and refreezing (1951). Another process theory describes how people in organizations react to changes imposed upon them.

Ethical, servant, spiritual and authentic leadership style

Servant leadership in the workplace is about helping others to accomplish shared objectives by facilitating individual development, empowerment and collective work that is consistent with the health and long-term welfare of followers. This is often seen as similar to ethical leadership (Trevino 1986). Greenleaf (1977) proposed that 'service to followers' is the primary responsibility of leaders and the essence of ethical leadership. Spiritual leadership describes how leaders can enhance the intrinsic motivation of followers by creating conditions that increase their sense of spiritual meaning in the work.

The definition of authentic leadership varies for different theorists, but they all emphasize the importance of consistency in their words, actions and values. Additional aspects of authentic leadership include positive leader values, leader self-awareness, and a trusting relationship with followers. The idea of authentic leadership has received a lot of attention in recent years and it provides another perspective on ethical leadership. The journal *Leadership Quarterly* published a special issue on authentic leadership in 2005 (see Avolio & Gardner 2005).

This overview and definition of the different leadership styles serves as a theoretical background for an analysis of the different directors of the National Museum of Art.

Director 1 – Sune Nordgren, the charismatic and visionary museum leader

> *I am an entrepreneurial person. I am interested in developing big projects, which can be spectacular, but spectacular in a long process where the main goal can be for instance a new museum. I am bad at administrative issues, here I need support (Sune Nordgren, Förvandlingens konst, Sveriges Arkitekter).*

The choice of the new director was controversial amongst the art curators. Sune Nordgren was Swedish first of all, and lacking academic degrees in the arts as he was a graphic designer. He had shown abilities to change smaller art institutions, but had no previous experience in leading a major traditional art institution. He was charismatic and had shown abilities to position 'art 'in a contemporary way and thereby attract audiences.

Sune Nordgren made important and remarkable changes in the standard exhibitions and installed new controversial ones. What provoked many was his change from the traditional hanging of art by time period in the National Gallery, and instead placed old and new art together. Most importantly the traditional room of Munch paintings within the Gallery was no longer solely devoted to Munch. He exhibited the traditional and most famous Norwegian artist in the same space with contemporary artists, inspired by the exhibition policy at the Tate Gallery of London. Changes to the exhibitions of Norwegian art heritage created a lot of controversy and negative public opinion. At the same time he developed and launched an architecturally 'froglike' installation on the parking lot behind the National Gallery. This temporary exhibition was called 'Kiss-the-Frog' and housed contemporary art installations where the new National Museum of Art was planned to be situated. This attracted a huge amount of visitors, and broke previous audience records. Nordgren also substituted the traditional security guards with 70 newly hired guides. They were young, arts educated, and had experience in the service sector.

There were many interviews and articles about Sune Nordgren and his leadership style:

> *Sune Nordgren was as a leader of Malmö Konsthall quite clear in everything he did. He had a definite identity, he expressed a clear vision, and he performed according to his vision. Those years he led Malmö Konsthall were the best in the 30 years long history of this institution … It is important with new challenges. The National Museum in Oslo can be that. I see it can be a complicated challenge he has taken there. But here too, is the old public enlightenment Nordgren in activity. The audience oriented, strong and clear Nordgren (Lars Nittve, Director Moderna Museet in Stockholm, Ukeavisen Ledelse 2009).*

The innovative and fresh approach to the old and traditional National Museum of Art by the director Sune Nordgren, and his ability to make changes quickly with the support of many of the employees, reveal that he is a charismatic and clear leader; some will call him even a visionary leader. He was a typical charismatic, visionary leader with clear ideas of where he wanted the museum to go. The research on charismatic and transformational leadership indicates that a clear and compelling vision is useful to guide change in an organization (Yukl 2010).

> *Sune Nordgren is missed by the Security employed people. He talked to everybody, was inclusive and visible (Security employee at the National Museum of Art 2011).*

Sune Nordgren can also be placed in the long Scandinavian tradition of participative and empowering leadership style (Bjerke, 1999). Participative leadership involves the use of various decision procedures that allow other people some influence over the leader's decisions. Other terms commonly used to refer to aspects of participative leadership include consultation, joint decision-making, power sharing, decentralization, empowerment and democratic management.

Although Sune Nordgren can be seen as a typical Scandinavian leader, he received a lot of criticism from the curators and art educated employees in the museum. They felt left out of the organization because the organizational structure did not leave room for them to influence and have a voice. Sune Nordgren's changes in exhibitions were not in accordance with the approach of the traditional curators; the core of the museum staff. So the picture of him being participative is blurred; he uses a participative leadership style with the administrative staff, but not with the curators who represented the traditional values and identity of the museum. Driven by his overall vision of the National Museum opening itself and its art to the audience, he wanted queues in front of the museum and achieved that with several exhibitions. After a lot of criticism from this small, powerful curator group allied with cultural critics in the major newspapers in Norway, and with little overt support from the board, he decided to leave the organization. His departure was discussed and grieved.

Director 2 – Allis Helleland, the authoritative and elitist museum leader

> *When I came to the State Museum of Art in Denmark 13 years ago, the museum was as bad as the National Museum of Art in Oslo, as dark and old*

fashioned (The incoming director of the National Museum of Art, Allis Helleland, Dagsavisen, 25 February 2007).

The debate about Allis Helleland and her leadership qualities started long before she was installed in Norway. Some claimed that she represented a mainstream art perspective and that appointing her would not benefit contemporary art in the newly integrated National Museum of Art. Others claimed that hiring her was unfortunate for a museum in crisis, because she had been a debated and criticized leader of the State Museum of Art in Denmark. She signaled early that she wanted to change the organizational chart completely and that she had the support of the board to do this. Employees were initially positive, despite her controversial leadership approach in Denmark, but their support diminished rapidly with the impulsive decisions Helleland took and the public verbal comments she made. The first unpopular and highly criticized move was to instruct all employees that all communication with the media should be controlled by her. This was understandable as the past internal controversies and conflicts were broadcast in the media weekly, but people reacted to her authoritarian approach and way of communicating. Journalists were in particular appalled by her decisions. This introduced a new period of negative publicity about the museum. Allis Helleland overrode the internal purchasing committee by buying a painting of the young female artist Unni Askeland. This action consequently enflamed criticism, both internally and in the media. Protest letters were written to the board. External influential people also wrote a letter to the cultural minister, demanding her resignation. An internal report about the working climate revealed that employees felt overseen, isolated, not treated with respect, and that they did not get any support from the director in their daily work (Salomo *et al.* 2008). There were also disagreements between the director and particular groups of employees, reflecting that they felt they were not consulted or treated in a professional way.

> *The National Museum of Art is in a severe crisis because it is led top-down. It is a destructive organization with no sensitive and listening leader, which again leads to negative premises for professional work. Good professional premises require functionally developed leadership lines. Such as the situation is now, the administration is ruling above the professionals. This is highly visible through the buying of new art (Ina Blom, Professor in Art History, Klassekampen, 28 February 2008).*

> *She came in as fresh air, being courageous and outspoken, but never managed to articulate clearly what she meant to do with the museum. Allis Helleland had little faith and belief in the leadership group, was both direct and impulsive in her leadership style as she went directly to the people in question when she wanted something to be done in the organization (Employee in the administrative staff, interview 2010).*

Allis Helleland started by over-ruling internal practices and discounting professional expertise. She was not afraid of being strong and decisive, using her power as director and from this perspective fitted well within an authoritative leadership style as described earlier. Decisions were implemented in an impulsive and direct way, without following professional, functional lines and established hierarchy. She had an elitist view of leadership as she did not involve employees in decisions. The museum needed a strong and dynamic director who could take charge of the difficult situation, but unfortunately she communicated in a manner that was interpreted negatively by both employees and media. She obviously had ideas for the Museum and wanted to change the organizational chart, but her impulsive behavior made it very difficult to install any changes in the stressed organization. It is difficult to place her directly in one leadership style, but it seems she belongs to the traditional autocratic leadership style.

During this period the Board Chair started to get attention and criticism, because some board members resigned and because he seemed to have a dominating and controlling style. The Board was also criticized for hiring Allis Helleland without checking out her previous controversial leadership style. The Board Chair also gave her a six year pay-out after she was dismissed, which provoked many in the community. The Board of Directors of the National Museum of Art in Norway has definitely played another important role throughout the turbulent times. Any discussion of structuring and leadership must inevitably address the issue of corporate governance, as Lapierre states (2001). It was clear that the Board in this case did not necessarily understand their role and were not effective in helping the leader set the agenda. When the Norwegian Ministry of Culture substituted the Board of Directors with completely new members in 2008, this was seen as an overdue decision. Malfunctioning art leaders, ineffective organizational structures, and wrong strategic decisions are the responsibility of the board of directors. Searching for scapegoats amongst the leaders, when organizational problems arise and the press is negative, is a wrong and destructive approach.

Director 3 – Audun Eckhoff, the leader creating stability

Visual art, design and architecture should be in the center for the interest of the National Museum of art, not how the museum is organized. I am first and above all, very happy to have got the job. I hope and believe I can contribute to create order in the museum and motivate for great effort towards the opening of the new museum building (Newly-appointed leader Audun Eckhoff, Klassekampen, 8 April 2011).

Since Audun Eckhoff became director of the museum, there has been a general positive attitude to him both as a director and leader. Some claim it is because he is Norwegian; others claim it is because of his previous relevant education in art history and his appropriate experience, first as curator in contemporary art, then as director of Bergen Kunstmuseum for several years; others again claim it is because he shows a calm, self-conscious and decisive attitude as a leader. Audun Eckhoff comes from a cultured family and he is well-positioned amongst the cultural capital élite, given his arts background. He is positively received by the previous critical curators in the museum, but is not overly participative towards the administrative staff. He obviously handles the media well as having previous experience as a journalist, so he remains 'untouchable' even if there is some report of little activity around the museum with few and insignificant exhibitions.

Audun Eckhoff is a courageous man and he gets good evaluations of the people who have worked with him. He dared to be open as applicant for the position twice, even after he lost when Allis Helleland got the job (Leader, Dagbladet, 28 January 2009).

Eckhoff represents first and most security, says Professor in Art History Bjerke, who characterize him as a relaxed, formal and correct person (Klassekampen, 27 January 2009).

I experience Sune Nordgren and Audun Eckhoff as diametrically opposed leaders. While Nordgren was clear, visionary, including and sharing, I experience Eckhoff as distant, elitist, and protective (Administrative employee at the National Museum of Art, Interview 2010).

Eckhoff is perceived as inclusive and participative towards the professional art employees and directors, whereas he is seen as élitist by general employees, as he keeps his door locked all the time. He changed the organizational chart immediately, reinstalling six functional art departments and appointing new directors for each of them. This decision was important and gave him the legitimacy he needed to start with, see Figure 8.2. He has also spent time recruiting new directors for the art functions and developing plans and architectural designs for the new museum building, to be located close to the city hall by the harbor in Oslo, and planned to be completed by 2016-2017.

General decisions are taken from the top and information is then given downwards, providing little possibility to influence. His leadership style is top-down without being totally authoritarian. He achieves legitimacy internally and externally because he represents values located around tradition and stability as well as art knowledge. This supports well the art leadership approach suggested by Lapierre (2001).

Figure 8.2 New organizational chart of the National Museum of Art

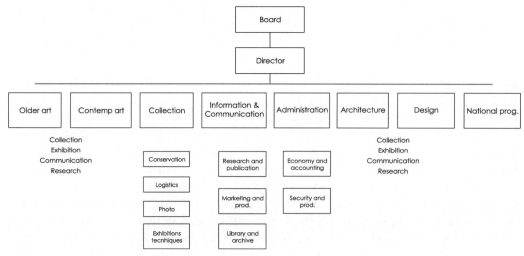

Conclusions

The leadership of changing art organizations can both be complex and controversial as the different examples of directors have shown. Leadership in the arts belongs to the artists and those with an arts education, but there are many ways of executing this leadership. In the first case, the charismatic and participative leadership style of Sune Nordgren was very positive in legitimizing change. Unfortunately, the first director implemented a series of rushed and wrong organizational decisions. Integrating the four previous museums quickly and tightly, implementing an organizational chart that did not include the art fields of each museum, marginalizing the art professionals, and not including any of the previous directors; all decisions that received criticism. Charismatic leaders are needed in a time of change, but they should have legitimacy and the support of the important art professionals. The second director, with an authoritative and élitist leadership style, also did a lot of harm to an exhausted group of employees. While it was the role of the Board to prepare her properly for the difficult task, she needed to handle the new responsibility with greater humility and respect towards all the employees. She would have needed professional assistance in organizational development because the employees were demoralized. In her defense, she had to face the responsibility and burden on her own. The Board Chair would interfere when problems arose, but in a directive way with the employees, overseeing her. Although the director had a controversial and negative leadership style, the directors of the board did not act in a responsible and professional way. They were all finally dismissed and a new board was installed. The composition and role of a board should be given high priority in all arts organizations, because they play a pivotal role in taking strategic decisions, hiring the top director, and assisting him or her through the implementation of change processes.

It may be concluded from the case analyzed that the third director is a good choice. Having a good institutional legitimacy amongst élites in the Norwegian art world and with a reasonable respect for employees without being overly participative, he seems to have a viable leadership style for an art institution in a period of change. Implementing a new organizational structure with functional art departments was a wise choice, but the cross functional collaboration in developing and setting up new exhibitions has appeared to suffer, as there is little activity going on. A matrix form of organizing with exhibition projects running across the functionally ordered units may be an answer to this, but it requires a dynamic and flexible organizational culture. Since the third director has only been in the position for three years when writing this, it is possibly too early to draw any conclusions about him being the successful leader of the three. He still needs to show more results and demonstrate active decisions in getting a new building constructed, developing actual and relevant art exhibitions, and so on. But judging after the overly positive external press coverage and evaluations, it seems that the symbolic importance of the leader is more important than the actual results. He has demonstrated that he can stabilize the institution, and gain both internal and external professional respect.

When summing up what can be learned from this case, the following propositions are put forward:

- Leadership of museums in a period of change require a well-composed board of directors taking responsibility and hiring the right leaders at the top;

- Leadership of museums in a period of change requires art leadership;

- Leadership of museums in a period of change is both about securing stability for the organization, creating visions for the future and empowering employees;

- Leadership of museums is the balancing of mixed interest groups and institutional expectations;

- Leadership of museums in a period of change is about conscious and professional handling of media; and

- Leadership of museums in a period of change require both legitimacy amongst the artistic professionals and balancing the need for change versus stability.

Questions

1. How did the amalgamation of the National Museum of Art in Norway come about? What factors involved in this process contributed to the problems that followed, and how could it have occurred differently?

2. Describe the different styles of leadership exhibited by the three directors of the National Museum of Art in Norway, and consider their strengths and weaknesses.

3. What leadership model would best suit the challenges present in the case study of the National Museum of Arts in Norway so that more successful outcomes could have occurred?

References

Avolio, BJ & Gardner, WL 2005, 'Authentic leadership development: Getting to the root of positive forms of leadership', *Leadership Quarterly*, 16 (3), pp. 315-338.

Bagdadli, S & Paolino, C 2006, 'Institutional change in Italian museums: Does the museum director have a role to play?' *International Journal of Arts Management*, vol. 8, no. 3, pp. 4-18.

Barnard, C I 1952, 'A definition of authority' In R. K. Merton et. Al. (Eds.), 1952, *Reader in bureaucracy* Free Press, New York.

Bjerke, B 1999, *Business leadership and Culture*, Edward Elgar, Cheltenham, UK.

Chekova, E 2004, 'Organizational structure of Russian state museums: Recent innovations' *International Journal of Arts Management*, vol. 6, no. 2, pp. 44-53.

DiMaggio, PJ & Powell, WW (Eds.) 1991, *The New Institutionalism in Organizational Analysis,* University of Chicago Press, Chicago.

DiMaggio, PJ & Powell, WW (Eds.) 1991, *The New Institutionalism in Organizational Analysis,* University of Chicago Press, Chicago.

Elstad, B and De Paoli, D 2008 *Organisering og ledelse av kunst og kultur,* Cappelen-Damm, Oslo.

Greenleaf, R K 1977, *Servant leadership: A journey into the nature of legitimate power and greatness,* Paulist Press, Mahwah, NJ.

Heller, F & Yukl, G 1969, 'Participation, managerial decision making and situational variables', *Organizational behavior and human performance,* 4, pp. 227-241.

Hersey, P & Blanchard, KH 1977, *The management of organizational behavior,* 3rd ed., Prentice Halls, Englewood Cliffs NJ.

House, RJ 1977, 'A 1976 theory of charismatic leadership' in J G Hunt & L L Larson (Eds.) 1977, *Leadership: The cutting edge,* Southern Illinois University Press, Carbondale, pp. 189-207.

Janes, R 1997, *Museums and the paradox of change,* 2nd Edition. Glenbow, Calgary.

Janes, R 1999, 'Seven years of change and no end in sight: Reflections from the Glenbow Museum' in *International Journal of Arts Management,* vol. 1, no. 2, pp. 48-52.

Lapierre, L 2001 'Leadership and arts management' *International Journal of Arts Management,* vol. 3, no. 3, pp. 4-12.

Lewin, K 1951, *Field theory in social science* Harper & Row, New York.

Meyer, JW & Rowan, B 1991, 'Institutionalized organizations: Formal structure as myth and ceremony' in William Powell and Paul DiMaggio (ed.) 1991 *The New Institutionalism in organizational analysis,* The University of Chicago Press, Chicago.

Rentschler, R 2001, 'Is creativity a matter for cultural leaders?' *International Journal of Arts Management,* vol. 3, no. 3, p.13 -24.

Salomon, R, Heen, H, Grimsmo, A & Enehaug, H 2008, *Arbeidsmiljø og arbeidsorganisering ved Nasjonalmuseet for kunst.* Arbeidsforskningsinstituttet.

Sandberg, L 2008, *Alle snakker om museet. Nasjonalmuseet for kunst fra visjon til virkelighet* Oslo: Pax Forlag A/S.

Trevino, LT 1986, 'Ethical decision making in organizations: A person-situation interactionist model', *Academy of Management Review,* 11, pp. 601-617.

Yukl, G 2010, *Leadership in organizations,* Pearson: New Jersey.

Weber, M 1947, *The theory of social and economic organizations,* Translated by T Parsons, New York: Free Press, New York.

Chapter 9

Cultural leadership and audience engagement

A case study of the Theatre Royal Stratford East

HILARY GLOW

Background

The Theatre Royal Stratford East's (TRSE) artistic director, Kerry Michael, initiated the Open Stage project, a comprehensive two-year consultancy with members of the East London community, to open a discussion with them about what they want to see on the stage. In particular, audiences and volunteers from the community will become co-programmers of the company's season in 2012.

The Open Stage project is dedicated to democratizing theatre, to listening to the voices and stories of those in the community who are not often heard, and to building a sense of empowerment and ownership of the theatre by the local community. And this process of empowering audiences involves, what the Artistic Director Kerry Michaels refers to, as 'giving up our power' by 'sharing it with people who want to come along to that party' (Michael interview 2011). By looking to their community and asking them what they want to see in the theatre, the TRSE is turning on its head the traditional cultural authority of the arts organization and the role of its creative leadership.

This chapter looks at the Open Stage project not as a manifestation of the individual accomplishment of the organization's Artistic Director, but as part of a whole-of-organization process, and as a critique of dominant patrician power relations that exist between many arts organizations and their audiences or communities. The Open Stage project, and the thinking that underpins it, can be seen as a critical response to a cultural and political context in which arts organizations may operate as effective apartheid entities, separating artists from audiences. Such a regimen is reinforced in the cultural sector through a cult of leadership; artistic directors are specialists, visionaries, holders of special knowledge and expertise, whose work is appreciated only by aficionados and those 'in the know'. In the arts and cultural sector there is a sense of the exaggerated agency of its leaders; exaggerated because it tends to be leader-centric and focused on the achievements of individuals. Rather, this chapter argues that the task of facilitating and developing the engagement of audiences in the performing arts, requires new thinking around networking and public participation which in turn requires new models of distributed arts leadership, leading to organizational renewal.

Romanticized leadership

The notion of the heroic or visionary leader comes from mainstream management theory and, in particular, theories of transformational leadership. In the arts and cultural sector, leaders tend to be in the transformational mode with a focus on charisma, inspiration, stimulation and individuality (Alimo-Metcalfe & Alban-Metcalfe 2005). Arguably, in considering the role of artistic directors and the gap that many arts organizations reproduce between artists/art-making and audiences, there is a tendency to romanticize arts leadership; artistic directors can be seen as having a quality of mystical allure. Research on romanticized leadership suggests that this occurs when there is a distance between leader and follower and where leaders maintain a 'magical' image of themselves that inspires 'follower worship' (Bligh and Schyns 2007, p. 237). As Fairhurst (2007) has argued, leader-centrism produces a view of dependent followers and the promulgation of the belief in 'the power of one' and the primary significance of individual action.

In her analysis of dominant notions of leadership, Sinclair (2007) identifies a range of conventional assumptions, including that leadership is about an individual performance despite the evidence that followers contribute to performance (2007, p. 28-29). The leadership in evidence in the current case study is of interest because it evidences a focus on followers. A recent contribution to theories of leadership has developed the notion of 'aesthetic leadership'. This is a shift away from thinking about leaders as charismatic and visionary individuals who identify and define meanings for followers, towards the notion of leaders creating events and opening up opportunities for felt-meaning ('sensory knowledge') so that those involved experience emotional attachment (Hansen et al. 2007, p. 545). The Open Stage initiative involves the creation of an opportunity, or series of opportunities, where the meanings that may be derived from participation are diverse, affective, and build attachment to the organization. Whether or not the leadership of this project is best encapsulated by the notion of 'aesthetic leadership', there is some evidence that the task of enhancing engagement in the performing arts through public participation requires new distributed leadership models. Jennings and Jones (2010) argue that there is an urgent need for such new forms of cultural leadership. As this case study evinces, leadership to enhance public participation in the arts needs to democratize the decision-making process, provide opportunities for dialogue, and enable audiences/participants to become involved in shaping the experiences on offer (2010, p. 25).

In opening up a dialogue with audiences and community members, the Open Stage project can be seen to be informed by both a UK cultural policy emphasis on the relationship between arts and social inclusion, and new discourses within arts marketing focusing on audience experience and engagement. Durrer and Miles argue that these two forces are inter-connected – that marketing for arts institutions, dedicated to attracting wider audiences, is an explicit response to 'the social inclusion agenda within British cultural policy' (2009, p. 225). In their study of UK arts managers working for institutions which address 'socially excluded' audiences, Durrer and Miles found that new approaches to marketing depend on 'a personalized approach that promotes dialogue, trust and relationship building and is maintained by...gatekeepers entrusted with the task of attracting 'socially excluded' individuals into arts institutions' (2009, p. 226).

However, to see the Open Stage project solely in terms of either social inclusion or as a marketing exercise, provides a limited and largely instrumentalist rationale. What is striking about this case study is that it suggests a new model for leadership based on a democratic (and ethical) understanding of the responsibilities of arts organizations to the individuals it serves.

Leadbeater (2009) describes how, in a commoditized world, organizations tend to do things *to* and *for* people based on a number of deeply-rooted assumptions: 'Knowledge and learning flows from experts to people who are dependent or in need. Organizations are hierarchies based on the power and the knowledge to make decisions. Authority is exercised top down. The aim is to define what people lack – what they need or want that they have not got – and then deliver it to them' (p. 3). In Leadbeater's admittedly generalized account of the way artists and cultural organizations tend to work, the artist is often seen as working in a field marked by 'separation and specialism' that allows an 'uncompromising vantage point outside everyday society' to produce 'special insight into the world he stands apart from'. Such a view is long and deeply held within a profession that often requires 'special training and self-belief', but 'often it seems modern artists are self-indulgently talking to a narrow coterie of followers' (p. 4). It often produces, he says, art that is 'done to us, as us and for us, but not *with* us'.

Leadbeater's point is to assert the collaborative potential of the web and its capacity to 'alter the way art is made and the roles of arts institutions, such as galleries' (p. 5). This current research is not concerned with the web, but rather with the ethos and the imperative of arts institutions to invite us to 'think and act *with* people, rather than *for* them, on their behalf or even doing things to them...to connect with other people with whom we can share, exchange and create new knowledge and ideas through a process of structured lateral, free association of people and ideas' (Leadbeater, 2009 p. 5). Rather than perpetuate the distance between artists/arts managers and audiences, TRSE demonstrates how new modes of arts leadership democratize the arts and open doors to new participants as part of organizational renewal.

Approach

The notion of distributed leadership is useful as a way of understanding the leadership style at TRSE. It has previously been used by Hewison and Holden (2011) to encapsulate the recent radical changes at the Royal Shakespeare Company (RSC). The RSC's move away from hierarchy ('with coercive, reward and information power concentrated at the top') towards a flatter and more organic management structure with an explicit shared leadership between artistic and management roles, provides a working example of a distributed leadership model (2011 pp. 38-40). As Hewison and Holden go on to show, distributed leadership is directed to the embedding of leadership within a wide group, and entails sharing leadership roles (2011 pp. 38-40). The TRSE's Open Stage project also exemplifies distributed leadership; Kerry Michael, as Artistic Director, has developed an agenda for the company around audience collaboration and dialogue; he has embedded this goal into the centre of the organization (rather than turning it over to a separate department such as marketing, education or community outreach), and he has facilitated the building of networks that allow for new ideas and information to flow in and through the organization. In this way, the leadership role entails articulating and maintaining the organization's core values, building a sense of shared purpose across all areas of the organization and identifying and facilitating connections between people and ideas.

Open Stage: Theatre Royal Stratford East

The TRSE began its life in 1953 as a political theatre collective called the Theatre Workshop, under the artistic directorship of Joan Littlewood. Dedicated to producing theatre for the working class, the TRSE repudiated the middle-class monopoly of theatre, and sought to produce popular politically informed plays under the banner: 'The great theatres of all time have been popular theatres which reflected the dramas and struggles of the people' (Eyre & Wright 2000, p. 261). For Littlewood a 'popular' theatre was one which reached non-metropolitan and non-middle class audiences and sought to inform and entertain them.

The TRSE continues to see itself in terms of its relationship to its community with the aim of 'reflect[ing] the concerns, hopes and dreams of the people of East London' (TRSE Annual Report 2008). East London's Newham Borough has a large immigrant community with over 100 languages spoken, and is London's youngest borough with a youth population of 68 percent (TRSE Annual Report 2009-10). Under the artistic directorship of Kerry Michael, the company sees itself in the role of empowering the communities it serves by 'giving voice to stories rarely heard', by developing young talent (including writers, directors and performers), and by producing new work which reflects the cultural diversity of the community (TRSE Annual Report 2008, p. 7).

In 2010, TRSE launched its Open Stage project – a two-year initiative designed to hand programming control over to the public to determine what will appear at the venue in the lead up to the London Olympic and Paralympic Games in 2012. The Open Stage project aims to 'research, devise, deliver and evaluate a new model of public engagement' through dialogue, the embedding of partnerships with local people and organizations, and the empowerment of new audiences (Handel 2010).

What would you like to see in Open Stage?

Open Stage began with recruiting 25 'co-progammers' and over the two years of the project this has increased to 50. Co-programmers are volunteers from the community whose roles involve the development of relationships with local residents and organizations. Volunteers are cross-generational and from diverse ethnic backgrounds, reflecting the diversity of the East London community. They were recruited through a range of channels including the theatre company's website and email list, community and volunteer organization contacts, and word of mouth. Once recruited, the team of volunteers has engaged in a range of skill development programs including interview and communication techniques and administering questionnaires. The questionnaires were drafted with input from the staff of the TRSE, including Front of House, Marketing and Youth Arts and Education departments and the volunteers. The questions changed during the course of the project as a result of volunteer feedback (Handel Interview 2011).

On the pilot weekend the team of volunteers went out in pairs into the streets of Stratford to interview the public about what they would like to see on stage. Interviews took place in commuter and shopping areas, the library, bus stations, cafes, bars and in the mall. A total of 229 people were interviewed (from a range of ages and ethnic backgrounds) and were asked a number of questions about their awareness of, and interest in, the work of the theatre. In particular, respondents were asked, 'What would you like to see in Open Stage?' Once people had been interviewed in the street they were invited to come into the building, to meet the volunteers and the staff of the organization (Handel interview 2011).

The responses of interviewees delivered some specific information about topics of shows they'd like to see but generally the feedback was in the form of suggestions of genres people wanted to see on stage – pantomimes, real-life stories, comedy and musicals were the most frequently mentioned. This has led to the development of partnerships with other arts organizations involved in producing or creating works for children and families, dance companies, and comedy and music producers.

Since the pilot weekend, the community has continued to be consulted through surveys, questionnaires, interviews and online engagement about the programming of the theatre in 2012. From November 2010 to January 2011 volunteers and staff asked around 1,000 audience members and local residents for their views on what they would like to see. In May 2011 the volunteers entered a phase of training in programming with the intention of using their research to curate a six-month season of works from January-July 2012. Their professional development included training in casting actors, licensing script rights, script development and collaboration with artists. In addition, facilitated sessions addressed decision-making processes, working as a team and project planning.

Specifically, the volunteers addressed the complexities of programming through skill development sessions with the artistic director. This involved a critical interrogation of the genre of musicals as this had been the most frequently suggested programming option that emerged through the consultation process. This process of interrogation meant that the volunteers were asked to reflect on the range of possibilities that the genre of musicals might include. At the same time, volunteers considered a range of operational issues such as budget and financial resources, facilities, target audiences, selling point and scheduling.

The excitement generated by the process also had the effect of encouraging TRSE staff to take ownership and build their active engagement in the project. Out of 33 staff members, 15 volunteered their time to take part in the project. They reported that spending time with the community volunteers was the 'highlight' of the experience. The feedback from staff generated an understanding of the importance of building the volunteers' sense of ownership of the building and the different spaces and activities that occur throughout it. Visiting directors and writers based at TRSE have been encouraged to give volunteers access to their rehearsal rooms and have invited the volunteers to participate in different stages of the creative process.

Challenges

Artistic directors and audiences

In an interview with this author, TRSE Artistic Director Kerry Michael identified a number of key contextual factors which informed the decision to undertake the project. In particular the TRSE is a major arts organization with the closest proximity to the 2012 London Olympics Games, and Michael and his team felt that they needed a project that would 'empower our community...to have some ownership of culture during [the Olympics]' (Michael interview 2011). By building and extending its community engagement, 'our conversations with the community', the TRSE would have a better understanding of the short and long term impact of the Olympics. While community engagement is a long-standing priority of the company, there is a need to 'put extra effort' into building community connection and outreach for the period following the Games, particularly in the light of the changing demographics of East London.

Beyond the immediate pressure of the Olympic games on the local community, Open Stage has been designed to 'test the organization's DNA' (Michael interview 2011). Michael sought to review the assumptions and practices of the TRSE; to 'not rest on our laurels' as an organization already well-known for its audience engagement: 'If you keep doing the same thing in the same way, actually how do you know it still works, and how do you know it's the right way of doing things? By doing this program we have to deconstruct all that shorthand and we have to explain it again...and just remind ourselves of what we're doing'. Michael also identified the need to provoke debate about the role of arts organizations and their publics: 'I wanted to do something that was big enough and significant enough [to cause] debate amongst our peers and our funding bodies, and our sector about who's here for whom? Who's here to serve whom? Who's our paymaster?' (Michael interview 2011). The development of Open Stage as a co-production project has been developed as a challenge to conventional assumptions around the role of arts organizations and their publics.

The notion of co-production is not in itself new. Brown & Novak-Leonard (2011) identify a raft of practices within the arts which encourage a 'more immersive and interactive experience' for audiences and where 'the line between creator and observer' is obscured (2011, p. 6). Within the museum sector, partnership projects, public consultation, and advisory groups have become an accepted way of working particularly in the UK. Although there is a range of interpretations of co-production, Davies (2010) writes that '...it differs from a traditional process of production in that the producers and consumers work together in a joint process of production' (2010, p. 307). There are a number of distinctive features to the TRSE's Open Stage co-production project: the use of volunteers as cultural intermediaries; the whole-of-organization approach to audience development; and, of particular relevance to this chapter, the role of network-building as a key component of the organization's activities. All these features suggest possibilities for a new model of cultural leadership. While Michael is a key figure in the process, he is not the sole driver of it; he has had a leadership role in conceptualizing and articulating the relationship between the values and mission of the project to those of the organization as a whole. Along the lines of distributed leadership models described above, Michael's role has been to facilitate the entry of both more lateral and external voices into the process of generating and selecting ideas.

It may be that new thinking around arts and cultural leadership is overdue. Bourdieu identifies how familiarity with high culture is a scare resource distributed along class lines (2000, p. 359). Following Bourdieu, scholars have noted the elitism of arts and cultural organizations where the gatekeepers facilitate entry for the like-minded: those who possess the cultural competence to decode works of art. It has been noted, for example, that within the cultural industries, and despite the variety of cultural forms and activities within the sector, the key decision-makers are frequently drawn from a narrow band or grouping, reflecting 'a very particular class background and habitus' (Negus 2002, p. 512). In his study of the British music industry, Negus found that the decision-makers are middle class white males who represent 'in condensed form, the preferences and judgments of a small, relatively elite educated, middle-class, white male faction'(Negus 2002, p. 512). In much the same way, Curran's (2000) study of the cultural values and social networks amongst magazine and newspaper literary editors, publishers and novelists finds a similar, relatively small but dominant network of gatekeepers and aesthetic arbiters. In the museum sector, Durrer and Miles find that museums and galleries are often traditionally elitist institutions accessible only to individuals with the 'appropriate' cultural, social and economic capital (2009, p. 226).

Bauman discusses the role of arts institutions in policing the boundaries of taste: '... bric-a-brac promptly turns into works of art once it is transferred to a gallery whose walls and gates separate good art from bad (and, for the cognoscenti, art from non-art) (2008, p. 209). Bauman's uncompromising metaphor sees the walls of arts organizations as part of the 'cage/shelter' that defines the 'difference between the 'inside' and the 'outside' in the arts' (2008, p. 214). The caging (or sheltering) of art (in Bauman's terms) can make arts organizations tend to turn inward. Sterngold identifies how over time, many mainstream organizations, 'become preoccupied with their products ... become overly dependent on aggressive sales and promotion efforts ...and have a tendency to become myopic and inward looking over time ...' (2010, p. 78).

The inward gaze of arts organizations also has consequences for audiences; as Bauman indicates, arts institutions work for the cognoscenti to differentiate 'art from non-art'. Dervin's research confirms that such insularity delimits the organizations' apprehension of audiences. The arts sector tends to focus on 'arts aficionados' who 'mirror the characteristics of the very same individuals who administer the arts ...white, highly educated, professionals, upper middle and upper class' (2010, p. 246). This means, Dervin suggests, that 'arts companies are putting their efforts into a group with whom they already share a worldview ... '[with] common perspectives and assumptions' (2010, p. 246). For Dervin, this is principally a problem of communication which the arts sector needs to engage with more effectively (along with other service providers competing for attention); arts managers are 'beset by challenges around communicating their offerings to publics whenever those publics are not among the initiated' (2010, p. 245). For Davies (2010), the issue in museums is that museum staff tend not to have the necessary formal and informal networks into communities and that therefore 'if the museum's workforce does not reflect the population that it seeks to serve it will be more difficult for the museum to make links with that population ... personal networks appear to play a role in determining who the museum works with [and] it seems probable that museums with workforces that are markedly different from the audiences they target will be at a disadvantage' (2010, p. 317). One of the key features of the Open Stage project is its engagement in the task of network-building. It is doing this by using both formal and informal networks to recruit and involve external parties.

Outcomes

Leadership and networks

Bauman points out that the network (unlike the hierarchical organization) is notable for its flexibility and the 'extraordinary facility with which its composition … tends to be modified' (2008, p. 13). Networks come about in the course of action and are repetitively recreated through iterative communications. Arguably, the kind of fluid, flexible, responsive and infinitely changeable nature of the networked organization is an antidote to the dominant view of arts organizations as places where information and ideas flow from the centre first downwards and then outwards; from cultural gatekeepers to the initiated. Rather, TRSE can be seen to respond to Holden's call for cultural institutions to shift their focus from 'product to people' and 'to put in place measures to attract, educate and listen to a wide public' (2010, p. 60).

In sociology the social network literature examines social phenomena as activity across a network of 'actors' with various ties between them. 'Actors' refers to individual people or groups, and 'ties' refers to relationships characterized by a flow of resources which can be material or non-material (Williams 2005). Previously it had been assumed that strong ties between individuals and groups lead to social cohesion, and conversely that weak ties lead to alienation. Sociologist Mark Granovetter (1983), a major contributor to the literature on network theory, theorized that strong ties by themselves generate fragmentation as sub-groups in a community become isolated from each other, and weak ties lead to community integration and provide connections between sub-groups.

According to social network theory, where strong ties bring social support, weak ties bring new information. Granovetter posits that 'weak ties' are those that form a low-density network around individuals and organizations. An individual or organization with few weak ties will be deprived of information from distant parts of the system, and the information he/she does receive will be localized and provincial, and as such insulate the individual or organization from new ideas. It is beyond the scope of this chapter to conduct an actor-network analysis of the operations of the TRSE; however my argument here, to extend Granovetter's approach, is that many arts organizations are focused on their strong ties; the intimate circle of stakeholders and cognoscenti (or fans) who understand and identify with the goals of the organization. The problem with this focus on strong ties and the absence of a more diffuse network of weak ties is that new ideas spread slowly and organizations can become inflexible and narrowly focused. This is relevant to the current case study which provides an exemplar of the diffusion of ideas through the connecting medium of weak ties, and shows the strength of weak ties in reaching socially distant and previously unknown targets. Many arts organizations place the Artistic Director at the top of a hierarchy with connections to the public through various departments such as education and marketing. The current case study suggests a different organizational model where the community volunteers sit within a network that reaches out to the Artistic Director, the Open Stage team and TRSE staff in all departments, visiting artists, residents, audiences, other arts organizations, community organizations and funders and philanthropic partners. Ideas flow in and around all the 'actors' in the network which, in turn, evolves to accommodate and build on the information it gathers and disseminates.

Looking at arts organizations in terms of their capacities as networks focused on the strength of weak ties may seem an unlikely application of Granovetter's research (1983) which was specifically addressed to the process of getting a job and the role of personal informal ties in helping to secure a position. However, weak ties are also an efficient means for the communication of cultural ideas and symbols. Theatre companies tend to operate within small, closed and intimate social circles; TRSE's Open Stage suggests that the opposite is not only possible but desirable if the goal is to deepen and extend the audiences' engagement.

Mintzberg sees a key role for new models of leadership to enhance the possibilities for networked organizations: 'A robust community requires a form of leadership quite different from the models that have it driving transformation from the top. Community leaders see themselves as being in the centre, reaching out rather than down' (2009, p. 142). Hewison and Holden (2011) have noted, in their analysis of the radical restructuring of the RSC that there is something of a paradox in having a new co-operative and non-hierarchical organizational culture that has relied on 'the direction and coherence' provided through organizational leadership. The same paradox could be identified in the case of the TRSE where leadership has been a key factor in the move towards a de-centered and networked organization.

Conclusion

Audience participation and engagement projects are not beyond criticism. Indeed, to be successful, such projects need to be underpinned by critical thinking and the testing of assumptions. Freshwater argues that the belief that participation empowers audiences has become a 'compelling orthodoxy' in theatre and performance studies, an orthodoxy that is often 'reductively and uncritically' applied (2009, p. 56). She gives the example of UK theatre critic for the Guardian, Lyn Gardner's description of the appetite of contemporary audiences for active engagement and its connection to political empowerment: 'The audiences are already storming the barricades, it is up to the rest of us to give them a helping hand because the revolution has already started without us ...' (Freshwater 2009, p. 56). For the current chapter the argument is not that there is an automatic equation of participation with empowerment or political agency, rather that the Open Stage project, in fostering the active participation of community members, is taking a leadership role in reviewing and reassessing the assumed cultural authority of arts organizations.

Just as there is nothing inherently politically radical about audience participation, there is no guarantee that all exercises in audience engagement are of equal quality. Lynch (2011) documents how in the museums and galleries sector, for example, there have been cases where community partnership programs have been unsuccessful. Lynch cites cases where insufficient effort was made to gather knowledge of local needs; in some cases community partners felt that the museum's claims of community collaboration were exaggerated or that they felt 'used by their museums...as a means to access further funding' (2011, p. 6).

In Lynch's research, key factors in successful community engagement projects are committed leadership, the active embracing of the values of the project by the whole organization, and the embedding of the organization within the local community whose members are understood not as beneficiaries but as active partners (2011, p. 7). Lynch's benchmarking of good practice underscores the quality of the Open Stage project; it is a long term commitment to produce not only an artistic product (in the form of a season of work in 2012) but also skill development for participants. The TRSE provides an example of the role of distributed or shared leadership. Following Mintzberg, the work of the leadership of the organization is, in effect, to embed a decentralized leadership across the organization; from its artistic director, to its project managers, and to the volunteers that are brokering relationships between the organization and its community. As Hewison *et al.* point out, such innovations in the leadership of an arts organization will help it to become 'sustainable, resilient, well-networked ...capable of growing its own capacity to act, and providing high-quality results for its customers, staff and funders' (2010, p. 117).

There is, finally, something poignant about the work of Open Stage coming to fruition at the same time and place as the 2012 London Olympics. Where the Olympics Games are defined by their appeal as an international showcase for elite, competitive, athletic performance, Open Stage sees its cultural role as explicitly local, aesthetic, participative and democratic. At this stage the benefits that might flow to the residents of Stratford East from the Olympics are not clear, however, it seems likely that those who have taken up the opportunity to participate in Open Stage at TRSE will have experienced an enhanced sense of community belonging. This is, surely, a good outcome for arts leadership.

Acknowledgements

I am grateful to Kerry Michael and Charlotte Handel from the Theatre Royal Stratford East for generously sharing their thoughts on the Open Stage project.

Interviews

Handel, C 2010, Manager Open Stage Theatre Royal Stratford East, interviewed 13 December 2010

Handel, C 2011, Manager Open Stage Theatre Royal Stratford East, interviewed 2 May 2011

Michael, K 2011, Artistic Director Theatre Royal Stratford East, interviewed 2 May 2011

Questions

1. Discuss the model of leadership that the author describes as dominant in the theatre, and how the model described in this case study differs?

2. The Theatre Royal Stratford East has undertaken a different approach to engaging its audience in the process of theatre making. Discuss this approach and what might be its strengths and weaknesses.

3. In this case study, arts leadership is described as acting within a model of exclusiveness and privilege. What does the author mean by this, how might this be demonstrated, and what are the implications for arts leaders?

References

Alimo-Metcalfe, B & Alban-Metcalfe, J 2005, 'Leadership: The time for a new direction? *Leadership*, vol. 1, no. 1, pp. 51-71.

Annual Report, Theatre Royal Stratford East, January-December 2008.

Annual Report, Theatre Royal Stratford East, January 2009-March 2010.

Back, L 2007, *The Art of Listening*, Berg, Oxford.

Bauman, Z 2008, *Does Ethics Have a Chance in a World of Consumers?* Harvard University Press, Cambridge, Mass.

Bligh, MC & Schyns, B 2007, 'The romance lives on: contemporary issues surrounding the romance of leadership', *Leadership*, vol. 3, no. 3, pp. 343-360.

Bourdieu, P 2000, *Distinction: A social critique of the judgement of taste*, Trans R. Nice. Harvard University Press, Cambridge MA.

Brown, A & Novak-Leonard, J 2011, *Getting in on the Act: How arts groups are creating opportunities for active participation*, James Irvine Foundation.

Davies, S 2010, 'The co-production of temporary museum exhibitions', *Museum Management and Curatorship*, vol. 25, no. 3, September pp. 305-321.

Dervin, B 2010, 'Hidden Passions, Burning Questions: The other side of so-called Mass audiences' in L Foreman-Wernet & B Dervin (eds) *Audiences and the Arts*, Hampton Press, Cresskill, NJ, pp. 243-264.

Durrer, V & Miles, S 2009, 'New perspectives on the role of cultural intermediaries in social inclusion in the UK', *Consumption, Markets & Culture*, vol. 12, no. 3, September pp. 225-241.

Eyre, R & Wright, N 2000, Changing Stages, Bloomsbury: London.

Fairhurst, GT 2007, *Discursive Leadership: In conversation with leadership psychology*, Thousand Oaks, CA, Sage.

Freshwater, H 2009, *Theatre and Audience*, Palgrave Macmillan, Basingstoke, Hampshire

Granovetter, M 1983, 'The Strength of Weak Ties: A Network Theory Revisited', *Sociological Theory*, vol. 1, pp. 201-233.

Handel, C 2010, Stratford East Open Stage Report, Theatre Royal Stratford East.

Hansen, H, Ropo, A & Sauer, E 2007, 'Aesthetic leadership', *The Leadership Quarterly*, vol. 18, no. 6, pp. 544-560.

Hewison, R & Holden, J 2011, *The cultural leadership handbook: How to run a creative organisation*, Gower, Surrey.

Hewison, R, Holden, J & Jones, S 2010, *All together: a creative approach to organisational change*, Demos, London.

Holden, J 2010, *Culture and Class*, Counterpoint, British Council, London.

Jennings, N & Jones, H 2010, 'Engaging hearts and minds: leadership and taking part' in S Kay & K Venner (eds) *A Cultural Leadership Reader*, Cultural Leadership Program, Creative Choices, London.

Leadbeater, C 2009, *The Art of With*, Cornerhouse Manchester, Creative Commons UK, http://www.cornerhouse.org/wp-content/uploads/old_site/media/Learn/The%20Art%20of%20With.pdf, Accessed August 2011.

Lynch, B 2011, *Whose Cake Is It Anyway? A collaborative investigation into engagement and participation in 12 museums and galleries in the UK*, Summary Report, Paul Hamlyn Foundation.

Mintzberg, H 2009, 'Rebuilding Companies as Communities' *Harvard Business Review*, vol. 87, no. 7, pp. 140-143.

Open Stage, Theatre Royal Stratford East http://www.openstage2012.com/?category_name=open-stage Accessed 10 July 2011.

Sinclair, A 2007, *Leadership for the disillusioned: Moving beyond myths and heroes to leading that liberates*, Allen & Unwin, Sydney.

Sterngold, A 2010, 'The over-selling of marketing rhetoric to nonprofit arts and cultural organisations' in L Foreman-Wernet & B Dervin (eds) *Audiences and the Arts*, Hampton Press, Cresskill, NJ, pp. 75-88.

Williams, KH 2005, '*Social networks, social capital, and the use of information and communications technology* ProQuest Dissertations & Theses' (PQDT).

Chapter 10

Leadership and transformation at the Royal Shakespeare Company

ROBERT HEWISON, JOHN HOLDEN & SAMUEL JONES[1]

Background

'The value of the RSC's story is as an example of a company in turnaround'.

Sir Christopher Bland, Chairman of the Board of Governors of the RSC 2004-2011, and former Chairman of British Telecommunications plc, February 2009

The Royal Shakespeare Company (RSC) is probably the best-known theatre company in the world, and has a long and distinguished history. It is a charitable, not-for-profit organization employing around 800 people (including full-time and part-time staff), and its purpose is to produce great work for the widest possible audience. Everything that it does is directed to this end. It brings to this task considerable strengths: Royal patronage, an experienced and committed Board, a proud history, an excellent reputation, a world-famous theatre building, and dedicated staff; many with years of experience in the craft and skills of the theatre. The RSC is itself a valuable and respected brand name – it is the most recognized theatre name in the United Kingdom – and enjoys considerable public support and affection.

Yet in spite of these strengths the RSC began the 21st century facing serious challenges to its operating model, compounded by leadership problems, internal dissension, and low morale. These issues became manifest in declining audiences,

---

[1] The following text is an edited version of a much lengthier pamphlet titled All Together: a Creative Approach to Organizational Change, published by Demos, London, and available at http://www.demos.co.uk/publications/all-together.

...r reviews and falling income. Many of the conditions that led to this situation ...pping for years, and were exposed when, between 1999 and 2002, ...nced a crisis that threatened to overwhelm it. At a Board meeting ...wly appointed Artistic Director Michael Boyd summed up the

> *...has suffered both historically and in the recent past from a remote ... hierarchical management approach which has led to a sclerosis in ...unication of authority, the misuse of information as power and a ...nitiative and management skills at departmental level (Boyd 2003,*

...facing Boyd at that point, which were also those facing the new ...ctor Vikki Heywood, can be summarized as follows:

- ...o rebuild the morale of the organization;
- ...o rebuild the critical reputation of the RSC, which was low;
- ...to restore the confidence of senior management;
- how to restore the staff's confidence in senior management;
- how to restore relations with supporters, sponsors, and funders, especially the main public funder, the Arts Council;
- how to deal with a looming financial deficit;
- how to handle the loss of a permanently available London theatre;
- how to manage the reconstruction of the Royal Shakespeare Theatre, for which the Arts Council had set aside £50 million in Lottery Funding, but which would cost more than double that;
- how to solve the long-term structural problems of the RSC, and rebuild an organization, while working with the grain of its dominant culture; and
- how to do all this, and continue to show artistic leadership by mounting critically successful productions.

Financially, and more importantly, creatively, the RSC has not only survived the crisis of 1999-2002, but has re-established its reputation, has opened a reconstructed main theatre in Stratford-upon-Avon and has taken on several major and ambitious new projects, including the World Shakespeare Festival as part of London's Cultural Olympiad. This achievement has happened because of a process of change and growth across the whole organization that is rooted in the concept of 'ensemble'.

In February 2007 we were invited, as members of the UK 'think tank' *Demos*, to conduct an observational study of the change process that the RSC had begun to undertake. Over a period of nearly three years we conducted interviews with members of the RSC at all levels, attended rehearsals, charted the course of critical response, and were present at workshops and meetings designed to further the change process. Having established a 'base-line' in terms of the company's understanding and acceptance of the company values represented by the term 'ensemble', we paid special attention to the formal and informal networks within the organization, and how they changed. Our conclusion was that by 2010, the general (but not complete) adoption of the 'ensemble' principle had helped to transform a failing organization into a successful and creative one.

Approach

The 'ensemble' principle

Historically the RSC has described itself as an 'ensemble' – a French word meaning 'together' or 'viewed as a whole'. In the theatre it has the specific meaning of a group of actors who work together in a collaborative fashion over a period of time. What Boyd and Heywood have done is to extend the principles of ensemble, as applied to the acting company, to the whole organization, both in its internal management and its external relations with audiences and other businesses. In the RSC's 2006 statement of its 'Purpose and Values' it makes a commitment:

> *To create our work through the ensemble principles of collaboration, trust, mutual respect, and a belief that the whole is greater than the sum of its parts (RSC 2006, p. 3).*

Ensemble should be thought of not only as a management tool, but as a set of moral principles that remains constant as a guide to leadership decisions and administrative actions. Ensemble is a value, as well as a description of a particular way of organizing people: a way of being as much as a way of doing. It is also a moving target, in that it can be re-articulated to meet changing needs and circumstances.

Organizational development guided by ensemble principles has helped the RSC to achieve artistic success, improved financial performance, more efficient operations and productions, and better morale, and leadership has played an essential role in aligning the values of ensemble with strategic objectives and organizational change. This has been achieved by employing rhetorical power and judicious intervention, and by balancing organic evolution, shaped by the staff as a collective, with an intentional program of change, shaped by Boyd and Heywood as leaders.

Some of the organizational changes that have happened at the RSC are conventional, though not necessarily easy to achieve: improved communications; delegated responsibilities; more transparency; greater resilience; accessible leaders; alterations in the physical environment of the theatre and its offices. Other aspects of the RSC's development are less conventional and offer useful lessons.

The challenges

Ensemble and leadership: The lessons learned

It is a paradox of ensemble that the organic development of a co-operative and empowered organizational culture nevertheless depends on the direction and coherence provided by leadership. The RSC's progress over the course of our research clearly demonstrates the need for effective leadership. What we mean by 'effective leadership' is the ability to marry rhetorical power with practical innovations so as to create a sustainable, resilient, well-networked organization, capable of growing its own capacity to act, and providing high-quality results for its customers, staff and funders.

The RSC story shows that it is not the titles and conventions of leadership that matter, but what leaders do and how they do it. Much of the rhetoric around leadership concentrates on the individual ('the right person at the top') but research shows that companies (in the creative sector at least) may have a single individual as the public face, but have strong teams acting as collective leaders (Leadbeater & Oakley 2001). At the RSC, and in theatre and the arts more widely, the model of explicit shared leadership between artistic and managerial roles is far from novel: Britain's National Theatre, for instance, has both an Artistic Director and an Executive Director. Other sectors should learn to think of leadership as embedded within a wider group, and as a flexible activity that can be successfully shared in many ways. The generally accepted term for this in Leadership theory is 'distributed leadership' (Bass & Stogdill 1990).

Leaders need to use the right language and metaphors

It has been important to find some word or term that both acts as a metaphor for distributed leadership and fits organizational culture. At the RSC it has been the term 'ensemble'. Other organizations will need to find a phrase, that fits their own culture and sector, but everyone needs a shorthand that sends the same set of messages: that people will have a voice, will take responsibility for each other and themselves, and will work to a common end. Whatever term is chosen, it needs to be adaptable to the way that the organization develops, and leaders must be alive to when the language needs to change.

Leaders need to embody the values that they promote

Strong and distinctive organizational cultures, resting on explicit values, have been recognized as a key factor in successful organizations (Collins & Porras 1994; Peters & Waterman 2004).

References to values and relationships are a constant feature in the RSC's ensemble journey. Boyd has repeatedly emphasized the need for honesty, altruism, tolerance, forgiveness, humility and magnanimity. One of the main tasks of leaders is to articulate and reiterate organizational values and link them in one direction to the individual and in the other to the wider world.

Sustainable organizational change can only come about if the rhetoric of the way the organization operates is matched by the quality of relationships that it produces. Any disparity between the rhetoric of values and what happens on the ground damages organizations – as Google found out when the gap between its corporate slogan 'Don't be evil' and its dealings with the Chinese government created a storm of protest (Battelle 2005). Equally, values need to connect inwardly so that they are apparent in everyday practices and the quality of relationships. When values expressed are disconnected from the norms of behavior within an organization it leads to cynicism, and poor morale and performance: it also discredits the leaders and the vision they develop.

But leaders cannot simply communicate values – they have to do more. In an organizational context, discussion of values can often seem artificial and remote from everyday life. Lofty pronouncements from a Board or CEO seem divorced from the pressures of getting things done. Leaders have to provide the spaces and places, and the time, for values to be explored, discussed, disputed, agreed, and internalized. They also have to 'walk the talk' and be personally responsible for living up to the organization's values.

Leaders need to lead the change process

Organizational change, wherever it is attempted, takes place in a context where the organization is busy and short of time, where external factors demand attention, short-term pressures distract from long-term vision and where there will be some internal resistance. Organizational development is easily set back by such obstacles, but all of them should be expected and anticipated by leaders who want to foster change, even though the particular forms taken will be unpredictable. Leaders need not only to demonstrate confidence in the change process but to be deeply involved in the minutiae of change, because sustainable change can only come from within; it cannot be imposed from without. They must also be committed to leading the change process: they can use external help and support, but change cannot be sub-contracted or outsourced.

Leaders must acknowledge emotions

A remarkable feature of the RSC's leadership and management style has been the regular and explicit reference to emotions. In a speech at the New York Public Library in June 2008, Michael Boyd used words like terror, daring, fear, empathy, compassion and 'love, which I say without any apology'. Indeed, he used the word 'love' ten times (Boyd 2008, p. 6).

Very few leaders in government or the corporate sector speak so openly about the emotions that everyone knows are a major feature of organizational life. There are exceptions. In the Institute of Directors' magazine, *Director,* of June 2009, Tim Smit of the *Eden Project* was described as 'an inspirational leader' partly because 'he marries vision and emotion with pragmatism'. Yet acknowledging emotions is still seen as odd and mysterious – the magazine article is titled 'Casting a Spell' (Simms 2009).

Leaders often avoid talking about the emotional life of an organization – it is seen as odd, embarrassing, and 'soft'. But emotions exist, and when harnessed in the right way, are powerful forces. As Linda Holbeche, an expert in organizational change says:

> Managing change effectively requires more than an intellectual understanding of the processes involved. It requires … real emotional, political and some would say spiritual intelligence on the part of those leading change (Holbeche 2007, p. 8).

Leaders should provide conceptual simplicity in response to organizational and contextual complexity

Every large-scale organization is complex, and every organization exists within a changing and multifaceted context. Difficult and demanding tasks need to be underpinned by clear and comprehensible concepts that everyone understands and can feel part of both intellectually and emotionally. A good example of an organization that got this right is NASA. When President Kennedy visited the NASA Space Center, he asked a cleaner what his job was, and the cleaner replied: 'Putting a man on the moon'. The RSC offers a more modest, but equally compelling case of a complex organization with a simple message: when asked what was the purpose of the RSC, our interviewees repeatedly expressed the same aspiration: to be the best theatre for Shakespeare in the world.

Leaders are at the heart of a network, not at the top of a pyramid

As the business academic Professor Henry Mintzberg puts it:

> A robust community requires a form of leadership quite different from the models that have it driving transformation from the top. Community leaders see themselves as being in the centre, reaching out rather than down (Mintzberg 2009, p. 142).

At the RSC, the shift in thinking from hierarchical to network models of leadership can be seen in two organizational diagrams, the first from 2007 (Figure 10.1) and the second from 2008 (Figure 10.2). These diagrams show how the RSC moved from visualizing the organization as a hierarchy (Figure 10.1) to seeing it more like a mind-map (Figure 10.2), with leadership placed as a central resource. Creating strong networks is one of the vital tasks of contemporary leadership.

Outcomes

Ensemble and the development of networks

Our study of the formal, informal and social networks of personal relationships within the RSC demonstrated how important it is to create and strengthen networks within organizations. There are numerous examples of how new and strengthened networks have helped the RSC to operate to better effect. Networks are important because:

Figure 10.1 RSC organogram, senior management structure 2007

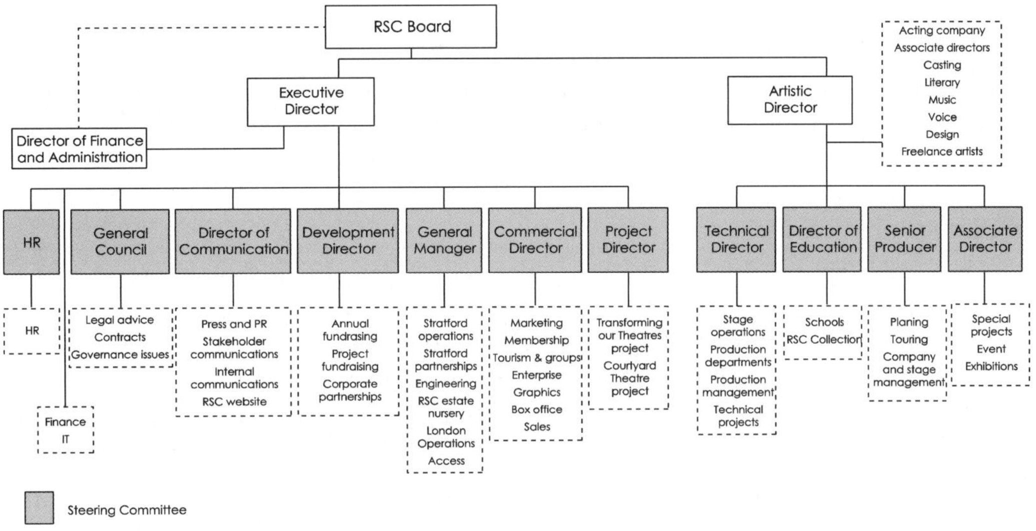

Source: Hewison, Holden, Jones 2010, p. 90

Figure 10.2 RSC organizational diagram, Senior management structure 2008

Source: Hewison, Holden, Jones 2010, p. 91 (adapted by Hewison, Holden & Jones)

Outcomes

Ensemble and the development of networks

Our study of the formal, informal and social networks of personal relationships within the RSC demonstrated how important it is to create and strengthen networks within organizations. There are numerous examples of how new and strengthened networks have helped the RSC to operate to better effect. Networks are important because:

- they encourage innovation: networks create links that allow things to happen – for example the commercial exploitation of a new lighting invention at the RSC became possible because of the newly forged relationships between half a dozen departments;

- they promote efficiency: networks produce collective, effective and speedy decisions;

- they make organizations resilient: networks enable self-organization and generate the capacity to respond to events in the right way;

- they promote individual welfare: networks allow individuals to flourish within a collective, because they provide support, and connection to a greater whole; and

- they stimulate communication and awareness: networks are vital in spreading knowledge and creating understanding about the organization as a whole.

Networks need a common language of words, metaphors and symbols

The words that leaders use have to resonate and have meaning across the whole organization. A common language helps networks to form and eases communication. Ensemble is a founding concept at the RSC, and the word itself appeals both to tradition and to the specialism of a particular discipline – the theatre. It thus helps to create unity. The words 'group' or 'team' could have been used instead of ensemble, but neither would have had the same resonance or the same sense of history. Networks grow organically, and it can also be helpful to use words, like ensemble, that are ambiguous, because that allows for development, creativity and exploration.

Within networks, seemingly small acts and moments can gain extraordinary potency – both positive and negative. Leaders need to have heightened sensitivity to the way that meaning gathers around symbols and metaphors and the way that people project big ideas onto the detail of their lives. For example, in addition to changing the way that networks operate through interaction in physical space, the new Royal Shakespeare Theatre building has become a powerful symbol of a renewed RSC. It is a multi-million pound metaphor for the way that the organization has changed not only itself, but its relationships with the outside world – from its audiences to its locality and to its supporters.

Networks are strengthened through learning and self-reflection

The RSC has created many formal and informal opportunities for people to learn not just about things that are immediately relevant to their jobs, but much more widely. This process has been managed by Human Resources, who have developed the concept of 'ensemble learning', through which members of staff learn from each other. Our conclusion is that not only is learning valuable for the individual, but also that it increases the number and quality of interactions in the organization, leading to more conviviality, better communication, and improved mutual understanding and respect.

One feature of the RSC's development over the last seven years has been continuous self-reflection. At various points on the path of changing the organization, leaders and larger groups of staff have taken stock of where they have come from, where they are and where they are going. The techniques used to undertake self-reflection have ranged from a consciously structured whole-company staff survey, through managerial or departmental gatherings, to one-to-one meetings.

Self-awareness within a network creates constant sources of feedback, which mean that corrective or beneficial action takes place more speedily, and can take the form of 'nudges' and 'tweaks' rather than sudden and violent changes of direction. An example is the way in which the use of the word 'ensemble' is itself being slowly dropped from written communications and discussions, because it has started to become over-used.

Networks need to be open and transparent

The RSC has moved from being a hierarchical organization steeped in secrecy, where information was closely guarded and decisions taken by individuals or small groups, to one that is much more open. This has been particularly the case in human resources, finance, and artistic planning departments. The beneficial effects of these changes and the resultant gains in efficiency have been made possible by the relatively free flow of data and information around the networked organization. The more information moves around a network, the more the network itself is strengthened.

Networks help overcome 'silos'

Studies attest to the fact that people work better, and are happier in their work, when they have a large degree of autonomy and control over what they do (Sennett 2008, Malone 2004). The experience of many companies confirms that flattening hierarchies, giving people more responsibility, and encouraging questioning improves performance.

However, the simple devolution of power risks creating silos and a series of units at war with each other. It can also lead to inefficiencies where disparate ways of doing things fail to mesh with each other. The desired state is therefore one in which autonomy, individual responsibility and collective responsibility all increase.

Combining individual action with systemic consistency across a networked organization (as opposed to directing action through a hierarchy) depends on people trusting each other. As Paul Skidmore puts it in *Network Logic:*

> *Leaders carry responsibility to preserve the trust on which their networks depend. In an unpredictable world in which some failures are almost bound to happen, that is a tough challenge. Acknowledging our interdependence with others, and the limited capacity of our leaders to manage it, will be a frightening experience. It is much more convenient to think that leaders will be saviors – and that we have someone to blame when things do not go our way. But if it wakes us up to the potential within each of us to solve our own problems, then so much the better (Skidmore 2004, p. 100).*

At the RSC, it is recognized that leaders cannot have all the answers, but there is a strong belief in the leaders' sincerity, and that they will always try to do the right thing. As one member of the team put it,

> *They [Boyd and Heywood and other senior managers], the powers that be, are trying to make it a positive and uplifting experience for everyone and I think that it is working.*

Sensitivity to individual perspectives and recognizing everyone's contribution increases a sense of belonging

The RSC has found a number of ways to accommodate the needs of individuals and has acted to make sure that those needs are met. One example is consideration of different standpoints on organizational decisions. As one interviewee put it:

> *You actually do matter … There is a genuine effort to make each person a valued member of staff.*

In addition, efforts are made to recognize everyone's contribution to the organization. For example, the RSC lists all staff alphabetically within their departments in its performance programs. This seemingly small idea is emblematic of something that is in fact very important. It demonstrates the RSC's ecological sensibility – that is, it shows an understanding that every part is needed to make a whole, and that every element is as vital as every other in creating a complete system. This is recognized in management theory:

> *In a context that is fast-moving, complicated and unpredictable, the notion of organizations as living, complex, adaptive systems seems particularly apt (Holbeche 2007, p. 12).*

It is also recognized in other successful companies, such as Pixar, where:

> *The technical people and the artists are peers with each other. We do not have one in a second class to the other, we don't think that one is more important*

than the other, rather they're all coming together for the purpose of the story (Catmull 2007).

Networks are powerfully affected by buildings and design

During the period of our research, different parts of the RSC moved premises, and people therefore did their jobs in different spaces and places, be that offices or theatres. They also worked in different cities, and at different times of the day.

The experience of the RSC shows that physical remoteness is difficult to overcome, and that it is easier to form working relationships when everyone is together in the same place at the same time. What is equally clear is that buildings and spaces have affects as well as effects. In other words, places have their own psycho-geography, and the quality of the relationships within a network is affected by the way that physical spaces encourage or inhibit contact and communications. The thrust stages at the RST and the Swan Theatre (the RSC's smaller theatre space in their new building) clearly demonstrate this understanding, as they are intended to transform the relationship between actor and audience.

Conclusions

Creativity and change

Organizational change is not easy – according to Linda Holbeche 'various reports suggest that 75 percent of all transformation efforts fail' (Holbeche 2007, p. 6). Leaders have to hold in balance, on the one hand, an organization's creativity and desire to change, and on the other its continuity, established culture and traditions (Hewison 2006, p. 43). The experience of the RSC shows some ways in which this can be done.

Crisis can provide an opportunity for change, but ambition and energy are what make change happen

President Obama's former Chief-of-Staff, Rahm Emanuel, is credited with saying: 'You never let a serious crisis go to waste. They are opportunities to do big things' (Emanuel quoted in Zeleny 2008). Bill George, Management Professor at Harvard says the same thing: '…never waste a good crisis' (George 2009, p. 75). The RSC's experience bears witness to the fact that people are more willing to accept radical change in times of crisis.

But once the need for change is recognized, the next step is to create a sense of coherence, so that effort can be directed to a shared set of long-term priorities rather than dissipated in a flurry of short-term, fire-fighting responses. The RSC's experience shows that big, ambitious priorities concentrate effort and energy.

Over the last five years the RSC has set itself a number of tasks that have stretched every fibre of the company, including the staging of *The Complete Works Festival, The Histories, Stand up for Shakespeare,* and the remodeling of the RST, its offices in

Chapel Lane and other parts of the organization's Stratford estate. It is the scale of the ambition and the clarity of the goals that have provided the context in which many different, detailed tasks have come together to produce the desired results. A big, shared ambition encourages collaboration. It helps generate responsibility and encourages communication and efficiency because people realize that the goal can only be achieved by working together.

The experience of the RSC shows that energy is needed to push organizational development forward. That energy can be injected by leaders (such as when Boyd and Heywood address meetings); it can come from external sources (such as outside facilitators); and it can come from creating 'pulse points' where the whole organization is stretched to achieve a specific goal.

Experimentation and constant small-scale innovations help change to happen

There are many advantages in undertaking organizational innovation on a limited but continuous experimental basis because such an approach:

- is less threatening than major change;
- can be retracted if the innovation proves problematic;
- is easier to slow down or speed up than large-scale change;
- is less expensive than wholesale change;
- creates momentum and stimulus;
- focuses energy;
- develops confidence;
- provides opportunities for celebration;
- acknowledges that different parts of an organization move at a different pace; and
- makes it easier for members of staff to recognize their own impact and that of others.

A good way to experiment with change is through inter-disciplinary, task-oriented, time-limited teamwork. The RSC set about addressing a number of issues, such as meetings, by setting up teams of people from across a range of departments to come up with suggestions for reform. These endeavors were not always 100 percent successful, and some people thought that too much time was spent on meetings and discussions through this process. Nevertheless, our view is that setting up teams of people who bring different experience and perspectives to a specific task which they have to achieve within a particular time (no more than three meetings) is a good approach. It works best where expectations of the process and the potential outcomes are set up in advance, and where there is a level of commitment to implement the suggested changes so that people don't feel they are wasting their time and effort.

Changing things depends on creating confidence and trust

Leaders need to develop the confidence of their staff that what they are doing is right and will work. The RSC did this partly by seeking outside advice and validation to affirm what they were doing, but they then understood that they needed to 'ride their own bicycle'. Implementing change is also helped when there is trust in leadership – not necessarily trust that leaders will always get it right, but trust that they will try to do the right thing, and always act in what they believe to be the best interests of the organization and the people within it. Creating and maintaining trust is a tough challenge, but is also one of the most important tasks of contemporary leadership.

Change needs to be tested internally and externally

One danger of change processes within organizations, with their accompanying concentration on internal focus and more frequent discussion groups, is that they can lose touch with external realities. Inspiring rhetoric and charismatic leadership, on their own are not enough. Once a company believes its own propaganda, it is in dangerous territory, as the case of Enron clearly shows. The RSC benefits from being unable to insulate itself from outside judgment – every play goes in front of the critics and the public – but it has also sought to test its own understandings by the frequent involvement of outsiders. Indeed, the commissioning of our (*Demos*) report provided one external check.

The realization of creativity rests on collaboration

As a successful cultural organization, the RSC lives and breathes artistic creativity. But every organization has to adapt, innovate, and be creative to some degree. The RSC's experience shows that creativity can only be realized through collective and collaborative endeavor, and the more that is facilitated – through good communications, a strong common culture, the creation of the right set of attitudes, and so on – the more likely it is that the organization will be able to experiment, and hence to innovate well, across its whole range of activities.

Organizations need to build systems that are not just optimally efficient in a specific set of circumstances, but systems that are capable of changing to meet new circumstances: in other words organizations need internally generated resilience. In turn, that resilience is generated by creating shared terms of engagement – they cannot be imposed – that govern the relationships between different people and functions. Instead of attempting the now impossible task of micro-managing specialized, knowledge-driven functions, leaders must pay attention to developing the norms of responsibility, honesty and trust within the organization that enable people to work together. Leaders must develop both organizational interconnectedness, and the capacity of individuals and departments to work together. The concept of the 'ensemble' addresses exactly these questions of instilling behavioral norms through strong values, while reconciling the individual's needs for creative expression, reward, and liberty, with the need to be part of a social system that is efficient, responsive and liberating rather than conformist, restricting and inefficient.

Questions

1. Describe what is meant by the notion of 'ensemble' in the context of the Royal Shakespeare Company and its present leadership. What impact do you think this new organizational model has had on the Company's operation?

2. Consider the situation that the leaders of the Royal Shakespeare Company faced at the beginning of the new millennium. Do you think their solution(s) addressed this successfully? If so, why? If not, why not?

3. Are the concepts of 'ensemble' and 'leadership' oppositional? Discuss what you understand by these terms, and how you think they might work together in a large organization such as the Royal Shakespeare Company?

References

Bass, BM & Stogdill RM 1990 *Handbook of Leadership: A Survey of Theory and Research,* The Free Press, New York.

Battelle, J 2005, *Search: How Google and its Rivals Rewrote the Rules of Business and Transformed our Culture,* Penguin, London and New York.

Boyd, M 2003 'Playing our proper role. The way forward for the Royal Shakespeare Company', typescript October 2003.

Boyd, M 2008b Speech to the New York Public Library June 20, 2008.

Catmull, E 2007, Interview with Iinovate, A podcast by students of Stanford University's Business and Design Schools, accessed online at http://iinnovate.blogspot.com/2007/02/dr-ed-catmull-co-founder-and-president.html, November 25, 2009.

Collins, J & Porras, J 1994 *Built to Last: Succesful habits of Visionary Companies,* Harper Business, London.

George, B 2009 *7 Lessons for Leading in Crisis,* Jossey-Bass, San Francisco.

Hewison, R 2006 *Not a Sideshow: Leadership and Cultural Value,* Demos, London.

Hewison, R, Holden, J, Jones, S 2010 *All Together: A Creative Approach to Organisational Change,* Demos, London.

Holbeche, L 2007 *The High Performance Organisation: creating dynamic stability and sustainable success,* Elsevier Butterworth Heinemann, Oxford.

Leadbeater, C & Oakley, K 2001 *The Independents: Britain's New Cultural Entrepreneurs,* Demos, London.

Malone, T 2004 *The Future of Work: How the New Order of Business Will Shape Your Organisation, Your Management Style, and Your Life,* Harvard University Press, Cambridge, Mass.

Mintzberg, 2009 'Rebuilding Companies as Communities', *Harvard Business Reviw,* (July-August 2009), pp. 140-3.

Peters, T & Waterman, R 2004 *In Search of Excellence*, Profile Books, London.

RSC 2006 *Royal Shakespeare Company Annual Report 2006*, London, RSC.

Sennett, R 2008 *The Craftsman*, Allen Lane, London.

Simms, J 2009 'Casting a Spell', *The Director*, June 2009, Institute of Directors, London, available at: http://www.director.co.uk/magazine/2009/6%20June/simms_62_11.html.

Skidmore, P 2004 'Leading Between' in McCarthy, H. (edition), *Network Logic*, pp. 89-102, Demos, London.

Zeleny, J 2009 'Obama weighs quick undoing of Bush', *The New York Times*, 9 November 2008.

Part IV

Leadership as an Artistic Process

Chapter 11

Learning from creative work processes in the theatre

Stepping into character

HELLE HEDEGAARD HEIN

Background

The role of creativity in the future economy

Looking to the knowledge society, the creative economy and the experience economy there is no doubt that the future labor market will be increasingly dominated by a highly specialized and creative work force engaged in complex problem solving and creative work (Florida 2004; Gardner *et al.* 2001). In many Western economies, creativity has been singled out as *the* critical factor in the future economy.

Existing research points to several prerequisites for doing creative work:

a) The possibility of undisturbed concentration on a complex problem for a considerable amount of time under moderate time pressure (Amabile 1996; Amabile *et al.* 2002);

b) The feeling of being on a mission; that there is a higher purpose for doing creative work which means that the task itself is perceived as meaningful (Amabile *et al.* 2002; Hein 2009);

c) The realization that there is no such thing as divine inspiration. Rather, inspiration and creativity is enabled through hard work and by establishing a framework and rigorous routines (Hein 2007; Tharp 2003);

d) The willingness to step outside one's comfort zone. Obtaining a higher level of performance until the point of mastery is seldom done without at some point feeling anxiety or frustration (Csikszentmihalyi 1997; Hein 2009); and

e) Useful ways of coping with the cognitive and psychological barriers of doing creative work, such as coping with anxiety of failure, procrastination, the fear of losing face, etc. Cognitive and psychological barriers come with the territory of creative work – the question is not how to get rid of them, but how to cope with them (Argyris 1991; Hein 2007; Sternberg & Lubart 2007).

Even though the main share of creativity researchers agree on the prerequisites for creative work mentioned above, transferring this knowledge to a business context still proves a challenge for leaders and other facilitators of creative work processes. Based on diary entries from creative workers, a research project showed that reports of creative thinking during the work day were extremely seldom (Amabile *et al.* 2002) meaning that a vast creative potential goes unrealized.

Thus, there is a great need for the development of managerial skills for facilitating creative work processes. One way of doing so is by learning from successful and professional facilitators of creative work processes. In this case we will look to successful stage directors at The Royal Danish Theatre in Copenhagen, Denmark.

Approach

The Royal Danish Theatre as a creativity laboratory

The research presented here is based on the findings from a major research project using The Royal Danish Theatre in Copenhagen as a creativity laboratory.

Using the method of grounded theory, the collection of data has taken place over a period of 3½ years, from 2005-2009, and has generated a vast amount of data, primarily collected through qualitative observations and qualitative interviews. A total of 30 productions within the Opera, Ballet and Drama departments have been observed (5 opera, 12 ballet and 13 drama), ranging from the observation of morning class (ballet), readings (drama) and ordinary rehearsals all the way through the rehearsal process ending with dress rehearsals and the premiere. The typical production has a duration of eight weeks of rehearsal, each rehearsal typically lasting four to six hours. Each production has been observed two to five times a week depending on the rehearsal cycle and the phases of the creative process. For each production, at least five performances have been observed. Furthermore, a total of 180 managerial meetings have been observed, ranging from executive meetings, department meetings, evaluation meetings, strategy meetings, etc.

Lastly, more than 100 qualitative interviews have been conducted. Interviews with artists comprise opera soloists, choir soloists and academy soloists, principal dancers, soloists and corps dancers and actors (full-time employed as well as freelance actors). Interviews with managers comprise stage directors, ballet instructors and teachers, producers, stage managers, directors' assistants, artistic directors, the managing director of the theatre, etc. In addition, numerous informal talks have added to the data material. The interviews were conducted in order to investigate how both employees and managers think, reflect, and explain their behavior. Later in the research process the interviews were also conducted with the objective of testing categories, hypotheses, etc.

It is important to stress that the main objective of the research project was to develop new motivation theory focusing specifically on highly specialized, creative employees (see Figure 11.2 below). Along the way it became clear that rather than developing a motivation theory to fit all, it made more sense to distinguish between four different archetypes of highly specialized, creative employees, each having their own distinct motivational profile and leadership needs. It also became clear that certain directors were much more successful than others, and the data already collected provided an opportunity to look into the factors that distinguished the successful directors from the less successful directors in terms of personal characteristics, leadership style, psychological insight, the capacity to facilitate creative work processes, etc. Thus, the findings presented here are a by-product of the original research objective.

One last note before turning the attention to The Royal Danish Theatre: When asking what leaders of creative work processes can learn from stage directors on facilitating creativity, I will focus on the lessons to be learned from successful stage directors, i.e. directors of successful productions. But how does one define successful in regards to creativity? Here, I draw on Amabile's consensual definition (Amabile 1996) and define 'successful productions' as productions where: 1) appropriate observers independently agree that the result is creative, i.e. the audience, the critics, the artistic director, the performing actors, and the stage director and 2) the rehearsal process prior to the end result (i.e. the production) is regarded as creative (measured by the performing actors' and the director's experience and judgment).

Cases

For the analysis, two productions (both plays) have been singled out as being the most successful productions of the 30 productions observed. Below, I will give a short introduction to both productions.

Production number 1:

This play was new, made especially for The Royal Danish Theatre. The female director (Director number 1) was famous for her untraditional way of making plays. The theme of the play was the modern man. There was no script – the script was made during the rehearsal process as a result of improvisations. Five male actors were picked for the production based on a preliminary analysis of which characters were needed: The divorced single parent father; the young father-to-be; the mid-life crisis man; the contemplative family man; and the gay, life-experienced man. By her side during the entire rehearsal process the director had a female assistant with whom she had worked a number of times.

As this director worked very differently from 'traditional' directors, I will give a short overview of the process: In the beginning of the rehearsal process the director and her assistant spent a week alone with each of the actors. Based on questions like 'What do you dream of?' or 'When do you find it most difficult to be a man?', the director would pick up on some of the answers and ask the actor to improvise a scene about that particular paradox, dream, situation, etc. All improvisations were recorded on video. After a week, the actor was given a gross list of possible monologues to work with. After five weeks – one week alone with each actor – the director gathered all the actors for one week for improvisations for common scenes. Thus, after 6 weeks of rehearsals, each actor had a long list of possible monologues and a list of possible common scenes – but still no script.

Then the 'real' rehearsal process began. On the first day of rehearsal, the director arranged a run-through of the play in front of a number of invited female guests and asked the actors to improvise their way through their entire list of monologues and common scenes. This is highly unusual in many respects. First of all, it is very unusual to start off with a run-through of the play. Secondly, it is very unusual to invite guests for the first run-throughs. Thirdly, it is unusual to ask for a run-through when there is no script or no order of monologues and common scenes, as run-throughs are often undertaken when the actors more or less know their lines. After the very first run-through the director met with her guests (without the actors) to discuss what they had just seen. The actors returned the next day to get notes.

The rest of the rehearsal process consisted of rehearsals (improvisations) of individual monologues and common scenes, run-throughs (always with the same invited guests), notes, more rehearsals, more run-throughs and more notes. From time to time, the director made a decision to cut a monologue or a common scene and exchanging it for another monologue or common scene on the list (all the time also cutting short the original list). As the improvisations and rehearsals progressed, the assistant made a working script for the players. However, changes in the scripts were made all the way through to the dress rehearsal. Approximately 4-5 weeks into the rehearsal process, the focus of the rehearsals shifted from improvisations to more traditional rehearsals of lines, positions, fine-tuning of the lines, etc. Run-throughs were made at least once a week. The order of the monologues and common scenes shifted throughout the rehearsal period, only to be settled for good a few days before the premiere.

The rehearsal process was not an easy one and took its toll on both the director and the actors. Conflicts arose on a regular basis, making this perhaps the most demanding rehearsal process out of the 30 productions observed. However, both the director and the actors agreed that it was also a very useful and inspiring process and reminded each other that a demanding rehearsal often leads to better results than a 'feel good' process. In the end, the play got rave reviews. It played for a number of weeks at The Royal Danish Theatre, went on tour and due to public demand it was later performed by the same actors at a smaller theatre in Copenhagen.

Production number 2:

Production number 2 was a classic play by Shakespeare picked to open the new Play House in Copenhagen. The director (Director number 2) was a successful Norwegian male director, who had directed a few plays in Denmark as well. The main character was played by one of the most well-known and respected young Danish actors (freelance actor) and most of the other main characters were played by full-time employed actors of The Royal Theatre. The supporting characters were mainly played by freelance actors.

This eight week rehearsal process was much more traditional, moving from an investigative, analytical and playful phase to more traditional rehearsals where focus was on position, learning the lines, playing through each scene, etc. through to the dress rehearsal and the premiere. Being a Shakespeare play, there was a script – however, the script was edited by the director and the dramaturge. Consequently, that set another kind of framework for the rehearsal process, though still leaving room for improvisations. The director gave notes every day, most often at the end of the day, but sometimes at the beginning of the rehearsal. Run-throughs of each act were scheduled from week 4, and run-throughs of the entire play were scheduled from week 6.

The end result was a moderately daring interpretation of the Shakespeare play and this production received rave reviews as well. Almost every performance was sold out.

Challenges

Creativity

In order to analyze the two cases, a model of distinguishing factors based on existing research was used as an analytical framework.

For the past decade, the literature and research on creativity has become abundant and the use of the word 'creativity' in everyday life has skyrocketed. Existing research points to several perspectives on creativity: A mental/motivational perspective; a sociological perspective; a learning perspective; a cognitive perspective, etc. Here I will draw on the so-called confluence perspective and add to that a leadership perspective. The confluence perspective states that creativity requires a confluence of several distinct but interrelated resources – most of which is at least partly the responsibility of the leader.

Amabile sums up the prerequisites for creative work by pointing to three defining characteristics of the creative person – all of which must converge in order for creativity to occur (Amabile 1998).

First of all, in order to be creative, expertise is necessary. Expertise encompasses knowledge and technical, procedural and intellectual skills.

Secondly, creative thinking is necessary. Creative thinking encompasses the capacity to put existing ideas together in new combinations, but it is also a question of adopting a work style that is fruitful for creative work.

Thirdly, an important factor in doing creative work is motivation. Amabile points to the fact that creative work is closely connected to intrinsic motivation, not to extrinsic motivation. Intrinsically motivated people engage in their work for the sake of the work itself. The use of extrinsic motivation factors such as the carrot or stick approach does not work well in creative work, and some studies show that the use of extrinsic motivation factors can inhibit creative thinking.

Sternberg also points to several prerequisites for creative work: intellectual abilities, knowledge, styles of thinking, personality, motivation and environment (Sternberg 2003, p. 94). The five first prerequisites overlap with Amabile's factors, but environment is an important addition, and thus, I will add environment to the confluence model below.

Thus, some of the important factors that must converge in order for creativity to occur are:

Figure 11.1 Creativity from a confluence perspective: A model of factors that must converge in order for creativity to occur

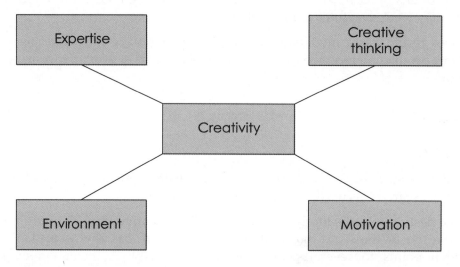

What then is the role of a leader in creating the above factors and making them converge? This will be the turning point of the chapter.

In my analysis of what leaders can learn from stage directors, I will disregard 'expertise'. Even though creative workers are expected to possess domain-relevant knowledge and technical skills, it is still fair to assume that the further development of such knowledge and skills is partly the responsibility of the artistic director and the theatre that employs the creative worker. Since the stage director doesn't carry the responsibility of an artistic director but functions more like a project manager, the further development of actors' knowledge and skills is not the responsibility of the stage director.

What do successful stage directors do in order to facilitate creativity?

The analysis will be divided into the three (leaving out 'expertise' from Figure 11.1) factors mentioned in Figure 11.1: creative thinking, environment, and motivation. Even though they are correlated, I will try to deal with them separately.

Outcomes

Creative thinking

Two factors proved especially important in spurring creative thinking from a leadership perspective: Establishing a clear framework and phase management.

Establishing a framework

Rephrasing the famous quote by Louis Pasteur, 'Chance favors the prepared mind', most artists (and scientists) will agree that creativity favors the prepared mind (Hein 2007). Preparation of the mind comes through rehearsing, sticking to a routine, studying, mastering, etc. – things that belong in the 'expertise' box in Figure 11.1.

But preparation of the mind also comes through establishing a framework. Contrary to common belief, creativity does not evolve in a vacuum or in an open, boundaryless space. Rather, it requires boundaries and a clear framework. As dancer and choreographer Twyla Tharp puts it: 'Before you can think out of the box, you have to start with a box' (Tharp 2003, pp. 78-79). Creativity requires boundaries: Boundaries of space, boundaries of time, boundaries of interpretation, boundaries of expression, etc.

Both directors made sure to establish a framework for the productions. This was done in a number of ways. One important factor is communicating the vision of the production. Both directors did that – not once, but numerous times during the eight week rehearsal period. In doing that, they both proved to be very eloquent about their vision and understood the importance of picking the right words to express a clear vision.

The vision works as an overall framework for the production. But both directors also set a precise framework for each scene by asking the actors to move within a limited space or by asking them to play the scene expressing certain emotions. They also frequently reminded the actors of the purpose of a particular scene in relationship to the entire play and the overall vision of the play, thereby not only creating a purpose and a vision of the play but also of the individual scenes and characters.

Phase management

Understanding the creative process and the different phases of the creative process is crucial to facilitating creativity.

Both directors were excellent 'phase managers', both on the macro and the micro level. On the macro level they divided the entire rehearsal process into different phases and knew when to move from one phase to another. Both productions were divided into three phases: 1) investigation/improvisation; 2) rehearsal; and 3) closing. On the micro level they knew when to stop a rehearsal of a specific scene and leave time for incubation.

The investigation/improvisation phase was characterized by a playful and investigative spirit. There were long discussions about a monologue or the meaning of a scene as well as discussions about the characters and the relationship between the characters. The actors were permitted to 'go wild' – laugh a lot, play a lot, discuss a lot, try different and somewhat extreme approaches to a scene or a character. 'No' was a seldom used word during this phase. Almost anything was allowed, and there was ample time to discuss and investigate.

The rehearsal phase was characterized by solving the puzzle. The pieces of the puzzle were made during the first investigative phase, and in the second phase it was time to put it all together. This phase was more analytical in the sense that the framework was not really debated. Scenes were rehearsed several times a day, using props and sometimes costumes. Investigations and improvisations were still welcomed, but the boundaries were narrowed significantly compared to the first phase. It was investigation within the framework. 'No' was a much more common word during this phase, and most of the time, 'no' would be accompanied by an explanation that related to the vision of the play and to the agreements made during the first phase.

Finally, the closing phase was characterized by numerous run-throughs of separate acts or of the entire play, most of the time as dress rehearsals. This phase was about mastering: mastering timing, mastering the characters, mastering positions, mastering expressions, mastering scene changes, etc. Only slight changes were made.

Entering a phase and moving from one phase to another phase wasn't announced – it was more of a covert, subtle announcement. For example, Director number 2 made use of symbols that underlined the spirit of each phase. During the first investigative phase, he would put on music before the rehearsal, so the actors would enter a room full of music. Entering phase 2, director number 2 didn't put music on.

In phase 1, both directors would invite the actors to join him/her around a table, seemingly acting like their peer. The leadership style was very democratic, and both directors allowed themselves to be goofy and relaxed and 'going with the flow'. They would both make a schedule for each day, but they didn't necessarily stick to the schedule but felt free to make changes on the spot. Entering phase 2 both directors would sit on a chair facing the actors, watching them rehearse, giving notes and corrections, commenting on their acting, etc. The leadership style shifted from democratic to authoritative, but most of the time polite (e.g. 'Could you try facing that way...' or 'What would happen if....', etc.). During this phase the schedule was much tighter. One hour was devoted to working on a specific scene, and when that hour was up, they would continue working on the next scheduled scene. Neither director kept working on a scene until they reached a point of clarity. Instead, they would stop when the time was up and sum up the solved and unsolved pieces of the puzzle and ask the actor(s) to think about a solution until the next rehearsal of the scene. This way, both directors made time and space available for incubation, thus spurring the 'illumination moment' for themselves as well as the actor(s) involved.

During the third (closing) phase, the directors would sit on the first row in front of the stage watching the run-throughs on stage. Both directors would be silent during the run-through. They would make notes and only speak when absolutely necessary. After a run-through they would give notes – sometimes explaining their notes, sometimes just ordering someone to make a change. Their leadership style was much more dictatorial. From time to time they would still take the time to discuss a problem with one or several actors if they felt that it was needed, e.g. if an actor was particularly unsure about a scene or a monologue – but they never wavered from their vision and from their directions. Instead, they took the time to listen and explain.

Environment

In establishing an environment that is supporting and rewarding creativity, three factors can be learned from the directors: creating a safe container; shielding leadership; and understanding flow and flow frustration.

Creating a safe container

For a number of reasons, creative work is sensitive work. It involves asking questions and suffering the frustration of not being able to come up with the answer, it involves mastering and learning and often includes divergent thinking, and values such as courage, discipline and curiosity.

In order for people to feel safe and secure in doing work that is sensitive by nature, it is important to create a safe container where hot and sensitive issues can be handled. Making suggestions, using yourself as a creative tool as an actor, running the risk of failing, etc., is highly sensitive. Therefore, it is important to encourage a behavior that is grounded in courage and curiosity. However, it is a fine line – it takes only a few minor mistakes to discourage that type of behavior.

Both directors were exemplary in that they succeeded in creating such a context/environment. During the first investigative phase, they never once ridiculed or laughed at a failed attempt to try something new. They never acted negatively if an idea didn't pan out or if a suggestion didn't prove feasible. Instead of discarding the idea and creating a negative atmosphere around ideas that proved 'wrong', they welcomed failures and crazy suggestions by saying 'yes' a lot, by laughing at jokes that weren't funny, by nodding vigorously even though something clearly didn't work, by going along with an idea in order to explore it, etc.

Both directors showed excellent praising and critiquing skills. They knew when, where and how to praise and criticize. 'Critique' as a process is highly sensitive for people engaged in creative work as the work itself is highly engaging, but also the individual is often personally engaged and passionate. This makes critique a highly sensitive task. Both directors always gave critique inside the rehearsal studio or on stage during rehearsal – never in the hallway or in the cafeteria. When given inside the work space, critique is made less personal. Also, both directors often found ways of making it clear that critique was not to be taken personally – for example, by referring to the character rather than saying 'you', they kept a distance between the actor and the character.

Likewise with praise. Oftentimes, praise given inside the rehearsal studio or on stage during rehearsal is often perceived as a ritual necessary for creating a safe environment and thus doesn't count as validation, recognition or praise *per se*. Consequently, praise that is actually meant as praise must be given outside the work space, e.g. in the hallway, in the cafeteria, etc.

Shielding leadership

For most professionals, there is a deep conflict between professional ethics (also known as duty ethics) and business ethics (also known as utility ethics) (Hein 2009). Moreover, many professionals feel that economics and management rhetoric constitute a threat to both their calling and their high standards. As a result, they often feel compelled to shield their calling and their higher purpose against the economic beast. For that reason, and many others, business ethics and a managerial vocabulary is often off-putting to many professionals and a prime reason for demotivation and frustration (Hein 2009).

Both directors showed a common trait in their leadership – a trait I suggest we call 'shielding leadership', where they shielded the actors from business ethics, managerial vocabulary, budget decisions, etc. Although deeply involved in discussions and decision-making concerning economy etc., they never once mentioned the economic reasons for their decision-making. They always argued from the perspective of art and focused on the higher purpose.

They both succeeded in shielding the performers from any kind of economic issues, establishing a small world in the rehearsal room where art was the only concern. They managed to move between the managerial sphere and the artistic sphere without mixing up the two spheres – they always kept them separate and never once made use of the managerial vocabulary once they entered the artistic sphere.

Understanding flow and flow frustration

Flow is an essential part of creative work. Csikszentmihalyi (1997) defines flow as a peak experience, where a person's capacity (in terms of body or mind) is stretched to its limits in an effort to accomplish something difficult or worthwhile. When an individual engages in this kind of extremely focused work, they may experience the feeling that their work is flowing effortlessly and they may lose track of time (Csikszentmihalyi 1997; Hein 2009).

However, flow is not always a pleasant feeling. Flow is experienced when dealing with highly complex problem solving and requires that the individual steps outside his/her comfort zone, which is obviously not always comfortable and may even be extremely frustrating. The paradox of flow is that people may feel very frustrated while at the same time enjoying themselves tremendously. Sometimes, there is a gap in the two feelings: Sometimes, the feeling of frustration is predominant, only to be exchanged for joy and happiness at a later stage (Hein 2009).

A common problem with 'flow frustration' at The Royal Danish Theatre was that, although they were highly experienced in the field of creative work, many directors and administrative employees mistook flow frustration for childish, immature behavior. When the artists were frustrated that they were not (yet) able to solve a problem or not (yet) able to master a skill, task, or scene, they would sometimes react in a very frustrated way (bickering, yelling, being unreasonable, crying, leaving the rehearsal studio, etc.) Yet, this was not childish behavior, but the result of deep frustration – only, the frustration was not demotivating. On the contrary, it was very motivating.

Both directors stood out in this respect. They were able to see past flow frustration, and they never reacted negatively when actors reacted in a seemingly unreasonable way. They embraced flow and flow frustration and remained calm, even when the actors were not. After rehearsal, when the actors had left, they would sometimes vent their frustration to their assistant or to the artistic director. But in facing the actors, they remained calm and collected during times of frustration.

Motivation

Motivating from an archetypical perspective

A major result of the research project was the development of a model describing the motivational profile of four archetypes of highly specialized creative employees. Figure 11.2 shows all four archetypes in brief and places them on a scale according to their willingness to make sacrifices. This is not a question of how much time (or overtime) one is willing to invest in one's work, but rather the degree of mental, physical and emotional energy one invests in work, and the degree to which one is willing to fight for what one believes in, regardless of the sacrifices that must be made to stay true to one's beliefs and values. Some archetypes are averse to sacrifice, while others see sacrifice as a means to a meaningful or valuable end.

There is no claim as to which archetype is best or most valuable, rather it can be argued that a combination of prima donnas, performance addicts and pragmatists is desirable, whereas pay check workers constitute a number of problems, the primary problem being that they are a substantial reason for the demotivation of the other archetypes as they tend to aim for a much lower standard than the other archetypes.

Figure 11.2 Four archetypes of highly-specialized creative employees (Hein 2009)

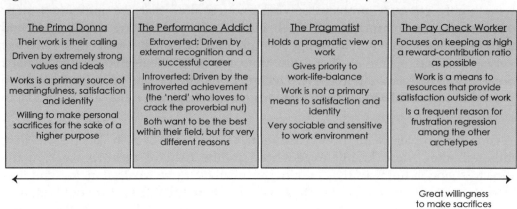

The Prima Donna	The Performance Addict	The Pragmatist	The Pay Check Worker
Their work is their calling	Extroverted: Driven by external recognition and a successful career	Holds a pragmatic view on work	Focuses on keeping as high a reward-contribution ratio as possible
Driven by extremely strong values and ideals	Introverted: Driven by the introverted achievement (the 'nerd' who loves to crack the proverbial nut)	Gives priority to work-life-balance	Work is a means to resources that provide satisfaction outside of work
Works is a primary source of meaningfulness, satisfaction and identity	Both want to be the best within their field, but for very different reasons	Work is not a primary means to satisfaction and identity	Is a frequent reason for frustration regression among the other archetypes
Willing to make personal sacrifices for the sake of a higher purpose		Very sociable and sensitive to work environment	

Great willingness to make sacrifices

Both directors intuitively handled the actors according to differences in their motivational profile. They knew when (and where) to praise or when to critique; they knew how to reward each actor according to his or her archetypical profile (by talking about the vision of the play, by co-nerding with them about Shakespeare, etc., by praising them in front of others, by respecting their need for work-life-balance, etc.) In contrast, some of the less successful directors handled the performing artists more or less the same, hanging on to their own preferred way of working so that the performing artists had to adjust to the director's way of working, whereas Director number 1 and Director number 2, while not straying from their beaten path, adjusted to each actor's needs as well.

Autonomy

The last lesson to be learned from the two directors is a lesson of autonomy. Each director gave autonomy to the performers in term of the means. But they didn't discuss the ends. Both directors were very clear about the goal of the performance: the story to tell, the interpretation of the play, the dramaturgy of the play – and they never wavered from that. They set clearly specified goals, but allowed freedom in how to reach the goal. They would happily engage in discussions about the goal, but they didn't do it in order to reflect on the goal or alter the goal – they did it to clarify the goal and to make a point about the vision of the play, thus instilling motivation and inspiration.

The directors set the framework for the process; they decided when it was time to move from one phase to another, but within each phase they granted the performers quite a bit of freedom and made room for their individual processes. Every performer was granted autonomy and freedom and also allowed to test the boundaries of the framework. But they weren't allowed to change the goal and the vision of the play.

Conclusion

A unique leadership

So what can leaders of creative work processes learn from successful stage directors when it comes to facilitating creative work processes?

Based on the two case studies working as examples of best practice, Figure 11.3 shows the skills and tools that can be distilled from the two successful stage directors used as exemplary case studies in this paper:

Figure 11.3 Creativity from a confluence perspective: Lessons learned from successful stage directors

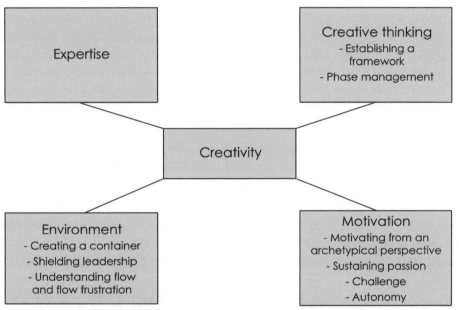

There are several prerequisites for doing creative work, and even though we know a number of these prerequisites very well, instilling them in an organizational business context still proves a challenge. This is no doubt partly due to the way we organize work in a business setting, seldom leaving time for concentration, focus and incubation. But this is not the only reason why a vast creative potential goes unrealized and why creative workers seldom report about doing creative thinking during their work day. Another important reason is that creative work and skills for facilitating creative work is lacking in leadership.

One major lesson to be learned from the two directors is that the way we perceive of effective leadership must be changed in a number of ways. Leaders must be willing to give up on control. They must dare exposing themselves – their vision, their passion, etc. Leaders must be courageous. They themselves must be willing to step outside their comfort zones. They must have the stamina to shield the creative workers from considerations (regarding budgetary decisions, strategic decisions, etc.) that leaders often (mistakenly) share with their employees. They must inspire. They must be willing to define leadership in a new way.

There is no doubt that fostering creativity and facilitating creative work processes is not an easy task. But it can be done. It may require changes in the way we organize creative work, but most importantly, it requires a unique set of skills on the part of the leader.

Questions

1. Discuss how leadership is demonstrated in this case study by the two different directors, and what outcomes this produced.

2. What impact would each approach to leadership in this case study have on the creative process of those involved in the making of the production?

3. Do you think that different approaches to leadership are needed, depending on the problems encountered by the leader, or could one approach to leadership work in every situation? Consider this question in the context of this case study.

References

Amabile, TM 1996, *Creativity in Context*, Westview Press, Boulder.

Amabile, TM 1998, 'How to Kill Creativity', *Harvard Business Review*, September-October.

Amabile, TM, Hadley, CN & Kramer, SJ 2002, 'Creativity Under the Gun', *Harvard Business Review*, August.

Argyris, C 1991, 'Teaching Smart People How to Learn', *Harvard Business Review*, May-June.

Csikszentmihalyi, M 1997, *Creativity Flow and the Psychology of Discovery and Invention.* Harper Perennial, New York.

Florida, R 2004, *The Rise of The Creative Class - And How It's Transforming Work, Leisure, Community and Everyday Life,* Basic Books, New York.

Gardner, H, Csikszentmihalyi, M & Damon, W 2001, *Good Work - When Excellence and Ethics Meet,* Basic Books, New York.

Hein, HH 2007, *Rutiner og rammer, kunst og kreativitet (Routines, Framework, Art and Creativity),* in Larsen, B & Hein, H H (eds), *De nye professionelle. Fremtidens roller for de veluddannede. (The New Professionals. The Future Roles of Knowledge Workers),* Jurist- og Økonomforbundets Forlag, Copenhagen.

Hein, HH 2009, 'A New Perspective: The Motivation and Management of Highly Specialized Creative Employees', *Paper for the 13th APROS Conference, Monterrey, Mexico, 2009.*

Sternberg, R J 2003, 'The Development of Creativity as a Decision-Making Process', in Sawyer *et al. Creativity and Development.* Oxford University Press, New York.

Sternberg, RJ & Lubart, TI 2007, 'The Concept of Creativity: Prospects and Paradigms', in R J Sternberg (ed), *Handbook of Creativity*, Cambridge University Press, New York.

Tharp, T 2003, *The Creative Habit. Learn It And Use It For Life*, Simon & Schuster, New York.

Chapter 12

Co-leading the creative process through collaboration

SUYIN CHEW

Background

Introduction

case study is to document the creative process of two artistic
artistic collaboration. The case study, located in Singapore,[1]
ment of collaboration during their artistic process led to a
ip for the subjects as both artists and leaders.

that governments support the arts for national glory, as an
ard, as a placebo, in the name of education, in the form of
mpensation, commercial value, and to assert its order and
ore, the government has been the dominant stakeholder in the
e arts landscape. In 1988, the then First Deputy Prime Minister,
announced the setting up of an Advisory Council for Arts and
. The report produced by the Council in 1989 became a major
fluenced the arts and cultural conditions in Singapore. It aimed to
apore from a cultural desert to a culturally vibrant nation and a

population of 4.987.6 million people. In 2008, the average household income of
the 80th to 90th percentile of earners was SGD$11,190 and SGD$20,240 for the top decile
(Singapore Department of Statistics 2009). The arts and cultural sector employs over 20 000
people and generates SGD$6 billion worth of operating receipts (Singapore Cultural Statistics
Report 2009). The country is known for its political stability, trade, manufacturing, finance and
service industries.

global city for the arts (Lim 2009). The strategy's primary focus was the development of an arts infrastructure in Singapore and recommended the building of performing arts venues, museums and libraries. This includes: the development of buildings such as the Esplanade Theatres on the Bay, the Singapore Art Museum, the Asian Civilization Museum, the Singapore Philatelic Museum and the National Gallery; the establishment of the National Arts Council, the National Heritage Board and the National Library Board; and funding and development for the Nanyang Academy of Fine Arts and the Lasalle College of the Arts to provide training/courses in both the performing and visual arts at the tertiary level.[2]

After the 1989 report, the subsequent papers constituted a series known as the *Renaissance City Reports*. The 1999 Renaissance City Report had a stronger and greater focus on developing the 'software' (i.e. the artists) as compared to the 1989 report, which was focused on the development of the 'hardware' (i.e. infrastructure). The speedy creation of an infrastructure plan in the early 1990s was a sign of the government's decision to support the arts and culture in the ways that governments know best (Bereson 2003, p. 5; Frey 2002; Pick 1989).

Twenty years later, Singapore has been transformed into one of the most dynamic cities in the Asia Pacific region. One reason used to explain this phenomenon is the proliferation of the various international arts festivals and activities as seen in the Singapore Cultural Statistics Reports over the past couple of years.[3]

Setting

Three lecturers at LASALLE College of the Arts[4] first met because theatre practitioner Elizabeth de Roza (E), visual artist Gilles Massot and choreographer Melissa Quek (M) worked together in the co-delivery of a collaboration class in which the tensions between photography and dance were explored to reveal notions about effort and effortlessness. The three artists were interested in exploring how inter-disciplinary work within an educational setting, could expand the boundaries of performance and performance research. This resulted in a short 15-minute student work that was performed at the College's Flexible

---

[2] In 2008, government funding for the arts stand at SGD$70 per capita and cultural philanthropy showed over SGD$90 million contributed. It also showed a 70 percent increase in tertiary arts courses over the last five years (Singapore Cultural Statistics report 2009, pp. 13, 17).

[3] According to the 2009 Singapore Cultural Statistics report, Singapore now has a vibrant arts scene and every day in Singapore there is a choice of over 80 arts and cultural activities that appeal to a diversity of preferences. Today, two out of five Singaporeans would have attended at least one arts or cultural event in the past 12 months. The Singapore Cultural Statistics (2004-2008) showed an increase in the attendance for ticketed performing arts activities. This refers to performing arts events that require a ticket for entry and the attendance of ticketed performance increased from 1,110,300 in 2004 to 1,538,000 in 2008.

[4] Founded in 1984 by De La Salle educator, Brother Joseph McNally, LASALLE College of the Arts is a specialist tertiary institution leading contemporary arts education in fine art, design, media and performing arts in the Asia Pacific (viewed 10 January 2012, http://www.lasalle.edu.sg/)

Performance Space in May 2010. The work received comments on the skilful way in which the various art forms were woven together instead of existing as separate ... s. Being inspired by the layers of complexity that were added with the ... ction of each additional view point, the artists wanted to explore this ... in another collaboration.

... gh Gilles Massot was instrumental in some of the key ideas for their next ... e did not see the work to completion. Later on two other key artists were ... in – Brian O'Reilly (musician) and Koo Chia Meng (video artist). Even ... these artists were also collaborators, they were not co-leaders of the ... as they were responding to the narrative that E and M had already ... Hence their roles were supportive in nature, and therefore this case study ... ow both E and M jointly led the creative and collaborative process. This ... then addresses this question:

... do dual artistic leaders lead the creative process through the element of ... boration?

...tistic leaders

Here is a brief background of the artist/leaders in this study:

After graduating from New York University's Tisch School of the Arts, Melissa Quek performed with the Ad Deum Contemporary Dance Company in Houston, Texas. Melissa also performed Kuik Swee Boon's *Silence*, at the 8th Asian Arts Festival in Beijing and in the SIDance Festival in Seoul. In terms of choreography, Melissa has choreographed and produced a number of full-length works including *No Strings Attached*, a 2009 M1 Fringe Festival Commission. Melissa is the Programme Coordinator for the School of Dance at LASALLE and dance reviewer for the *Business Times*.

Elizabeth de Roza, on the other hand, specializes in movement-based performances, drawing from traditional Asian theatrical training/performing methods and contemporary practices. Over the last couple of years, she has been invited to present her solo works and working methodology at four major international Magdalena theatre festivals: Rhode Island USA (2005), Singapore (2006) Santa Clara, Cuba (2008), Transit – Odin, Denmark (2009). She presented a performance installation exhibition, *Un-written* in Belgrade, Serbia in Real Presence 2008 and attended and presented a performance cum lecture, *The Karang Guni Man imagines Utopia* at the 15th Performance Studies International (2009) in Zagreb, Croatia. Elizabeth is currently the Programme Coordinator for the BA (Hons.) Theatre Arts programme at LASALLE, and completed her Masters of Arts (Fine Arts) in 2008.

Approach

The creative work

The creative work was originally entitled *Traces*, and used the image of a thumbprint to unpack concepts of identity and personhood. The reading of a thumbprint would reveal everything or nothing about a person, and thumbprints are traces of evidence that existed in that time and place. Therefore, although created to be a performance experience, the set from *Traces* also stands alone as an interactive installation artwork that allows the audience to leave their mark on it. *Traces* is about interacting with the space and uniting with the audience to create a performance experience. The combination of the diverse disciplines makes this work unlike any of the individual works previously created by the artists.

The desired outcomes by the dual artistic leaders (i.e. M and E) were to create:

- a work that blurs the lines between Performance and Visual Art;
- a break in the barrier of audience perceptions about their understanding of contemporary art, as the sensory experience would make the performance both different and more accessible;
- an increased awareness of and appreciation for interdisciplinary performance works; and
- art that is made more accessible to the audience.

Subsequently, the final work was re-titled as *RE:gina is Dead* because the narrative was developed by E and M into a murder mystery and the audience were suspects to the crime. This then became a play about the death of a fictional person where the murder victim represents the loss of identity, history, etc. Hence the question is raised – who is responsible for this loss? This essentially became the essence of the work.

The Substation's performance call 2010[5]

The Substation is Singapore's first independent arts centre that focuses on contemporary arts. Established in 1990 by the late Kuo Pao Kun, it is known for its pioneering and experimental arts programming, and as an incubator for emerging Singaporean artists. Noor Effendy Ibrahim, The Substation's artistic director, says:

> *The Substation needs to acknowledge the artistry and creativity of the emerging artists who apply themselves in the performative arts. Performance Open Call is exactly that platform which we hope will expand the scope of The Substation's support for these artists.*

> *For Performance Open Call 2010, The Substation selected* RE:gina is Dead! *by Melissa Quek and Elizabeth de Roza to be staged at The Substation Theatre from 17 to 19 September 2010. Effendy further explains that for Performance Open Call:*

> *...the first work chosen to be presented needs to be one that sets the tone: exciting, thought provoking, interactive, progressive.* RE:gina is Dead!, *livingly, is all that and more.*

---

[5] The information for this section is extracted from the Media Release on 4 Aug 2010 by The Substation – Performance Open Call 2010 – *RE:gina is Dead*! by Melissa Quek, Elizabeth de Roza & Gilles Massot.

One of the artists behind *RE:gina is Dead!*, choreographer and dancer, Melissa Quek, explains the show as:

> … *a combination of visual art and performance. We hope to break down the barriers between performer and spectator, to tell the audience that it's alright to think for themselves, and that they can construct meaning based on their own experiences and understanding.*

With this project, the artists depart from the conventional audience-performer relationships and explored performance as a holistic sensory experience, making the audience member a participant rather than a viewer. The performance was an interactive journey where audience members learned to sense performance rather than just wat~~ch it.~~

[text obscured by note] …ive experience was inspired by the television [text obscured] …ke *Cluedo*. Audience members watching the [text obscured] …p clues to determine the details of the murder, [text obscured] …os such as chalk and clue cards to participate in [text obscured] …s. The performance was executed in episodic [text obscured] …as paper, overhead projectors and mirrors were [text obscured] … murder. The performers/artists moved from [text obscured] …ged 'room' to another, delivering minimal [text obscured] …al dialogues through dance movements, and [text obscured] …y inviting the audience members directly into [text obscured] …artists not only involve the audience in the [text obscured] …t also provoke them to piece together their own [text obscured] …uch novel contemporary performance work. [text obscured] …ee evenings, from 17-19 September 2010. Each [text obscured] …uration, and only 15 to 20 audience members were allowed to attend per show.

[Handwritten note: "is this audience leading to more authentic participation / experience / learning?"]

Research methodology

The documentation of this case is significant as there is little written on interdisciplinary works that explore content relating to the history of Singapore. This particular creative work had only received one newspaper review and one critical essay written about it.[6] Besides the content of the work, it was also important to document best practices and evaluate these practices, so that the success may be repeated.

A good case study will gather data from a range of sources (Yin 2003) such as documents, interviews and observations. The use of multiple source of evidence is a key characteristic of a case study, and having a range of data sources and a number of case studies, will allow for triangulation to improve the validity of the data (Hammersley & Atkinson 2006).

---

[6] The essay by Richard Chua may be viewed at www.substation.org/regina-is-dead-artists-intervention-into-the-authoring-of-singapore-an-history.

The data collection methods for this case study include:

- primary data from semi-structured interviews, and
- secondary data from archival documents.

The data gathering from the dual artistic leaders (i.e. M and E) occurs through a multi-layered process. Individual interviews, as well as a combined interview with the duo, were conducted in December 2011. After the interviews, the author compared the interview findings with archival documents (Edelenbos & Erik-Hans 2006, pp. 437, 439). The data from the archival documents was multi-level and included the following:

- newspaper preview in the *Business Times*;[7]
- video of performance;[8]
- publicity information;
- journal notes from the choreographer/performer;
- project proposal to the Substation;
- media/press release of the production; and
- critical essay of the production by Richard Chua.[9]

After the data had been collected, it was coded and categorized into themes (Tharenou, Donohue & Cooper 2007, p. 83). Then the author analyzed the coded data/themes (Stake 2006, pp. 45, 49), by establishing a chain of evidence and pattern matching (Yin 2003, p. 34). This data analysis technique commonly known as 'thematic analysis technique' is widely used in qualitative research (Bryman 2004).

Challenges

Literature

Challenges for the project to achieve a successful creative outcome are embedded in the natures of both dual leadership and collaboration. Thus reviewing these two fields of literature is directly relevant to developing an understanding of the challenges involved and are considered below.

Dual leadership

The characteristics of dual leadership are similar in its definition and description to shared, participative, distributed and co-leadership practices. Shared

---

[7] Koh, N 2010, 'Interactive work kicks off new open call', *Business Times*, 10 September, p. L6 Arts 2010.

[8] *Re-gina is Dead!* 2010, video recording, Melissa Quek.

[9] Chua, R 2010, *RE:gina is Dead!: Artists' Intervention into the Authoring of Singapore (-an) History*, Substation, viewed 28 Dec 2011, www.substation.org/regina-is-dead-artists-intervention-into-the-authoring-of-singapore-an-history.

leadership is when influence such as cultivating motivation, providing direction and support is distributed among team members (Carson, Tesluk & Marrone 2007; Pearce & Manz 2005). According to O'Toole, Galbraith, and Lawler (2003 p. 252, cited in Eckman 2006, p. 90), shared leadership occurred among 25 firms in their study. Nhamo (2009, pp. 475-476) notes that the co-leadership model is a hybrid leadership model, as dual leadership is defined as two leaders in an organization that share executive power and have equal rank. de Voogt (2006, p. 17) says that dual leadership is not just about two people having equal rank in the organization, but the fact that they are brought together to solve a management crisis. Heenan and Bennis (1999, pp. 5-8 cited in Nhamo 2009, p. 475) notes that the dual leadership model provides recognition to both leaders who undertake the real work. This differs from other models whereby the leader is often the only visionary. Heenan and Bennis's (1999, p. 3 cited in Nhamo 2009, p. 474) view of leader and co-leader are that they are complementary in their skill and expertise. For example, the leader would be the visionary and the co-leader would lead the management and operations of the organization. Pierce (2000, cited in Eckman 2006, p. 91) observes that in the schools system where two principals are needed: one oversees the academic curriculum, while the other manages the school.

Eckman's (2006, p. 98) findings note that the co-leadership model is a way 'to provide stability and fill a void'. de Voogt (2006, p. 21) says that the practice of dual leadership whereby two leaders have equal power, is a special case that takes place when the person in charge does not have the full knowledge and skills to do the job required. He adds that the practice of dual leadership imposes a restriction on the power of the original leader. Conflicts naturally surface in any relationship and in Reid's & Karambayya's (2009, p. 1073) research, they examine the conflict between the artistic director and the managing director and how their conflict impacts on the organization's ability to function. Eckman's (2006, p. 89) findings show though that the application of the co-principal leadership model in schools has led to strong job satisfaction among both leaders.

The application of dual leadership is also seen in other writings: Etzioni (1965, p. 688) attempts to integrate the theory of complex organizations with the Bales Parsons model of small groups; Nhamo (2009) examines the possibility of adopting a co-leadership model to address the issues of climate change; while de Voogt (2006, p. 19) applies the dual leadership model to two Dutch art museums. Eckman describes the challenges faced in the practice of co-leadership, noting:

> *Problems in communicating, defining responsibilities, developing trust, presenting a unified front, and being 'played against each other' [by the other stakeholders], endless negotiation and a waste of precious time (2006, p. 102).*

In addition, Brickley (1997, p. 2009) found that it was difficult to evaluate the individual performance of dual leaders and provide the right incentives, as reward and recognition is usually given for good individual performance (Nhamo 2009, pp. 475-476). Brickley's (1997, p. 189) paper also examined the challenges and costs involved when organizations want to separate the titles and responsibilities of its dual leaders. He argues that the costs of separation are larger than the benefits for most large firms. Some of these costs include those related to information, such as having the organization change their succession processes and those incurred by inconsistent decision making when authority is divided among more than one person (Brickley 1997, p. 195).

Collaboration

According to Wondolleck and Yaffee (2000, p. xiii), collaboration 'involves individuals or groups moving in a situation in which no party has the power to command the behavior of the others'. Collaboration has also been described as 'the pooling of resources . . . by two or more stakeholders to solve a set of problems which neither can solve individually' (Gray 1985, p. 912, cited in Legler & Reischl 2003, p. 55). Marinez-Moyano (2006) emphasize that collaboration is a process where two or more people or organizations work together to realize shared goals and that most collaboration requires leadership.

Gajda (2004, p. 65-66) found these definitions of collaboration to be ambiguous, because of the difficulty for organizations to put collaboration into practice and evaluate its success. This is despite the fact that it is increasingly considered as the foundation and the means by which outcomes will be achieved. Legler & Reischl (2003, p. 55) explained that:

> When resources are scarce, or when mutual problems are too large for any one stakeholder to address independently, the potential for cost sharing or ensuring access to limited resources can motivate stakeholders to collaborate.

Therefore, collaboration is described as an emergent process where stakeholders are interdependent – solutions emerge by dealing constructively with differences, joint ownerships of decisions are involved, and stakeholders assume collective responsibility for future directions (Gray 1985, cited in Legler & Reischl 2003, p. 56). One of Gajda's (2004, pp. 67-69) research questions was focused on the level/breath of collaboration that is needed to achieve particular outcomes. This question among others, led to the following principles and description of collaboration:

- Collaboration is imperative and is known by many names;
- Collaboration is a journey not a destination; and
- Collaboration develops in stages and the personal is as important as the procedural.

Black *et al.*'s (2002) paper explores the elements of collaboration, trust and knowledge sharing in the design and implementation of a new information system. They found that as participants become more involved with the project, it led to an increase in collaboration and productivity. Etzioni (1965, p. 688) said that the likelihood of collaboration among leaders would decline if they do not hold organizational positions holding similar levels of ranking and accountabilities to the organization.

Creating common goals is an important step in collaboration and allows for institutionalization of collaboration (Lauber *et al.* 2011). Sharma and Kearins's (2011, pp. 168, 180-182) study investigates inter-organizational collaboration and sustainability and found that people start to collaborate with the intention of minimizing costs, but they soon discover that collaboration can be an extremely tense, frustrating and time-consuming process due to diverse expectations and agendas. Other problems with collaboration include distrust of others and lack of commitment to the collaboration due to previous negative collaboration experience. The benefits of collaboration include learning, relationship building, joint problem solving, joint innovation and value creation, efficiency, resource sharing, cost saving, capacity building and survival (Sharma & Kearins 2011, pp. 191, 193).

Legler & Reischl (2003, pp. 61, 64) have said that the elements necessary for successful collaboration are interdependence/resource sharing, diversity, communication, planning/coordination and the right climate. Once these elements exist and are acknowledged, collaborators will become motivated to work towards shared goals (Legler & Reischl 2003, pp. 64-65). Archer and Cameron (2008) list the qualities for successful collaborative leaders as those who:

- have a personal reason for collaborating;
- have the ability to enable their staff to understand complicated situations;
- know how to handle conflict;
- are aware of who they can work with and are fearless and bold in action;
- are able to balance the delivery of outcomes with bonding that is built with the other collaborators;
- are able to share recognition and rewards;
- are confident in one's own leadership style; and
- are able to discuss and work though tough and sensitive issues while building significant partnerships.

In the evaluation of collaborations Legler & Reischl (2003, p. 58) added that:

One way to measure the effectiveness of collaboration would be to measure the amount of activities in which coalitions engage to address their mutual problems.

When disagreements and conflict occurs, individuals may be reluctant to cooperate due to a fear of compromising their values (Bryan 2004). This can be problematic, as studies have shown that many successful collaborative attempts are dependent on a willingness to compromise (Selin & Chavez 1995).

Although Eckman (2006, p. 103) said that the co-leadership is one model that uses 'a collaborative method to leadership', the gap in the literature shows that that there is little written that discusses dual leadership models with collaboration to show how dual leaders lead the creative process through collaboration. The concept of dual leaders leading through collaboration is also supported by Nhamo (2009, pp. 474-475) who said that:

thumbprint would reveal everything or nothing about a person, and thumbprints are traces of evidence that existed in that time and place. Therefore, although created to be a performance experience, the set from *Traces* also stands alone as an interactive installation artwork that allows the audience to leave their mark on it. *Traces* is about interacting with the space and uniting with the audience to create a performance experience. The combination of the diverse disciplines makes this work unlike any of the individual works previously created by the artists.

The desired outcomes by the dual artistic leaders (i.e. M and E) were to create:

- a work that blurs the lines between Performance and Visual Art;
- a break in the barrier of audience perceptions about their understanding of contemporary art, as the sensory experience would make the performance both different and more accessible;
- an increased awareness of and appreciation for interdisciplinary performance works; and
- art that is made more accessible to the audience.

Subsequently, the final work was re-titled as *RE:gina is Dead* because the narrative was developed by E and M into a murder mystery and the audience were suspects to the crime. This then became a play about the death of a fictional person where the murder victim represents the loss of identity, history, etc. Hence the question is raised – who is responsible for this loss? This essentially became the essence of the work.

The Substation's performance call 2010[5]

The Substation is Singapore's first independent arts centre that focuses on contemporary arts. Established in 1990 by the late Kuo Pao Kun, it is known for its pioneering and experimental arts programming, and as an incubator for emerging Singaporean artists. Noor Effendy Ibrahim, The Substation's artistic director, says:

> *The Substation needs to acknowledge the artistry and creativity of the emerging artists who apply themselves in the performative arts. Performance Open Call is exactly that platform which we hope will expand the scope of The Substation's support for these artists.*

> *For Performance Open Call 2010, The Substation selected* RE:gina is Dead! *by Melissa Quek and Elizabeth de Roza to be staged at The Substation Theatre from 17 to 19 September 2010. Effendy further explains that for Performance Open Call:*

> *...the first work chosen to be presented needs to be one that sets the tone: exciting, thought provoking, interactive, progressive. RE:gina is Dead!, livingly, is all that and more.*

---

[5] The information for this section is extracted from the Media Release on 4 Aug 2010 by The Substation – Performance Open Call 2010 – *RE:gina is Dead*! by Melissa Quek, Elizabeth de Roza & Gilles Massot.

One of the artists behind *RE:gina is Dead!*, choreographer and dancer, Melissa Quek, explains the show as:

> *... a combination of visual art and performance. We hope to break down the barriers between performer and spectator, to tell the audience that it's alright to think for themselves, and that they can construct meaning based on their own experiences and understanding.*

With this project, the artists depart from the conventional audience-performer relationships and explored performance as a holistic sensory experience, making the audience member a participant rather than a viewer. The performance was an interactive journey where audience members learned to sense performance rather than just watch it.

The interactive visual-performative experience was inspired by the television programme *CSI* and games like *Cluedo*. Audience members watching the performance were able to pick up clues to determine the details of the murder, and they were invited to use props such as chalk and clue cards to participate in the performance as it progresses. The performance was executed in episodic moments. A variety of props such as paper, overhead projectors and mirrors were used to recreate scenarios of the murder. The performers/artists moved from scene to scene, from one staged 'room' to another, delivering minimal monologues, carrying out physical dialogues through dance movements, and presenting mysterious symbols. By inviting the audience members directly into these scenarios, the performers/artists not only involve the audience in the resolution of a murder mystery, but also provoke them to piece together their own thoughts and feelings towards such novel contemporary performance work. Three shows were staged over three evenings, from 17-19 September 2010. Each show was about 45 minutes in duration, and only 15 to 20 audience members were allowed to attend per show.

Research methodology

The documentation of this case is significant as there is little written on interdisciplinary works that explore content relating to the history of Singapore. This particular creative work had only received one newspaper review and one critical essay written about it.[6] Besides the content of the work, it was also important to document best practices and evaluate these practices, so that the success may be repeated.

A good case study will gather data from a range of sources (Yin 2003) such as documents, interviews and observations. The use of multiple source of evidence is a key characteristic of a case study, and having a range of data sources and a number of case studies, will allow for triangulation to improve the validity of the data (Hammersley & Atkinson 2006).

---

[6] The essay by Richard Chua may be viewed at www.substation.org/regina-is-dead-artists-intervention-into-the-authoring-of-singapore-an-history.

Teams of capable and dedicated leaders and co-leaders working in collaboration are required to get the job done.

Eckman (2006, pp. 102-103) said:

By sharing problems and responsibilities and collaborating on decision-making, the co-leaders are no longer the single isolated leader of their organizations. There is always someone to "brainstorm with about same site issues". The co-[leadership] is one model that utilizes a more distributive and collaborative approach to leadership.

Thus, the process of analyzing and documenting the practice of dual leadership through collaboration will need further exploration in this case.

The elements of developing trust (Eckman 2006; Sharma & Kearins 2011), shared decision-making (Brickley 1997; Eckman 2006) and the impact of conflict on the leaders' ability to function (Eckman 2006; Legler & Reischl 2003; Reid & Karambayya 2009) have emerged through the literature as challenges faced in both the dual leadership and collaborative processes. Therefore a question raised with the dual leaders during the interview process includes finding out how trust between them and their collaborators was established, demonstrated, retained and increased. It is also important to understand their decision-making process, how they came to a consensus with their artistic vision, their aesthetical approach and the methodology they used in creating the work. In terms of conflict, questions were framed about if they experienced any conflict while working together and how they handled that conflict. The data collected from the questions shows further details on how the dual leaders cope with these challenges during their collaboration.

Outcomes

The findings show that the elements of collaboration are embedded in the dual leaders creative process. These elements have surfaced through the interviews and review of the various documents described earlier, such as press releases, the video of performance etc. These elements are important as they contribute to the successful collaborative relationship of the dual leaders. In order for the dual leaders to be able to repeat the success of their collaborative relationship, the author has analyzed and defined how the elements appear, take shape and develop.

Shared vision and ownership

Effective vision can be achieved by dual leaders (Reid 2009, p.1096) and this was necessary for effective collaborations. M wanted to work on interactive experiential performance whereby the audience is not passive but engaged and E was interested in the influence of multi-disciplinary and cross disciplinary work as well as the active participation of the audience. The artistic leaders came together because they were interested in exploring similar ideas and concepts. E said:

> *It was not a forced collaboration; we really wanted to work together.*

This supports Heenan and Bennis's (1999, pp. 5–8 cited in Nhamo 2009, p. 475) findings that dual leaders share aspirations and the desire to work together.

As a dancer/choreographer, M could have left the narrative to E but M did not want to be told what to choreograph so she played an equal role in shaping and influencing the narrative. M said:

> *There is less ownership if I left the narrative to someone else.*

This brings the collaboration from the peripheral level to a higher and deeper level. It also enabled both artists to have a shared vision which led to their ownership of the shared creative process and outcomes.

Trust and risk

Trust is a necessary element in any collaboration (Bachman & Zaheer2008 cited in Sharma & Kearins 2011, p. 173) and both E and M had already started to build this trust prior to working on this project as they were colleagues at work and their students had worked together before. Therefore, they had the prior opportunity of observing each other's working styles. E said:

> *There was a lot of trust – we were just going to do it. And the trust has increased after working together on this and there will be more future collaborations with each other as this is an interesting way of working.*

The process of collaboration was very much based on risk taking and trust on the part of the leaders. This was achieved through a balance of task oriented vs. process-oriented collaboration in this case. This is similar to what Etzioni (1965, p. 689) advocated – there are two kinds of leaders in a group: one who is expressive (social, emotional), while the other is instrumental (or task oriented). From the findings on this case, task oriented collaboration was focused on collaborative decisions that had to be made and these collaborative decisions had mainly to do with resources and its allocation (e.g. finances), logistics, and operational issues. M was mainly responsible for these decisions. She was the contact point for the Substation. But even though decisions were operational and administrative, this was still discussed by both of them. Process oriented collaboration on the other hand allowed for experimentation and discussion of the creative ideas and concepts through dialogue (i.e. meetings and rehearsals).

The duo recognized that their collaborative experience has enabled them to increase their trust in each other thereby allowing them to share knowledge and skills. This was a necessary first step because dual leaders need and rely on each other's skills and knowledge to complement one another (O'Toole, Galbraith & Lawler 2003, p. 254, cited in Eckman 2006, p. 90).

Shared decisions and roles

M who was the initiator of the project provided the leadership for the formation of the partnership (Legler & Reischl 2003, p. 57) and convinced the other stakeholders of the need to collaborate. Subsequently, E became an equal collaborator and artistic leader in every sense as decisions made were joint decisions and E had the power to influence the creative outcomes as well. Both of them demonstrated traits of leadership as they were each willing to accept the consequences of decisions and actions (Philips 2009, p. 4, Stogdill 1974, p. 81, cited in Nhamo 2009, p. 469). E said:

> It's more exciting to share the decision-making process as it's effective.

Eckman (2006, p. 102) also found that respondents in her research highlighted that the strength of the co-leadership model was the ability to share the decision-making process and outcomes with an equally respected peer. What makes E and M dual leaders is also the willingness to share their roles. E said:

> In terms of artistic and creation, we shared that by defining the parameters of our co-leadership.

Building upon the trust that they already had and the understanding of each other strengths, they were able to share their leadership roles. This meant that where M was allowed to work directly with the musician, E worked with the video artist. M was in charge of the movement/dance while E directed the happenings that took place in some of the rooms (For example she looked into what each room represents, what props are to be in the rooms, what will happen in the rooms, etc.). This sharing of roles approach complemented and completed their working relationship.

Conflict, problem solving and communication

The probability for conflict among dual leaders is higher, as there are two leaders rather than a single leader. E said:

> Our conflict was not aggressive. It was due to the different aesthetics and different choices that we wanted but we knew that conflict was necessary for the work that we produced…disagreements were always resolved by talking it through and we were comfortable to do that. Criticisms were not taken personally.

M said:

> The way we resolve disagreements was to ask each other to just try it and to go for it because with aesthetics, we can only imagine what is going to happen, but it does not always work that way, so the only way is to try it out and if it doesn't work, to abandon the idea and not hold it against each other.

Even at the rehearsals, E said:

We spent most of the time talking and it had to be done. This is one of the first few times (working on a piece) that I spent most of the rehearsal time talking.

During the numerous meetings where brainstorming, negotiation, consensus seeking and validity of creative ideas took place, the dual leaders talk and discuss extensively about what is the journey that the audience will take.

M said:

The process of talking (i.e. discussions) was laying the groundwork so that it leads towards the same direction.

The artists were confident of their own rigor and craft and the process of discussions showed that they had to confront similar problems (Turcotte 2000 cited in Sharma and Kearins, 2011, p. 171). Their problems were solved through discussions and improvisation, as they did not want to compromise on the quality of the content. M and E secured the collaborative process through high levels of interaction with each other (Chrislip 2002). In their discussions, they identified and defined the issues, generated options, and agreed on the creative criteria before evaluating options and reaching an agreement. Eckman (2006, p. 102) says that good communication skills, similar to those needed in a marriage, are needed for the co-leadership model to work. Their conflict was resolved quite easily, as they were both willing to act as both mentor and student when required (Heenan & Bennis 1999, pp. 64–273 cited in Nhamo 2009, p. 478), and asked each other for input, guidance, and opinions. They understood each other's role and were interested to listen and embrace each other's values while working as individuals as well as a team. Eckman (2006, p. 93) comments that:

The personal and professional attributes affect the role dimensions of role conflict and role commitment, which in turn contribute to or affect job satisfaction.

Future: Stakeholders as collaborators

Another element for successful collaboration is having a climate that is supportive of collaboration. M said:

Substation was supportive of the risks that we were taking.

Substation provided the environmental structure and climate that supports collaboration and experimentation (Rubin 2009). This was in addition to Substation being the producer and funder of the work. As the work was dependent on the audience participation and response, the audience became an important stakeholder as they too influenced the outcomes of the work for each show. The artists also indicated that they are serious about taking the audience views into consideration for the re-staging of the work in the future.

The supporting collaborators were also stakeholders. E said:

> *The integration of video and music was at the peripheral level as it was merely highlighting what was being created.*

Therefore, the duo is interested in the future to include other collaborators on the same leadership levels in terms of influence and power. This would change the dynamics of the dual leadership model as they move towards a multiple leadership model, with the inclusion of more leaders.

Conclusion

M and E had a shared understanding about the nature of collaboration and the variations and complexities that surround it (Gajda 2004, p. 68). In addition, they went through the stages of collaborative development from the assembling and forming of their team. They had to go through the storming (discussions/ conflict) and order before moving into the norming and performing stage and finally to the final stage of transforming and adjourning, as described by Gajda (2004, p. 70).

M and E shared their decision-making; they shared the responsibility, authority, accountability and recognition of the process and outcomes, and this did not lead to inconsistency in outcomes as Brickley (1997, p. 195) had found, but rather it heightened the quality of the relationship among the dual leaders and the content of the outcomes.

E said:

> *Collaboration is the way to work in the 21st century because the work is pushed to another level.*

M and E understood the concept and strengths of power sharing and delegation (Heenan & Bennis 1999, pp. 5-8, cited in Nhamo 2009, p.475). They were able to manage their egos and take their bows together (O'Toole, Galbraith & Lawler 2003, p. 259, cited in Eckman 2006, p. 90).

None of the difficulties that could arise through a dual leadership relationship was seemingly present. For example there were no power struggles, no unequal workload, no inconsistent messages, no inconsistent work ethics, no inconsistent decision-making with shared authority (Brickley 1997, p. 218) because their leadership styles were compatible and interactions and communication with each other throughout the process was consistent. This enabled the collaboration process to be mutually beneficial (Legler & Reischl 2003, p. 56).

Finally, M and E's collaboration led to mutual learning and value creation (Sharma & Kearins 2011, p. 172) as the outcome was an integrated performance. It cannot be defined as a dance performance or a theatre performance. The work has truly exemplified their working style and collaborative efforts and approach, which was shared and integrated at all levels. This requires co-operation, co-ordination and collaboration (Gajda 2004, p. 69). They have managed to move from being single discipline artists to multi-discipline until their final work was inter-disciplinary.

E said:

> *The two art forms dance or theatre can't be identified. You can't call this a theatre or dance performance as the work had moved beyond one genre to another.*

This concurs with the highest level of collaboration known as integration described by Gajda (2004, p. 71) – unification whereby a single structure is formed.[10]

Even though both artistic leaders started with differing aesthetical backgrounds and experiences, their ingredient for success was their ability to share the same wavelength about their creative work and its outcomes. By constructively dealing with their challenges, they have managed to mesh their contrasting talents to find the same thread and commonality. Given their success, this could be the start of a collaborative relationship that has the potential to become both on-going and highly beneficial to both artists. There are indeed already examples of brilliant artistic partnerships such as the collaboration between Martha Graham and Isamu Noguchi or John Cage and Merce Cunningham, so there is no doubt the process can work to everyone's advantage.

Questions

1. Discuss how the creative process can be monitored and its outcomes evaluated through a collaborative process. What are the advantages and disadvantages of the collaborative approach in achieving a successful creative outcome?

2. If collaborative creative relationships can be fostered, discuss what leadership approach is best suited to achieving this and why? Discuss this in the context of the case study.

3. How does a successful collaboration occur within an arts practice? What are the approaches required to achieve both a successful collaboration as well as an artistic success?

References

Amaratunga, D, Baldry, D, Sarshar, M & Newton, R 2002, 'Quantitative and qualitative research in the built environment: Application of mixed research approach', *Work Study*, vol. 51, no. 1, pp. 17-31.

Archer, D & Cameron, A 2008, *Collaborative leadership – how to succeed in an interconnected world*, Butterworth Heinemann.

Bereson, R 2003, 'Renaissance or Regurgitation? Arts Policy in Singapore 1957-2003' *Asia Pacific Journal of Arts and Cultural Management*, vol. 1, issue 1, December, pp. 1-14.

---

[10] The levels of integration begin with level 1-networking, level 2-co-operating, level 3-partnering, level 4-merging, and finally level 5- Unification (Gajda 2004, p. 71).

Black, LJ, Cresswell, AM, Luna, LF, Pardo, TA, Martinez, IJ, Thompson, F, Andersen, DF, Canestraro, DS, Richardson, GP, Cook, M 2003, 'A dynamic theory of collaboration: a structural approach to facilitating intergovernmental use of information technology' in *Proceedings of the 36th Annual Hawaii International Conference on System Sciences*.

Brickley, JA, Coles, JL & Gregg, J 1997, 'Leadership Structure: Separating the CEO and Chairman of the Board' *Journal of Corporate Finance*, vol. 3, pp. 189-220.

Bryan, TA 2004, 'Tragedy averted: The promise of collaboration', *Society and Natural Resources*, vol. 17, pp. 881-896.

Bryman, A 2004, 'Qualitative research on leadership: A critical but appreciative review', *The Leadership Quarterly*, vol. 7, pp. 729–769.

Carson, JB, Tesluk, PE & Marrone, JA 2007, 'Shared leadership in teams: An investigation of antecedent conditions and performance' *Academy of Management Journal*, vol. 50, pp. 1217-1234.

Chrislip, D 2002, *The Collaborative Leadership Fieldbook - A guide for citizens and civic leaders*, Jossey Bass.

Chua, R 2010, 'RE:gina is Dead!: Artists' Intervention into the Authoring of Singapore (-an) History', Substation, viewed 28 Dec 2011, http://www.substation.org/regina-is-dead-artists-intervention-into-the-authoring-of-singapore-an-history/

de Voogt, A 2006, 'Dual leadership as a problem-solving tool in arts organizations' *International Journal of Arts Management*, vol. 9, no. 1, pp. 17–22. HEC Montréal, Canada.

Eckman, EW 2006, 'Co-principals: Characteristics of dual leadership teams', *Leadership and Policy in Schools*, vol. 5, no. 2, pp. 89-107.

Edelenbos, J & Klijn EH 2006, 'Managing Stakeholder Involvement in Decision Making: A Comparative Analysis of Six Interactive Processes in the Netherlands', *Journal of Public Administration Research and Theory*, vol. 16, no. 3, pp. 417-446.

Etzioni, A 1965, 'Dual Leadership in Complex Organizations', *American Sociological Review*, vol. 30, no. 5, pp. 688-698.

Frey, BS 2002, 'Creativity, Government and The Arts', *De Economist*, vol. 150, no. 4, pp. 363-376.

Gajda, R 2004, 'Utilizing collaboration theory to evaluate strategic alliances', *American Journal of Evaluation*, vol. 25, no. 1, pp. 65-77.

Gillham, B 2000a, Case Study – Research Methods, Real World Research.

Gillham, B 2000b, The Research Interview, Real World Research.

Hammersley, M & Atkinson, P 2006, *Ethnography Principles in Practice, 2nd edition*, Routledge, New York.

Hartley, JF 1994, 'Case Studies in Organizational Research', in C Cassell & G Symon (eds), *Qualitative Methods in Organizational Research*, Newbury Park, CA: Sage Publications, pp. 208-229.

Koh, N 2010, 'Interactive work kicks off new open call', *Business Times*, 10 September, p. L6 Arts, 2010.

LASALLE College of the Arts home page viewed 10 January 2012, http://www.lasalle.edu.sg/.

Lauber, TB, Stedman, RC, Decker, DJ, Knuth, BA & Simon, C 2011, 'Social network dynamics in collaborative conservation', *Human Dimensions of Wildlife*, vol.16, pp. 259-272.

Legler, R & Reischl, T 2003,'The relationship of key factors in the process of collaboration', *Journal of Applied Behavioral Science*, vol. 29, no.1, pp. 53-72.

Lim, J 2009, 'Blueprint for the Arts', 10 August, viewed 14 December 2009 http://julianalim.wordpress.com/

Marinez-Moyano, IJ 2006, 'Exploring the Dynamics of Collaboration', in Interorganizational Settings', in Schuman (ed), *Creating a Culture of Collaboration*, Jossey-Bass, p. 83.

Media Release, 4 August 2010, The Substation -Performance Open Call 2010- Re-gina is Dead! Singapore.

Nhamo, G 2009,'Co-Leadership in Climate Change: An Agenda to 2013 and Beyond',Politikon, *South African Association of Political Studies*, vol. 36, no. 3, pp. 463-480.

Pearce, CL & Manz, C C 2005,'The new silver bullets of leadership: The importance of self- and shared leadership in knowledge work', *Organizational Dynamics*, vol. 34, pp. 130-140.

Pick, J 1989, *The Arts in a State: A Study of Government Arts Policies from Ancient Greece to the Present*, Bristol Classical Press.

Re-gina is Dead! 2010, video recording, Melissa Quek.

Reid, W & Karambayya, R 2009, 'Impact of dual executive leadership dynamics in creative organizations', *Human Relations*, vol. 62, no. 7, pp. 1073-1110.

Renaissance City Reports, viewed 19 August 2010 www.nac.gov.sg/sta/sta02.asp

Rubin, H 2009, *Collaborative Leadership: Developing Effective Partnerships for Communities and Schools*, Corwin Press.

Selin, S & Chavez, D 1995, 'Developing a collaborative model for environmental planning and management', *Environmental Management*, vol. 19, pp. 189-195.

Sharma, A & Kearins, K 2011, 'Interorganizational collaboration for regional sustainability: What happens when organizational representatives come together?', *The Journal of Applied Behavioral Science*, vol. 47, no. 2, pp. 168–203.

Singapore Cultural Statistics (2004-2008), 2009, National Arts Council, Ministry of Information, Communication and the Arts, Singapore.

Singapore Department of Statistics, 'Statistics Singapore: Total Population of Singapore' viewed 10 August 2009, http://www.singstat.gov.sg/

Stake, R E 2006 'Multiple Case Study Analysis', The Guilford Press.

Substation home page, viewed on 10 January 2012, www.substation.org/.

Tharenou, P, Donohue, R & Cooper, B 2007, *Management Research Methods*, Cambridge University Press.

Wondolleck, J M & Yaffee, S L 2000, *Making collaboration work: Lessons from innovation in natural resource management*, Island Press, Washington, DC.

Yin, R K 2003, *Case Study Research: Design and Methods, 3rd edition*, Sage Publications.

Chapter 13

Thriving or surviving

Artists as leaders of smaller arts organizations

Jo Caust

A leader is best when people barely know he exists, when his work is done, his aim fulfilled, they will say: we did it ourselves (Lao Tzu, 6th century BC).

Background

Artists are highly adaptable. They need to be if they are to survive. They have to deal with insufficient funding (or none at all), high costs, public criticism if what they do is not well received, and the overall 'politics' of the arts. When these factors are combined within the context of smaller arts organizations, where just surviving day-to-day can be daunting, the role the artist plays as 'leader' is one of continuous challenge. In this study the leadership practices of three artist leaders are explored. Each of them leads a small arts organization: one in dance, another in theatre, and a third in community arts. The artist leaders of these organizations are asked how they deal with their challenges while still trying to do their best artistic work, and the solutions they have found to survive and thrive nevertheless.

The most recent survey of artists in Australia by Throsby and Zednik (2010) emphasizes the need for artists to have time to do their work but lack of money usually limits their opportunities. So being an artist is not necessarily a desirable aim in life for those who want to have an easy existence. It frequently involves struggle. Robinson (2010) emphasizes the need of artists to understand the system that they operate within, thereby increasing their resilience for survival.

Artists are sometimes framed as having enormous egos, being difficult to work with, and behaving like children; so, it is argued, leading a group of artists in this context requires incredibly finely honed skills (Thomas 2008). Artists as leaders are also drawn as ego-driven, narcissistic individuals who exploit others to make their own work (Fitzgibbon 2001). Moreover, Fitzgibbon (2001) argues that leadership in the arts is often not 'shared' or 'collaborative':

> Not only is leadership dominant and tending at times towards the autocratic, but also in each instance, structures are skewed, albeit to varying degrees, to ensure the centralisation of power (Fitzgibbon 2001, pp.169).

However Hewison and Holden (2011) argue that contemporary creativity models depend on collaboration rather than competition. At the same time they acknowledge that a creative process often involves conflict, so they argue there is an interesting dialectic present in the process of creation with collaboration. This is a different framing to Fitzgibbon where conflict as part of the creative process is interpreted negatively. Thorn (1990) acknowledges the complexity of making art but asserts it requires good organization and collaborative skills to succeed. He argues that the separation between artists, management, and boards in contemporary arts organizations has served to marginalize artists from the business of running their own enterprise. Instead he believes that artists are good at managing and organizing because of the very nature of their own work processes. Beirne and Knight (2002) comment that there are many artists and arts managers who see the workplace as entirely interconnected and so the separation between management and arts making, is not an issue. In fact, Lapierre (2005) frames management as creating and argues that this aspect of management should be embraced in the training of managers.

Certainly the capacity for strong leadership is a pre-requisite for survival in the world of the arts. This quality of strength is not about a leadership style (e.g. autocratic or directive) but recognizing that the individual leader needs to embody a set of values that reflect confidence and a passionate belief in what they are doing. This approach to leadership is noted by Drucker (1990) when he talks about the qualities needed for leaders in the 'not-for-profit' sector where they must have a high degree of commitment to their organization, putting the interests of the organization before any self-interest.

In considering then the challenges of artists as leaders, there are issues around process, environment and outcomes that are important to explore.

Approach

This research focuses on three individual artist leaders and how they interpret their roles and work practices; it does not address the views of those who work with the individuals. The three individuals were chosen by the researcher as interesting research subjects because of their different approaches to their work, their different art forms, their obvious passion and commitment to their work, the respect from the arts community towards them, their individual achievements, and their receptivity to talking with the researcher about their work. All the individuals were comfortable with their real names being used in the context of this research.

Interviews were undertaken by the researcher late in 2011 and early in 2012. Other information about the work of the companies concerned was gleaned from public documents such as websites and printed material produced by the company.

The focus here was on smaller companies, rather than larger ones, to see what leadership approaches and solutions were needed within the context of limited funding, few resources and high levels of pressure. There is an exploration of what the organization is about as well as the processes of the individual leader in relation to their everyday work and process.

Leigh Warren

Leigh Warren and Dancers, as the name suggests, is a contemporary dance company. Its founder and artistic director is Leigh Warren and he set up the company in 1993. The interview with Leigh Warren took place in his rehearsal studio at the top of a former factory building, now known as the Lion Arts Centre. The company's offices are next door to the studio in the same building. Warren had previously been a leading dancer for 12 years with the Nederlands Dance Theatre in Holland, under the artistic directorship of Jiri Kylian. He returned to Australia in the late eighties and then became the Artistic Director of the Australian Dance Theatre (ADT). He notes though that when a new Board of the ADT was appointed early in 1993 they:

> ... decided that I was not the 'right' person ...and so I was no longer employed ... I decided then with that experience that I would set up a company where I would work with the board and not for the board (Warren in conversation, December 2011).

As Warren explains:

> The group of people who had come on <the Board> had very little understanding of the artistic enterprise that I was engaged in ... they just wanted to put their corporate stamp on it. ... they wanted to change everything because they can then control it ... however they are transient... This is not necessarily the best way for an artist to evolve or develop (Warren 2011).

So conflict with a new board with a different set of priorities to his own forced Warren to address how he wanted to work. He then decided to set up his own company driven by his own particular vision. But he did this a little differently to existing models of arts companies then prevalent in Australia. He bought a 'shelf' company, changed the name of the company to Leigh Warren and Dancers and then invited people he thought could make a contribution to be members of his Board. He has kept the size of the Board quite small (6 including himself) and he made it clear to the Board members at the outset that their role was to support his vision. As he owned the company he had the capacity to do this — in a sense he was employing the Board (although not paying them anything), rather than the reverse. He says:

> *I was getting back to my own need to create work. It was also about providing a model of continuity. We need continuity. We need one generation connecting to the next (Warren 2011).*

Warren emphasizes many times in the interview his belief in continuity and stability so that artists can learn from each other to continue to develop and prosper. He believes his company has played an important role in this respect in Adelaide by supporting generations of new dancers who go away for periods of time and then return to the company to share their experiences. He talks about the positive advantages of working with the same creative team over many years; how this enables trust and good communication to develop that supports positive collaborations and artistic risk taking. He says you are able to have healthy conflicts (necessary for creation) without causing tension in the relationships. He describes his leadership style as:

> *...to be completely engaged as well as utterly disengaged at the same time. I found that works very well (Warren 2011).*

He thinks it is essential to be at a personal distance from your colleagues to engender and maintain their respect, especially given the physical intimacy that dance as an arts practice involves. He is also clear about boundaries and appropriate behavior when working together, which he emphasizes when he talks to all new personnel:

> *...we do not yell at each other here, even when we disagree. Artistic temperament is the affliction of amateurs (Warren 2011).*

Nevertheless this does not mean he is un-demanding in the rehearsal studio. He says that with more experience over the years he has recognized that:

> *I think you can always push people a little bit further. I am inclined to do that more in recent years (Warren 2011).*

His views on artistic collaboration are also quite clear. He talks about how he has had both good and bad experiences when collaborating on someone else's vision. Where he has been treated with respect and engaged from the outset he says the relationship has worked tremendously and this is reflected in the outcomes. But when he has been treated in a 'mechanistic' manner, merely there to provide some dance moves and not essential to contribute to the overall vision, the relationship and outcomes has been compromised. Therefore he thinks that if you are working with others you need to get them involved from the beginning, if you want them to commit to your vision.

> *People buy the idea and start contributing to it and you are all heading in the same direction. They then own the outcome if they are truly involved from the outset (Warren 2011).*

Warren expresses some frustration that he has to do a lot out of the rehearsal studio that he thinks ideally could be managed by others. On the other hand he thinks that the expectations of the role of administrator/ general manager are complex and not likely to be found in one human being. Ideally he likes to work with a 'producer' when he is developing a new piece – someone with whom he can also collaborate with, in getting the work up, appropriately presented and sold. When talking about the role of the artistic director versus that of the general manager he believes that, as the CEO, it is also his role to liaise with funders and negotiate the most critical external relationships. While he says it would be nice not to have to do this, he believes that he is the person generally people want to relate to, and his skills are now quite fine-tuned in this regard. He comments that:

> For the most part we have quite a good relationship with all the 'political' parties. Our attitude is bi-partisan. I don't care who is in power. We can't be worried about who is in power (Warren 2011).

In late 2011 Warren heard that *Leigh Warren and Dancers* were likely to lose their long-term triennial funding from the Australia Council. This was due to a change in policy at the national level that was re-directing all dance funding to projects of 'national 'significance. The interpretation of 'national' was problematic as it was not clear how this was defined and if regional companies are likely to be at a disadvantage in this regard. Despite this drama, Warren was remarkably sanguine. He said that he believed all artistic companies had a 'limited life' and maybe his company had come to the end of its life. However he was also disappointed that this was occurring when the company was getting more international invitations than ever before and, in his view, doing their best work. He notes in this context that:

> This is when politics becomes problematic. People are backing everything that gives them marketing success. They are not investing in the arts at all levels and they do not understand the ecology of the art form. They are relying on information that doesn't come from the field (Warren 2011).

His final comment was a little rueful.

> The Australia Council needs a really good shake up re its role. It's dangerous for all art forms to be in this position. It needs re-shaping. It needs a reality check (Warren 2011).

It seemed as if this resonated with the beginning of the conversation in a way, with the role of boards. So, in the end, perhaps it is an issue of who calls the shots? Should it be artists themselves, bureaucrats, peers or outsiders relatively uninformed in the arts? It also raises questions about the connections between political, artistic and funding decisions.

Lisa Philip-Harbutt

Eight years ago Lisa Philip-Harbutt was appointed Director of the Community Arts Network South Australia (CAN SA), a peak body that plays a multi-faceted role in supporting and enabling community arts practice (or community cultural development, depending on which title you prefer) in the South Australian community. CAN SA is located in a single story building in the city and shares its spaces, including a large rehearsal studio, with two other small arts and community organizations.

CAN SA is an advocacy body, a training organization, an initiator of arts projects, a support network for artists working in community, a home for marginalized communities and/or marginalized arts practice and engages in research as well as publication. Perhaps, in some ways, it is also an organization that re-invents itself every few years in response to its environment, as well to the restrictions placed on it. At a time of hostile funding environments for community arts and its associated practices, and where similar organizations across the nation have gone under, CAN SA has survived[1]. It may not be doing everything it would like to be doing, as well as operating on reduced funding and mostly part-time staff, but it is still active and engaged. Its Board is elected by its members and plays a significant role in determining the direction and activities of the organization, as well as supporting the Director in fulfilling her role. The majority of the Board's members are drawn from the community to which it serves: community cultural development and community artists.

Philip-Harbutt defines herself as an artist. But embracing this title hasn't been without its challenges.

> I was really self-conscious about saying I was an artist, I think because I didn't come from an arts background and I was aware of the general community perception of artists. I came from the bush – my parents were prospector/miners, the notion of an artist was someone who was élitist', and that wasn't me (Philip-Harbutt in conversation in February 2012).

She recognized early on though, that she was different and saw life differently to other people. At the age of five she first said to her family that she was an 'artist'. But as an adult, naming herself as an artist was confronting, given her preference for collaborative practices and her discomfort about the image of the artist as an élite' individual. She trained as a sculptor and worked in the theatre as a designer while continuing her own arts practice. At the age of 40 she decided to re-embrace the title of 'artist'.

> I have tried to not be an artist, I have been called a lecturer and I have tried to be different things. I have had other titles, but all the time I know that my brain is thinking like an artist. It is who I am (Philip-Harbutt 2012).

When she came to CAN SA as its Director she saw the role in an artistic framework. She says:

> I came to CAN SA thinking that the work could be just like learning another art medium; I wondered if it was possible to use the creative processes that I

---

[1] In December 2004 the Australia Council disbanded the Community Cultural Development Board (CCD) without any consultation with the field. More recently the CCD Board was replaced by the Community Partnerships Committee at the Australia Council. Peak Organizations such as CAN (SA) are no longer annually funded at the National level.

had always used and the collaborative processes that I knew well in another format, and I think it is (Philip-Harbutt 2012).

Philip-Harbutt says she always sees problems from an artist's perspective and tries to work how to shape an entity from the material she is given. CAN SA is a membership organization so she has a responsibility to meet the needs of its members. But she is herself a member, as well as a member of the Board, and the Director of the organization. She says she enjoys wearing different hats and changing them to whatever the situation demands. She says she addresses 'conflict of interest' by announcing to the Board or other staff which 'hat' she is wearing at the time. This seems to work and it appears no one doubts her integrity in the situation. Her particular love at present is undertaking and presenting research, having completed a research degree a few years ago about decision-making in the arts. She sees this as part of her arts practice where she gets to presents provocative ideas to an international audience. In this context she sees herself as an artist presenting something ephemeral that may nevertheless resonate with her audience much later after the event – her ideas may get them thinking differently or see something in a way that they hadn't before. She wants continuity for her work and hopes that whatever she does might have an ongoing life.

> *I might leave a pattern on the sand; someone else finds it and goes, oh, what's that? There is always the possibility of the art continuing after I leave it (Philip-Harbutt 2012).*

When talking about how CAN SA works Philip-Harbutt says that they always work in partnership with someone else and they work *with* people not just *for* people. She describes how CAN SA see their mandate:

> *…the circus coming to town is often a really important event, but we're like the workshop around the circus; we want to leave the skills, so that the kids learn how to be the circus performers themselves. … we want to make sure we are also empowering people to take on a larger role than audience, so that things have the potential to continue when we leave, so they are not depressed when the circus leaves the town (Philip-Harbutt 2012).*

Thus CAN SA is determined that their contribution is ongoing and sustaining. Philip-Harbutt also applies this model of empowerment to the people who work in CAN SA. She comments that many individuals who have worked for CAN SA go on to other roles, often as leaders, in other organizations. Rather than being concerned about people not staying with CAN SA, Philip-Harbutt says that she is proud that CAN SA is seen as a successful training ground. She is also conscious that this process means that CAN SA has an extensive network throughout the arts sector and therefore its philosophical influence is considerable. Philip-Harbutt says:

> *I don't believe that there's one truth, I think there are multiple truths and therefore multiple solutions. And given that, to lead well, you have to start with a solid idea but then give people opportunities to find their place within*

whatever it is you're working towards, and as a leader you need to be open enough to recognize other paths when they appear (Philip-Harbutt 2012).

Philip-Harbutt is articulating perhaps a less individually focused notion of arts leadership. While she acknowledges herself as a leader and as an artist, the focus is not on what *she* produces but on what either she creates with others or what others produce, achieve or do. In fact she admits that:

I found making art by myself very lonely, because I couldn't try out everything that was going on in my head all the time. And so, that's why collaborative art making is so important to me, because having a good tussle about an idea with somebody else, really pushes things along (Philip-Harbutt 2012).

Working with people in whatever way she can, is fundamental to Philip-Harbutt's approach. CAN SA is an organization that is about empowering people. So there is a good fit between Philip-Harbutt and the organization that she leads. CAN SA is inclusive and embraces difference while giving the possibility for people to change their lives through the process of making art. Philip-Harbutt interprets her leadership role as there to enable other people to reach their potential – this includes those who work with her in the team at CAN SA as well as those she works with on CAN SA projects from other communities.

Andy Packer

*Slingsby i*s a small theatre company founded by Andy Packer in 2007 to do work primarily for young people. Recently the company leased premises at the top of a renovated Victorian building in the middle of the city. The space has only three rooms but is spacious and light. Rehearsals occur in a space elsewhere. Not long after Packer founded *Slingsby* in 2007, and before they had produced any work, he received funding for the company. This in itself was unusual but reflected Packer's track record, his vision for the new company and his success in leveraging funding from multiple sources. Before this happened however there were important events/influences that contributed to his vision and his approach.

Packer worked for several years doing theatre for young people in various ways. He worked at the Adelaide Fringe Festival, the Come Out Festival (an arts festival for young people) and at Carclew Youth Arts Centre, so he had an understanding of how the funding system worked, as well as the possibilities for touring work. The first company he was part of was called *Ricochet*, and it was co-founded with several other artists to tour small scale work for schools around the country. It was initially self-funded by the participants until it made enough income to support the players. Packer said this early experience made him realize the possibilities of touring to small regional centres as well as ways of doing the work you believed in, albeit on a small scale. Packer began, as many others had before, doing everything; acting, writing, directing and carrying the sets. Within their small group the *Ricochet* members were allocated different tasks. Over time Packer became the one with the funding responsibility. This taught him that he actually liked this aspect of the work; working out budgets and making the books balance.

By 2006 he was the programming manager at Carclew[2], working with up to 14 people to organize Carclew's activities. During this period he had a kind of 'epiphany' when he went to the Montreal ASSITEJ Festival and saw there the work of the Danish theatre company, *Teatret Gruppe 38*, and their production of *Little Match Girl*. After weeping profusely at its beauty and depth he then:

> *...realised that that was the sort of theatre that I always wanted to make (Packer in conversation 2012).*

He came back to Australia determined to do just that. He describes this as:

> *... the vision was to make work that was emotionally complex for a niche audience...which was sort of 10 year olds and up ... to make it on a scale that could be presented both in a professionally equipped theatre and then also in a remote community, a school gym or town hall, but with the same production values. So the challenge ... Yorke Peninsula (rural South Australia) one day and New York the next. That was really the vision (Packer 2012).*

Packer then approached a former Executive Director of the Adelaide Fringe Festival and colleague, Jodi Glass, to work with him on this vision as the newly formed *Slingbsy's* executive producer. Simultaneously the State Government announced a new fund for theatre development – the first time new money had been available for setting up theatre companies for many years, where interested groups were invited to put in a tender. By getting the regional arts funder Country Arts SA on side as well, the newly-created *Slingsby* was successful in winning one of the three tenders available, receiving then A$115,000 annually for the next three years from the State government. To be eligible for funding however they had to incorporate as a company and establish a board for governance purposes. They undertook this process carefully using the advice of the local representative of the Australian Business Arts Foundation. She recommended several people after they described the kind of skills they would like on their board. Their preference was for non-arts people such as an accountant, lawyer, etc., but they wanted to keep the size of the board small. They then interviewed various individuals and pitched their idea for the company. This resulted in a committed board of six people including Packer, which meets four times a year and at other times is kept in contact about the company's activities through email. Packer is clear what he expects from them:

---

[2] Carclew Youth Arts is a multi-art form and cultural organization dedicated to artistic outcomes by and for people aged 26 and under. It provides young people with opportunities to try different art forms, supports emerging artists to develop their craft and advocates for youth arts practice.

...they're there for governance, they're not there to run the business. They trust Jodi and me to make decisions about strategic direction of the company (Packer 2012).

Incredibly their first production, *The Tragical Life of Cheeseboy*, was an overwhelming success. After its first showing in January 2008 it was invited to a return season in May 2008 when ASSITEJ[3] was being hosted in Adelaide. This gave the production access to an international audience as well as international producers resulting in immediate invitations for *Cheeseboy* from around the world. As noted on their website, *Cheeseboy* has since performed in 26 venues in 13 cities on five continents including the Children First Festival in Singapore, Festival Teatralia in Madrid, Imaginate Festival in Edinburgh, The Egg at Theatre Royal Bath, the Sydney Opera House as well as the desired regional tour in South Australia.

The creative process at *Slingsby* involves Packer working with several collaborators. Packer has an idea which he then develops as the director with a writer, designer and composer and other artistic collaborators. For their first three productions, the core group working with Packer have, all been the same people: Quincy Grant (composer), Geoff Cobham (designer) and Finegan Kruckemeyer (playwright). Other designers, musicians and performers are also engaged. However Packer acknowledges that he is providing the original vision and the collaborators are in a sense working with him to achieve it. He feels he says quite 'humbled' by this; the willingness of his artistic collaborators to buy into his vision and work with him to realize it. He describes this process as:

it's my job to set the road map… this is the challenge, this is the story we're trying to tell (Packer 2012).

But then he works with the others, particularly Cobham and Grant to devise the piece including the music. At this stage in the process everyone throws in ideas and no one is precious about which role they may hold.

…we're all in the room working together … the approach we have is that it's usually not the expert that has the best ideas…the work never winds up being what I first had in my head at all, because the metaphor behind it is usually still there, but how we get there and what it becomes is due to the collective, but we are not a collective in the sense that I'm the director and it's more me shaping things … the work is a result of everyone (Packer 2012).

Packer says there are four stages in their creation process where the ideas are continually re-worked until the final piece is created. The final stage involves four weeks of rehearsal but the whole creative process may have occurred over 18 months. The performers are also involved in getting to this end with often the

---

[3] ASSITEJ is the *Association Internationale du Théâtre de l'Enfance et la Jeunesse*, or, in English, the International Association of Theatre for Children and Young People.

actual actors being selected before the writing process begins, so that the piece is developed with that particular actor in mind. This means that the performer/s have a strong identity with the part they are playing. This is taken further given that Packer recognizes how closely the actor may have identified with a part. Packer notes:

> *I said to Steve <the original actor> right from the start with Cheese Boy, the show is yours for as long as you want to do it (Packer 2012).*

Packer plays a 'hands on' role with administrative aspects of the company as well, seemingly without feeling any resentment or tension about this. He enjoys the process of budgeting for instance and sees most aspects of the administrative side as 'creative' also. He seems to relish being involved with all aspects of the company although both Glass and Packer take on specifically different tasks at times. Glass for instance does the contracting but they develop the budget together. However, as the only full-time employee of the company, Packer has no choice to but to immerse himself in the many administrative tasks. But this is not a disadvantage as he notes:

> *…what I find is interesting is I am artistic director, and I am an artist, but I am also a CEO, so I think strategically from an artistic perspective (Packer 2012).*

He thinks this makes him different from other artistic directors, but also enables him to participate in conversations with funders about international marketing strategies, without feeling patronized. He observes that one drawback of getting more money from government has meant that the amount of reporting required has increased, which is very time consuming. The company currently receives around A$300,000 in annual grant funding and earns around another similar amount annually.

How *Slingsby* progresses from here will be interesting.

> *…we're very clear that if I decide to leave, the company will be wound up (Packer 2012).*

Slingby's funding conditions from the Australia Council are reliant on Packer being involved. Whatever happens in the future, Packer has successfully pursued an artistic vision and created the conditions for the kind of work he wants to do.

The challenges

The broader environment

In all these case studies the individual plays a leadership role but does it within restrictions imposed from both outside as well as within. For instance all three organizations receive funding from government bodies at the state and national level. To receive this they need to adhere to conditions of funding related to accountability, performance, reporting and evaluation. Two of these organizations are currently experiencing funding crises. While it can be argued that arts organizations are fortunate in Australia because they do receive funding, there is also a challenge in receiving funding because the funders determine the rules of the engagement. This, as Warren suggests, is not necessarily in the interest of the art form concerned, but may be influenced by broader political concerns.

Being an artist

Phillip-Harbutt shows ambivalence about even embracing the title of 'artist' yet recognizes there is no other way to describe who she is and how she fits in the world. In the end she has used it to frame every part of her working world and that now works well for her. Warren has lived the life of an artist always, and so for him, there was no other choice. But he was an artist who wanted to do more than interpret other peoples' work. He wanted to make his own work but he realized he needed do it within his rules. This is not an easy path but he has achieved it nevertheless even if it is now under threat. Packer has worked as an arts manager as well as an artist but his 'epiphany' about the work he really wanted to do shaped his decisions from then on. He recognized that to do the work that he believes in he must create a framework that supports who he is and how he wants to do his work. This has brought him recent rewards but the journey getting there has not necessarily been smooth.

Management and arts leadership

All of the leaders have management responsibilities. In Packer's case, he seems to almost delight in them. This does not mean that the responsibilities involved are not frustrating and time consuming whoever does them. Packer does comment though, that because he is on top of the budget and works collaboratively with Glass on all aspects of the company's management, he believes he receives more respect from the funders. Warren expresses some frustration that at times he has to do things he wishes someone else would or could do, but even so he acknowledges that he must be responsible for key relationships if the company is to survive. He is the company leader. Phillip-Harbutt recognizes that there are administrative tasks she has to do to keep the organization functioning but uses artistic metaphors to achieve them, interpreting them as creative endeavors.

Governance and structure

Both Warren and Packer talk about their company's legal structure and the need for a Board. They discuss how they chose their Board and what they expect from it. It is not hard though to see the complexities the role of the Board raises for the artists. As there is a direct link between receiving funding and being able to demonstrate accountability, governance is naturally emphasized as part of this compact. However, it could be concluded that there is a need for arts leaders, even in small entities, to spend large amounts of their time reporting to boards, as well as writing copious evaluation reports for funders, and this has the potential to exhaust limited resources and take time away from the actual art making.

Outcomes

Collaboration

An interesting aspect of all three artist leaders is their approach to collaboration. For all of them it is a part of their process and essential to achieving successful outcomes. They do not reflect the stereotype of the difficult guru arts leader who is driven by a pure (perhaps selfish) ego to achieve their vision, as is sometimes observed in the literature (Fitzgibbon 2001, Thomas 2008). In fact they all prefer to work with others to do their work and believe that collaboration with other artists enriches everything they do. This corroborates Hewison and Holden's (2011) view about the way artists and arts organizations rely on successful artistic collaboration to get good creative outcomes.

Warren notes how important it is to get others to buy into the vision from the outset so they all feel ownership of the outcome. Warren also notes how critical it is to leave ego and temperament outside the door, so that the creative process is positive and rewarding for everyone. On the other hand he describes a process where conflict is integral to the creative setting. He talks about why he likes to work with the same group of artists to enable this conflict to occur in a constructive manner. Yet Warren also describes collaboration with other artists where he felt he was treated in a 'mechanistic' way, so he sees collaboration as more than just 'artists working together'. He believes that collaboration has a quality of its own that involves mutual respect, 'give and take', and validation.

Packer describes a creative process where everyone involved contributes ideas and they all work at problem-solving without reference to their role in the group. He describes the process of creation as a 'collective' process; as artists and collaborators the work is their shared goal. Phillip-Harbutt notes that CAN (SA) always works with partners to do their work. That relationship is essential to their process. She also talks about the pleasure she gets from working with others to solve creative problems. She describes the process as a 'tussle' but an enjoyable one. In fact she feels both her leadership and the work is a success if others own the outcomes as their own.

However, while Packer and Warren both demonstrate that their processes are highly collaborative in development, the reality is they set the vision in the beginning and it is their name which is listed as director or choreographer at the end. Their process is definitely collaborative but is the outcome acknowledged as such? Warren certainly usually records that the final piece has been developed with members of the company. Packer acknowledges here that the actor owns the part until they decide to let it go. Everyone involved in the creation is credited and Packer is just one player in that regard. So while they are the acknowledged leader of the process they are generous and respectful in ensuring that everyone who contributes is appropriately recognized. This is not a mechanistic leadership relationship or a manipulative one; it is about exchange, collaboration, and respect.

Management and the artist

Phillip-Harbutt and Packer say here that the administrative work is also creative as Lapierre (2005) asserts. In addition the way these leaders talk about their roles supports Thorn's (1990) view of artists who have a deep understanding of the needs of organization and management. Warren also recognizes that he must engage in all aspects of the company's operation for it to survive. There is no evidence of separation here for any of them between different aspects of the company's operations demonstrating the inter-connectedness that Beirne and Knight (2002) infer. They also all recognize how important it is for themselves and their company to understand the system that they are working in (Robinson 2010). Given that they are all dependent on funding they need to work with government agencies, political parties and other stakeholders to promote their work and get everyone's understanding and support for it.

Leadership

All three individuals nevertheless demonstrate a great strength of character that perhaps separates them from others who do not take on these leadership roles (Drucker 1990). They have weathered many obstacles before they reached their positions. Perhaps developing resilience (Robinson 2010) and the capacity to fight back, is a sign of a leader. For the leader of an organization that has to fight to survive, the personal costs can be high. Phillip-Harbutt has weathered these struggles but it is no doubt stressful to continually justify the raison d'être for what you are doing. Perhaps because Warren has already been through many battles to survive as an artist, and is now approaching his sixth decade, he is philosophical about the nature of these battles. But nevertheless they take their toll and valuable energy that should be focused on creating good work is frequently spent dealing with the politics of the arts. Both Warren and Packer have taken control of their vision by structuring a company that supports it and having a Board whose role is also supportive. Packer's clarity of vision is allowing him to do the work he believes in – he has done everything expected of him by the funders at this juncture and he clearly works hard at communicating successfully with them. If there is artistic failure along the way, let us hope there is enough good will from all the significant stakeholders for Packer and *Slingsby* to ride it through.

Conclusions

This study addresses the challenges of being an artist-leader in a small arts organization. While these are different organizations and different art forms, the approach of all three leaders demonstrates a collaborative approach to both the creative process and to leadership. Whether the approach of artist leaders is different to that demonstrated in other sectors is not addressed here. What the study does address is how collaboration is significant for leaders to achieve successful outcomes in the arts. While these examples demonstrate the artists' approach to creativity, they also show leadership that is generous, wise and highly productive; perhaps providing a lesson for those outside of the arts. They do not do this by coercion but by getting everyone involved to commit to a process and then own the outcomes.

The subjects of the study demonstrate highly developed relationship and communication skills where they acknowledge constantly the roles of others in helping them to make the kind of work they want to do. Working with others to do the work, seems for each of them, a pleasurable journey where they use different approaches to do the work that matters to them. Rather than resent the engagement of others in owning the outcomes they feel that this result is a sign of their successful leadership.

Interviews

Packer, Andy 2012, Interview conducted on February 1, 2012

Phillip-Harbutt, Lisa 2012, Interview conducted on February 7, 2012

Warren, Leigh 2011, Interview conducted on December 15, 2011

Acknowledgements

The author would like to thank Leigh Warren, Lisa Phillip-Harbutt and Andy Packer for the generous giving of their time for this research.

Leigh Warren and Dancers can be contacted at: www.lwd.com.au.

Community Arts Network (SA) can be contacted at: www.cansa.net.au.

Slingsby can be contacted at: www.slingsby.net.au.

Questions

1. Discuss how collaboration is understood by the different arts leaders in this case study, and consider if and why there are differences in their approach.

2. Is artistic collaboration necessary to a particular art form or artistic practice, or does it reflect a particular philosophic perspective? Discuss this in the context of the case study.

3. Making new artistic work and leading an arts organization are both challenging and complex roles. Consider the challenges faced by the leaders represented in this case study and consider the effectiveness of their different approaches.

References

Beirne, M & Knight, S 2002, 'Principles and Consistent Management in the Arts: Lessons from British Theatre' *The International Journal of Cultural Policy* Vol 8, No 1 May 2002.

Cray, D, Inglis, L & Freeman, S 2007, 'Managing the Arts: Leadership and Decision Making under Dual Rationalities', *Journal of Arts Management, Law and Society*, vol. 36, no. 4, pp. 295-312.

Drucker, P 1990, *Managing the non-profit organization*, New York, Harper Collins.

Fitzgibbon, M 2001, *Managing innovation in the arts*, London, Quorum Books.

Lapierre, L 2005, 'Managing as Creating', *International Journal of Arts Management*, volume 7 (3), Spring 2005.

Morris, M 2001, 'Genius at work – a conversation with Mark Morris', *Harvard Business Review*, October, pp. 63–8.

Robinson Mark 2010, *Making Adaptive Resilience Real* Arts Council England.

Sutherland, I & Gosling, J 2010, 'Cultural Leadership: Mobilizing Culture from Affordances to Dwelling' *The journal of Arts Management, Law and Society* 40: pp. 6–26, 2010.

Thomas, MT 2008, *Leadership in the Arts; An Inside View,* Author House, Bloomington, USA.

Thorn, George 1990, 'Cultural Darwinism: survival of the smartest', in Nello McDaniel and George Thorn *Rethinking and restructuring the arts organisation*, New York, FEDAPT.

Throsby, D & Zednik, A 2010, *Do you really expect to get paid? An economic study of professional artists in Australia* Sydney: Australia Council.

Chapter 14

The art of collaborative leadership in jazz bands

PATRICK FURU

Background

I was about 45 when I realized something amazing: The conductor doesn't make a sound. The conductor's power depends on his ability to make other people powerful. That insight changed everything for me. I started paying attention to how I was enabling my musicians to be the best performers they could be. My orchestra noticed the change immediately. They asked, 'What happened to you?' (Orchestra conductor Benjamin Zander quoted in LaBarre 2007)

Global business today is fundamentally anything but business as usual. The methods, business models and approaches that worked well in the past no longer work as well, if at all, today. This has become well known to most managers already. The popularized slogan goes: 'What got you here won't get you there' (Goldsmith & Rentas 2007). While this is true, the change is more dramatic, requiring something more than only adjusting managerial methods and tools.

As Porter and Kramer (2011) claim, companies are 'trapped in an outdated approach to value creation that has emerged over the past few decades' (p. 64). The focus is more on short-term results than future sustainability of the business (Avery & Bergsteiner 2011). Business leaders are therefore turning to new sources of inspiration to deal with the constant changes. There is a strong indication that the economy of the future will require a lot more collaboration and artistic creativity. Austin and Devin (2003) are advising modern business leaders to 'look to collaborative artists rather than to more traditional management models if they want to create economic value in this new century' (p. xxii).

The requirements on leadership have become, if possible, even more apparent. Based solidly on his studies of group behaviour in the 1960s, Warren Bennis identified a number of factors for future leadership. He claimed: 'All leaders have the capacity to create a compelling vision, one that takes people to a new place' (Bennis 2009, p. 188). Similarly, DePree (1990) claims that the most important responsibility of the leader is to define reality for the organization. In today's competitive environment, leaders must take us to places we haven't been before (Barry & Meisiek 2010). However, many of the traditional management tools and models fail to provide business leaders with adequate support for taking their organizations to new territory. The traditional tools rely mostly on logic and rationality, which postulate that we are able to predict and know the world. Springborg (2010) argues that the traditional kind of inductive and deductive thinking is based on yesterday's sense-making, which is poorly suitable for navigating fresh territories. In contrast, the leader is recommended to look to the artists – actors, dancers and musicians – for alternative, more effective methods. The purpose for artists throughout the ages has been to 'navigate unchartered territories and reveal the difficulties as well as the glories lurking within them' (Ladkin & Taylor 2010, p. 236).

The idea of artists having much to give to business leaders is not new. In fact, Harvard Professor Abraham Zaleznik (1977) argued 35 years ago that business leaders have much in common with artists and other creative workers. However, it is now clear that the scarce and critical resource in business is not analytical business skills – it is creativity, foresight and innovation (Ladkin & Taylor 2010). 'Creating the next great thing demands constant innovation; it's a design task, not merely an analytical or administrative function. Historically, such creativity has been the primary competence of artists, not managers' (Adler 2006, p. 490).

What is striking about modern organisational life is the rise of a networked, distributed form of organising, in contrast to a hierarchical form. On the corporate level, we see growth in global strategic alliances, joint ventures, cross-border mergers, acquisitions and partnerships. On the sub-organisational and team level, the comparable phenomena are cross-company project teams, social networks, and virtual and internationally dispersed teams. Despite the popularity of these phenomena, success of these forms has not been great (Adler 2006). It is obvious that the crucial skill required for successfully operating these modern forms of organising is that of *collaboration*. In fact, IBM's latest study of over 1,700 CEOs globally reveals that '[the CEOs] are creating more open and collaborative cultures — encouraging employees to connect, learn from each other and thrive in a world of rapid change. *Collaboration is the number-one trait CEOs are seeking in their employees*, with 75% of CEOs calling it critical. […] The emphasis on openness and collaboration is even higher among outperforming organizations' (IBM 2012, p. 6-7, italics added).

Collaboration is found in many art forms. Indeed, actors, dancers and musicians who regularly perform as ensembles have mastered team-based collaborative competence to a much greater extent than have most managers (Adler 2006). It is therefore interesting to study closely this type of artistic collaboration to understand the power of this collaborative competence.

Benjamin Zander's experiences with symphony orchestras (see opening quotation above) indicate that much of the power in artistic collaboration is in releasing the latent competence and strengths within the individual musicians. This approach to collaboration seeks to answer the question 'what could be?' rather than 'what is?' The task of the leader then is transformed to that of an *enabler* of talent to blossom, instead of the traditional task of assigning pre-determined tasks to team (or orchestra) members.

An improvising jazz band, with its focus on collaboration and its highly fluid organisational form, is an excellent example of collaborative competence in action. In such a jazz band, a stream of innovative ideas are expressed, encouraged and tested continuously. This artistic process, which is firmly grounded in collaboration, provides an appropriate collaborative leadership model for teams and organisations. This chapter describes and analyses the constituents of collaborative leadership that is typical of improvising jazz bands during their performance. The practice of distributing leadership responsibility among band members has proven to be one aspect of the jazz band's effectiveness over time.

The challenge

The Golden Age of Jazz refers often to the era of late 1930s to early 1940s. In other words, jazz is not a new art form. The organisational form of improvising is nearly a century old. Nevertheless, the improvising jazz band has been hailed as the future form of organising (e.g. Barrett 1998; Hatch 1998, 1999; Peplowski 1998). There is a natural explanation of an apparent paradox in an organisational form of at least half a century old being the way to organise in the future. Tung (2006) argues that one of the distinctive features of art and artists is that they transcend time. Often great artists and art are ahead of their time, and their appeal grows with time. Thus, early jazz improvisers seem to have been way ahead of their time in terms of influencing the world's business organisations.

The focus in much of the leadership discourse has been on the individual leader. The vast majority of leadership studies and popular literature emphasize the individual leader's characteristics to achieve results. Recently, however, a growing interest in shared and distributed leadership has emerged (Carson *et al.* 2007; Day *et al.* 2004; Gockel & Werth 2010; Manz *et al.* 2010; Pearce *et al.* 2010; Pearce & Conger 2003). This is related to a more collaborative view of leadership, where the focus is on the *function* and not so much on the *person*. In fact, already Gibb (1954, p. 884) has argued that we should perceive leadership as a 'group quality [...] a set of functions which must be carried out by the group'.

The form of collaborative leadership found in art, and in particular in improvising jazz groups, is capable of innovative and creative outcomes. There are two main constituents to this type of leadership according to Manz *et al.* (2010). Firstly, within the whole team there must be a mutual commitment to maintaining a creative process. There can be no exceptions to this commitment. Secondly, the organization must recognize every stakeholder as a valuable contributor. In other words, everyone in the team must be mindful of everyone else's ideas, initiatives and strengths. When these two constituents are present in the team's operations, a collaborative form of leadership takes form. In this form, 'everyone is involved in the leadership process when and where they are most needed' (Manz *et al.* 2010, p. 216-217). It is important to note that the two above-mentioned constituents of collaborative leadership are necessary, but not sufficient, for such leadership process to take place. In any case, collaborative leadership seems to be based on a collective sense of responsibility for the goals of the team.

Collaborative leadership is not only associated with teams and team performance, although that has been the main focus of studies on this subject. As it has to do with influence and responsibility, collaborative leadership concerns teams, workgroups, organisations and any units that attempt to fulfil their goals. Follett (1951) introduced the notion of the *law of the situation*, meaning that influence should be given to the person with the most knowledge and experience in any given situation, regardless of rank or hierarchical position. This suggests that, as situations change, different leaders emerge.

Jazz improvisation has been used as a metaphor for organising for creativity and innovation in recent organisation theory (Hatch 1999; Kamoche *et al.* 2003; Newton 2004; Weick 1998). More specifically, the metaphor of jazz improvisation has applied to situations in organisations in which there are no formal structures and control mechanisms, or that these fail to support organizational activity. However, the novelty is that it has been used to explain the resulting success rather than failure (Lewin 1998). DePree (1993, p. 9) claims that 'We [business executives] have much to learn from jazz-band leaders, for jazz, like leadership, combines the unpredictability of the future with the gifts of the individuals'. There is arguably a more horizontal and collaborative type of leadership in this kind of artistic organisation, and jazz bands may provide a model of collaborative leadership that informs discussion of this phenomenon in other organisations and contexts. For this reason, the author of this study has sought to explore more fully the nature of collaborative leadership in jazz bands.

Approach

The phenomenon of collaborative leadership in improvising jazz bands was observed, discussed and analysed in seven executive education workshops involving a live jazz band. The purpose of the workshops was to bring a jazz band into the management education classroom to demonstrate in practice how an improvising jazz band operates. The focus of these workshops, which lasted between 1 hour and 45 minutes to 3 hours and 15 minutes, was on leadership, teamwork, and the concept of strategy implementation. All seven workshops were videotaped with one video camera for further analysis.

In each of the seven workshops, there was a band of five professional jazz musicians. The band was different in each of the workshops, and the musicians had not played together in that particular assemblage before. The purpose of this procedure was to demonstrate the universal professionalism of jazz musicians and the ability of this organisational form to take on any musical task without prior rehearsal and team building.

The total number of jazz musicians in the seven workshops was 22, implying that some musicians participated in more than once. The musicians represented six different nationalities: Finland, the Netherlands, Singapore, Sweden, USA, and the UK. The age of the musicians ranged from 32 to 75, thus testing whether the collaborative model of the jazz band stretches over generations.

The concept in the workshops was to give a task, i.e. a simple musical arrangement previously unknown to the musicians, and ask the band to implement it first without improvising and then with adding their professional creativity and improvisation to it. In reality, the band performed several alternative versions of the same original task with different variations, as well as totally new tasks that emerged through the discussion and analysis with the executive audiences. The bands' improvised and non-improvised performances were discussed and analysed interactively with the author as a facilitator.

Assembling five musicians who have not previously played together as an ensemble is common in the jazz tradition. In fact, musicians frequently play in a large number of different bands and regularly 'jam' with different jazz musicians (e.g. Berliner 1994; Eisenberg 1990; Kao 1997). A jam session is a gathering where basically any musician can enter the stage and play with whoever happens to be playing there. The jamming tradition effectively develops the player's musicianship through exposure to different styles, contexts and personalities, as well as expands and deepens their networks. All 22 musicians in this study were frequent participants in this kind of jam session.

Outcomes

The first outcome of the analysis of the jazz band model of working is that professional competence – the craft – is a prerequisite. Without being able to play your instrument, teamwork in a jazz band is impossible. In a sense, this observation is related to Follett's (1951) proposition that competence or knowledge is a basis for influence in a given situation. Furthermore, as all members of the group are competent they all, at various points in time, influence the direction of the performance. However, being able to master an instrument is a necessary, but not sufficient, condition for collaborative leadership. In order to understand the collaborative leadership model at work, we need to look more closely at how some of the basic concepts of art are applied in the jazz band's performance.

In their synthesis of studies on leadership as art, Ladkin and Taylor (2010) identify key motifs that reconceptualise leadership in general. From their discussion, three concepts appear central to understanding collaborative leadership in jazz bands. They are 'holding contradictions', 'craft vs. art', and 'meaning-making', which will be elaborated on below.

Holding contradictions

The famous quotation by F Scott Fitzgerald goes: 'The test of a first-rate intelligence is the ability to hold two opposing ideas in mind at the same time and still retain the ability to function'. In a sense, the same applies to the arts. Great art integrates contradictions, or ideas that at first sight seem to be contradictory, but after being brought together, appear natural. Thus, Ladkin and Taylor (2010) argue that 'containing and working with contradictions and paradox is indeed central to most artistic endeavours' (p. 238).

The jazz musician's ability to resolve and synthesize dilemmas and contradictions together is remarkable. The following sequence illustrates a reconciliation of an apparent contradiction:

> Trombonist: 'Should we take it as a swing? I could then play long arches behind the melody.'

> Bassist: 'Sure, a standard intro? One-six-two-five[1] twice?'

> Saxophonist: 'Or what would you say about latin? Wouldn't that work?'

> Drummer: 'Ok, let's start with an eight-bar vamp.'

> [after playing the tune]

> Facilitator: 'One of you said 'swing' and another 'latin'. How did you choose which one you were going for?'

> Drummer: 'Well, I thought it'd be nice to have them both. We started with a latin groove, and then in the first solo went to swing, and then came back to a swinging latin beat. So we chose both.'

Even though 'latin' and 'swing' are different – and even somewhat contradictory – rhythms in their pure forms, the jazz band was able to contain both of them in the same tune. Whereas a normal reaction to such juxtaposition would be to choose one or the other, the jazz musicians ask themselves: what will it take to have both of them? They find the resolution in contradictions instead of dismissing them. The reason is that within contradictions lie the potential for creating something unique, something that has not been done before, something that intrigues their artistic minds. Many of the musicians make it a habit to deliberately introduce potential contradictions for the benefit of fellow musicians.

> Guitarist: '[sometimes]… I don't play what everyone's expecting […] I want to play an odd thing, a chord […] maybe a chromatic scale that introduces dissonance to what's going on. […] makes it more exciting.'

---

[1] 'One-six-two-five', or more frequently expressed as 'I-vi-ii-V', refers to one of the most common chord progressions in music, thus being standard knowledge of every musician.

In other words, for the musicians, contradictions mean a source of creativity. Another contradiction that resulted in a creative resolution was witnessed in a tune called 'Stella by Starlight'. It is a jazz standard in 4/4 time. However, while playing the head (i.e. the melody), the band extemporaneously switched from 4/4 time to 3/4 (popularly known as the waltz rhythm). Nobody had planned it, they had not agreed on it. It just happened on the spot. If 'latin' and 'swing' are remotely related and resolvable styles, playing 3/4 and 4/4 spontaneously in the same tune is definitely contradictory.

What is especially intriguing about the switch from 4/4 to 3/4 is that the musicians could not tell whose idea it was to make that switch. Many identified the drummer, whose natural role it is to keep the beat running. However, the drummer had a different point of view:

> Drummer: 'No, no. You [the bassist] played that triplet just before and it gave me the idea to go into threes.'
>
> Bassist: 'I did?'
>
> Drummer: 'Yeah, you did, and [the pianist] was reacting to that so that's where we went.'

All the musicians were unanimously celebrating this resolution as one of the best moments in their playing together. It was creative, surprising, but still sounded good and it was the most natural turn in that tune. The musicians seem to enjoy this type of situations and episodes as they appeal to their creativity. Thus, contradictions seem to be related to a move away from standard operating procedure, which is felt as exciting. On these occasions, music is moved to a higher state, to something that is unknown but enthusing. Thus, music then becomes art.

Craft vs art

In discussing art-of-leadership literature, Barry and Meisiek (2010) distinguish between art-as-craft on the one hand, and fine art on the other. They argue that there has been a confusion of these concepts. This confusion has led to a usage of 'art' as referring to basically 'anything (i.e. any craft, occupation, practice, branch of learning, etc.) in which skill may be attained or displayed' (p. 333). They continue by claiming that most of the present leadership and art literature is concerned with the perception of art as craft in a more technical sense, in which 'technical' represents systematic skill. From this perspective, leadership is a set of systematic skills ('craft'). In contrast, an arts-oriented perspective of leadership draws on 'contemporary notions of fine art, playfully inviting multiple perspectives and interpretations' (p. 333).

In the jazz band context, both forms of 'art' are present. The *craft* is evident in the mastery of the instrument, the skill of playing. The technical aspects of playing an instrument are something that professional musicians try to improve throughout their careers. One of the most senior musicians explained:

I try to practice every day. I rehearse the scales up and down, and try to vary from day to day. You are never a master of your instrument. But that's not the only thing. When I've grown older, I've started to think more and more about the whole. Then it's not enough to play by yourself, you need other [musicians].

Another part of the craft is the conventions in jazz. Professional jazz musicians are trained in these conventions, both as part of their formal education and as part of the practice of playing together. These conventions form a universal jazz culture that is shared by professional musicians around the world.

Pianist: 'There's an awful lot of theoretical studying you have to do, and a lot of listening also [...] even if you learn from a book everything perfectly, you have to be able to be in that experience that you are listening to jazz music a lot and you learn from that. [...] and then you have to play, play with others.'

A fundamental aspect of the craft is the common terminology and language shared by jazz musicians. This shared language consists of verbal, body and musical language. The verbally spoken language consists of concepts that provide a common ground for the musicians to play together. For example, the concepts of 'heads and tunes', 'soloing', 'comping', 'trading fours' and 'groove and feel' are common in jazz language and are part of the cultural heritage in jazz improvisation (Hatch 1999). Jazz musicians need to know this terminology in order to be effective in their collaboration.

Drummer: 'I think [the pianist] said "latin", and then [the bass player] added on and suggested "maybe calypso". Then we agreed that the rhythm section starts the tune with a vamp for a couple of bars and then the horns kick in.'

Saxophonist: '...and I didn't know how the calypso would start so I waited to hear how it would turn out.'

Bassist: 'Right before we started I checked with the pianist if he was going to play a more percussionist type of comp or a melodic one.'

In this dialogue, a lot of implicit knowledge is embedded in the language. Simple words, such as 'latin', 'vamp' or 'comp' carry a lot of meaning for the musicians. The dialogue also reveals how the 'inviting multiple perspectives and interpretations', i.e. the fine art dimension, emerges in the band's work process. It is clearly a more collaborative dimension of skill or competence.

However, the words and concepts are not unambiguous. In fact, there are many cases in which the musicians are not exactly sure what the others are trying to communicate. In the workshops when musicians had little time to agree on the style, tempo, roles, intro and ending, etc., they just started playing and sorted things out as they played. The following sequence illustrates this:

Pianist: 'Should we try it as a gospel?'

Bassist: 'Sure, in the original key?'

Saxophonist (partly talking over others): '…a drum and bass vamp in the beginning, you know, funky style, then horns play the head…'

Trumpeter: 'Let's just start playing. Piano intro?'

Drummer (replying to saxophonist): 'You mean in three? A bit like this [illustrates silently one bar of comp]?'

Pianist (partly interrupting): 'I mean like a bluesy gospel…'

Saxophonist (mainly to drummer): 'Yeah, that's okay. Then bass riffs with…'

Pianist (talking over saxophonist): 'I could show… like… [plays chords]… this way.'

Trumpeter: 'Let's start guys.'

Bassist: 'I'm not sure, but yeah man, go ahead.'

Pianist: [starts with a bluesy gospel intro]

Surprisingly, despite the starting point, the performance went so well that it received a raving applause from the audience. The *craft* was there. The musicians all knew the concepts and the tune. However, they did not get it together during the planning phase, but only after they started playing together. That requires that the musicians listen actively and attentively to each other, and support each other's musical ideas. In other words, the characteristic that transforms the craft and skills to true jazz seems to be the art and the practice of 'playfully inviting multiple perspectives and interpretations' (Barry & Meisiek 2010, p. 333).

Even if some musicians, such as the pianist in the example above, are more influential in making decisions up front, all band members share the responsibility of the whole. In this collaborative operational form, leadership is a *function* that is performed by all band members, but at different points in time. The following quote describes this rotation of leadership responsibility.

> *Drummer: '…people talk about [passing] the ball. It's […] who's holding the ball [who has the lead], […] then pass it to somebody else, and […] somebody takes a leading role in that situation – gives the guidelines for the others.'*

Meaning-making

Woodward and Funk (2010) propose that 'leading is viewed as largely meaning-making' (p. 301). According to this view, when people lead they are in a continuous act of making meaning from real life experience from and in the world. In addition to meaning making, leaders must also have the ability to reflect on and learn from this continuous process. A leader, then, can be viewed as 'a seeker, a questioner and crafter of meaning' (p. 301).

The jazz band's members engage in collective meaning-making as they take turns in improvising solos, while others give support to the soloist. Playing solo means to take responsibility for the overall direction of the band. It is an act of crafting the current vision on the spot, given the information and the resources at hand. One of the musicians describe improvised soloing in the following way:

> Pianist: '...a bit like being in a group of people, and you're improvising a story [...], you're creating something. But also [...], everyone that's around you is giving you ideas for the story [...] to where you can bring your story. You don't have to take all of the ideas. But maybe you take some of them, and you try to create something. [...] and you are responsible for creating a coherent story of it.'

The quote resonates perfectly with Ladkin and Taylor's (2010) argument that musicians have 'the ability to hold what has been heard in the past, in order to anticipate the future and understand the present' (p. 238) and that this is an important characteristic of leadership.

The jazz musicians discussed this aspect of musicianship extensively. They claimed that the dynamics of this meaning-making in jazz improvisation is the essence of jazz music. It requires not only the craft of knowing the scales and harmonies on which to improvise, but – more importantly – also the art of active listening to all the ideas, suggestions, musical phrases and contextual factors that the other musicians, the audience and other stakeholders are presenting.

This very central element of art, i.e. using whatever is at hand to project into the future, demands collaborative leadership. Collaborative in the sense that every single musician bears the responsibility for meaning-making, and they take turns in who has the 'chief meaning-maker' role at the moment. However, not only the soloist is making meaning, but also the other musicians engage in meaning-making simultaneously. They constantly interpret the soloist's actions and try to support him or her with appropriate means.

In fact, when collective meaning-making is taking place, the musicians are *unable* to identify whose idea (i.e. meaning-making) was driving the music forward. The concentration on the performance is so intense that each musician is in a heightened state of consciousness. Even though one might think that they would be in a better position to identify each other's ideas, this is not the case. On the contrary, their concentration is focused on the main purpose, which is to make good music. Therefore, the question of who is making what contribution is secondary. Those who succeed at making best sense of all the ideas are effectively moving the band closer to the goal. In the best case, everyone is in that position, i.e. 'chief meaning-makers', at some point.

This meaning-making and creating-the-future-as-you-go does not, however, always produce great results. It entails taking a risk. Sometimes it pays off better than at other times. We must remember that the musicians do not know in advance the direction the song and the improvisations are taking. Therefore, setbacks occur occasionally. The jazz musicians admitted that they make many mistakes, most of which go relatively unnoticed – even by the other band members. Certain mistakes, though, are more blatant and they affect the whole and the end result. Nevertheless, musicians are experienced in dealing with these situations. As Ladkin and Taylor (2010) state, they can 'read significant aspects of a context, and make wise choices about where they should concentrate attention' (p. 238). When setbacks happen, the musicians' focus is tightly on the way forward, as is apparent in the following comments:

> Saxophonist A: 'The thing that is important when something happens... is, what happens next [...] Think about the next steps!' [...]

> Drummer: 'Sometimes things don't go the way you would like them to go. But you have to just... forget everything that went bad and try to look forward and enjoy what's good, and be on the spot and make sure to make it good.' [...]

> Saxophonist B: 'Yeah, my personal slogan is "Deal with it!"'

In sum, meaning-making in the improvising jazz band is a collective venture. Each musician is making sense of the situation, context, the musical ideas, etc. continuously. It is only through the collaborative mind-set of the musicians that these different meaning-making processes overlap enough so that the music they create becomes great.

Conclusions

Oscar Peterson, the late Canadian jazz pianist, once said: 'It's the group sound that's important, even when you're playing a solo. You not only have to know your own instrument, you must know the others and how to back them up at all times. That's jazz.' This statement captures much of the collaborative leadership model in the jazz band.

Even though jazz music is a North-American art form, it is interesting to note that the collaborative jazz leadership model seems to be quite universal. The jazz musicians participating in this study represented six nationalities located in four different countries of the world. Therefore, there is reason to believe that art originating from mainly one country can have a more universal effect on leadership.

In the jazz band, leadership is a collaborative function performed by all members of the band. However, collaborative leadership does not mean that all decisions are made together, or that everyone's input is required before anything can be done. On the contrary, in the case of jazz bands, collaborative leadership means that there is normally one leader *at any given point of time*. When the situation changes, for example when a new soloist takes over, the leadership position and responsibility changes. In other words, in the jazz band it is standard practice that the leadership role (the 'chief meaning-maker') rotates.

Figure 14.1 Elements of the collaborative leadership process

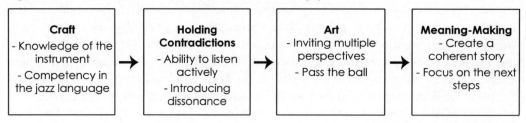

The collaborative leadership process can be summarized with the help of the three (in practice four) key concepts identified by Ladkin and Taylor (2010), namely 'holding contradictions', 'art vs craft', and 'meaning-making' (see Figure 14.1). It starts with the prerequisite, the craft. Musicians need to be able to play their instrument, know the scales, internalize the vocabulary and understand the conventions. That, however, is not yet art or leadership.

The second element and the first real part of the collaborative leadership model is the ability to hold contradictions. Opposing views are not turned down. Instead, every member of the band embraces them and potentially even introduces dissonance, as they are potential sources of creative solutions and inspiring end results.

The third element of the collaborative model is 'art'. In this context, art refers to 'playfully inviting multiple perspectives and interpretations' as Barry and Meisiek (2010, p. 333) rightfully put it. Jazz musicians rotate the responsibility for direction among themselves in order to seek novel solutions and to make sure that enough perspectives are presented.

The fourth element is 'meaning-making', which refers to the musicians' skill in creating coherence and meaning from all the diverse perspectives, ideas and the context in the moment to project into the future. Jazz musicians use whatever that has been said and is being said and mold that into a 'story', a solo, that takes the band forward and inspires consequent action.

In this collaborative leadership model, responsibility for the leadership function is carried by all members of the band, but at different points in time. In the end, all members of the band need to work for a common goal. As one of the musicians stated: '… *No matter what I do, the music is still my client, and I have to serve my client the best way I can.*'

Acknowledgements

The author gratefully acknowledges the financial support from the Foundation for Economic Education that has made this research possible.

Questions

1. Discuss how leadership works within a jazz band. What is different about it in terms of conventional models of leadership?

2.   Is the approach to leadership within a jazz band applicable to other fields? Why/How?

3.   What are the key characteristics of leadership in a jazz band, that support the making of art?

References

Adler, NJ 2006, 'The arts & leadership: Now that we can do anything, what will we do?', *Academy of Management Learning & Education*, vol. 5, no. 4, pp. 486-499.

Avery, G & Bergsteiner, H 2011, ''Sustainable leadership practices for enhancing business resilience and performance', *Strategy & Leadership*, vol. 39, no. 3, pp. 5-15.

Bansal, P 2002, 'The corporate challenges of sustainable development', *Academy of Management Executive*, vol. 16, no. 2, pp. 122–131.

Barrett, FJ 1998, 'Coda—Creativity and Improvisation in Jazz and Organizations: Implications for Organizational Learning', *Organization Science*, vol. 9, no. 5, pp. 605-622.

Barry, D, Meisiek, S 2010, 'The art of leadership and its fine art shadow', *Leadership*, vol. 6. no. 3, pp. 331-349.

Berliner, PF 1994, *Thinking in Jazz: The Finite Art of Improvisation*, University of Chicago Press, Chicago.

Bennis, W 2009, *On Becoming a Leader* (20th edition), Basic Books, Philadelphia.

Berns, M, Townend, A, Khayat, Z. Balagopal, B, Reeves, M, Hopkins, M & Kruschwitz, N 2009, 'The business of sustainability: Findings and insights from the first annual business of sustainability survey and the Global Thought Leaders' Research Project.' *MIT Sloan Management Review*.

DePree, M 1990, *Leadership is an Art*, Dell Publishing, New York.

DePree, M 1993, *Leadership Jazz*, Dell Publishing, New York.

Eisenberg, E 1990, 'Jamming: Transcendence through organizing', *Communication Research*, vol. 17, April 2, pp. 139-164.

Follett, PM 1951, *Creative Experience*, Peter Smith, New York.

Gockel, C & Wert, L 2011, 'Measuring and modeling shared leadership: Traditional approaches and new ideas', *Journal of Personnel Psychology*, vol. 9, no.4, pp. 172-180.

Goldsmith, M & Reiter, M 2007, What Got You Here Won't Get You There: How Successful People Become Even More Successful, Hyperion, New York.

Hatch, MJ 1998, 'Jazz as a Metaphor for Organizing in the 21st Century', *Organization Science*, vol. 9, no. 5, pp. 556-568.

Hatch, MJ 1999, 'Exploring the empty spaces in organizing: How improvisational jazz helps redescribe organizational structure', *Organization Studies*, vol. 20, no. 1, pp. 75-100.

Haugh, HM & Talwar, A 2010, 'How do corporations embed sustainability across the organization?', *Academy of Management Learning & Education*, vol. 9, no. 3, pp. 384–396.

IBM 2012, *Leading Through Connections – Insights from the Global IBM CEO Study*, IBM Global Business Services,   Somers: New York.

Kamoche, K, Cunha, MP & Cunha, JV 2003, 'Towards a theory of organizational improvisation: Looking beyond the jazz metaphor', *Journal of Management Studies*, vol. 40, no. 8, pp. 2023-2051.

Kao, J 1997, Jamming: The Art and Discipline of Business Creativity, HarperCollins.

LaBarre, P 2007, 'Leadership – Ben Zander', *FastCompany*, December 19.

Ladkin, D, Taylor, SS, 2010, 'Leadership as art: Variations on a theme', *Leadership*, vol. 6, no. 3, pp. 235-241.

Madson, PR 2005, *Improv Wisdom: Don't Prepare, Just Show Up*, Bell Tower, New York.

Manz, CC, Manz, KP, Adams, SB & Shipper, F 2011, 'A model of values-based shared leadership and sustainable performance', *Journal of Personnel Psychology*, vol. 9, no.4, pp. 212-217.

Marsalis, W (with GC Ward) 2008, *Moving to Higher Ground – How Jazz Can Change Your Life*, Random House, New York.

Newton, PM 2004, 'Leadership lessons from jazz improvisation', *International Journal of Leadership in Education*, vol. 7, no. 1, 83-99.

Pearce, CL 2004, 'The future of leadership: Combining vertical and shared leadership to transform knowledge work', *Academy of Management Executive*, vol. 18, no. 1, pp. 47-57.

Pearce, CL & Conger, JA (eds) 2003, Shared Leadership: Reframing the Hows and Whys of Leadership. Sage, London.

Pearce, CL, Hoch, JE, Jeppesen, IIJ & Wegge, J 2010, 'New forms of management: Shared and distributed leadership in organizations', *Journal of Personnel Psychology*, vol. 9, no. 4, pp. 151-153.

Peplowski, K 1998, 'The Process of Improvisation' *Organization Science*, vol. 9, no. 5, pp. 560-561;

Porter, ME & Kramer, MR 2011, 'Creating shared value', *Harvard Business Review*, vol. 89, no. 1/2, pp. 62-77.

Springborg, C 2010, 'Leadership as art – leaders coming to their senses', *Leadership*, vol. 6, no. 3, pp. 243-258.

Sveiby KE & Skuthorpe, T 2006, Treading Lightly: The Hidden Wisdom of the World's Oldest People, Allen & Unwin, Sydney.

Weick, KE 1998, 'Improvisation as a mindset for organizational analysis', *Organization Science*, vol. 9, no. 5, pp. 543-555.

Zaleznik, A 1977, 'Managers and leaders: Are they different?', *Harvard Business Review*, vol. 55, no. 3, pp. 67-78.

Index

marketing, 11, 46, 60, 61, 134
master-apprentice, 47
meaning-making, 219
Melbourne Symphony Orchestra, 74
merchandising, 11
Mikhaïl Piotrovsky, 4
Mira style, 25
Mira Trailović, 19
mission, 8, 85, 121, 138
missions, 116
morale, 146
motivation, 168, 184

N

National Gallery of Australia, 73
National Gallery of Victoria, 73
National Museum of Art in Oslo, 115
not-for-profit, 196
not-for-profit organization, 145
Nouvelle Compagnie Théâtrale, 97

O

Open Stage, 132
Opera Australia, 71
operating model, 145
opportunities, 8
oral culture, 27
Orchestra Victoria, 75
organizational change, 116, 147, 149, 155
organizational culture, 23, 29, 67, 129, 141, 148
organizational infrastructure, 61
organizational structure, 58, 90, 127, 128
organizational values, 116
organizing, 29

P

participative leadership, 116, 122, 125
pay check workers, 173
performance addicts, 173
persuading, 29
phase managers, 170
philanthropy, 10
Pierre Rousseau, 96
positive working relationship, 61
PR machine, 24
pragmatist, 173
pressure points, 64
    capacity, 66
    communication, 64
    staffing, 65

prima donnas, 173
primary leadership behavior, 60
principles, 116
private initiative, 24
private interest, 24
process leadership theory. *See* transformational
professional development, 19
programming, 60
progressive arts, 23
promotional campaigns, 27
public engagement, 136
public relations, 43, 61
purpose and values statement, 147

R

radio drama, 22
Rémi Brousseau, 96
re-organization, 10, 44
revenue, 6, 10, 66, 87, 102
risk taking, 188
role relationships, 121
romanticized leadership, 133
Royal Shakespeare Company, 135, 145

S

season selection, 66
seizing opportunities, 63
self-awareness, 153
self-improvement, 47
self-management, 21, 28
self-reflection, 153
senior management, 146
servant leadership, 123
Shakespeare Theatre, 59
Shanghai Audio Visual Press, 84
Shanghai Music Book Store, 87
shared leadership, 76, 142, 184
shared vision, 62
shielding leadership, 171
small arts organization, 208
Sochi, 41
social networks, 150, 152
sole leadership, 71
sole management, 73
solo leaders, 72
specific organizational cultures. See organizational culture
spinning, 24
spiritual leadership, 123
sponsorship, 76
staff involvement, 116